BLACK PLANET

Also by David Shields

Fiction
Dead Languages
Heroes
A Handbook for Drowning (stories)

Nonfiction
Remote

BLACK
PLANET

Facing Race During an NBA Season

DAVID SHIELDS

CROWN PUBLISHERS

NEW YORK

Published by Crown Publishers, 201 East 50th Street, New York, New York 10022.
Member of the Crown Publishing Group.

Random House, Inc. New York, Toronto, London, Sydney, Auckland
www.randomhouse.com

Crown is a trademark and the Crown colophon is a registered trademark of Random House, Inc.

Printed in the United States of America

Design by Leonard Henderson

Library of Congress Cataloging-in-Publication Data
Shields, David.
Black planet : facing race during an NBA season / David Shields.
—1st ed.
1. United States—Race relations.   2. African-American basketball players—Social conditions.   3. Basketball—United States—Sociological aspects.
4. Basketball fans—United States—Social conditions.
5. Shields, David—Diaries.   I. Title.
GV889.26.S55   1999
796.323'64'08996073—dc21   99-13084
ISBN 0-609-60452-X

10 9 8 7 6 5 4 3 2 1

First Edition

For Natalie

ACKNOWLEDGMENTS

I owe a great debt to the following people, who generously offered their encouragement and advice: Joel Drucker, Roger Fanning, Sloan Harris, Robin Hemley, Jennifer Hunt, Norma Logan, Allan Nicoletti, Doug Pepper, Ross Posnock, Laurie Shields, and Milt Shields. Particular thanks to Paul Bravmann, Leo Daugherty, and Michael Logan, who allowed me to use a few phrases and anecdotes from their correspondence; and to Peter Bailey and Jonathan Raban, who rescued me more times than I can count.

Each of us, helplessly and forever, contains the other.
—JAMES BALDWIN

CONTENTS

During the 1994–95 NBA season, I attended nearly all of the Seattle SuperSonics' home games; watched on TV nearly all their away games; listened to countless pre- and post-game interviews and call-in shows on the radio; talked to or tried to talk to players, coaches, agents, journalists, fans, my wife; corresponded with members of the Sonics newsgroup on the Internet; read articles and articles and articles. Although I'm a passionate basketball fan and Sonics fan, when I was writing the book I wasn't interested in the game per se—who won, who lost, the minutiae of strategy. I was interested in how the game gets discussed. By the end of the season, I'd accumulated hundreds of pages of often illegible notes, the roughest of rough drafts. Over the last three years, I transformed those notes into this book—a daily diary which runs the length of one team's long-forgotten season and which is now focused, to the point of obsession, on how white people (including especially myself) think about and talk about black heroes, black scapegoats, black bodies.

What John Edgar Wideman calls "our country's love/hate affair with the black body" can be seen nowhere more clearly than in the National Basketball Association, which is a photo negative of American race relations: strong young black men have some of the power, much of the money, and all of the fun. The NBA is a place where, without ever acknowledging it—and because it's never acknowledged, it's that much more potent and telling—white fans and black players enact and quietly explode virtually every racial issue and tension in the culture at large. Race, the league's taboo topic, is the league's true subject.

Listen:

1

AMERICA UPSIDE DOWN

11.5.94—My initial impression, as I stand next to the Seattle SuperSonics in the locker room an hour before the first game of the season, is that they're twelve utterly unconnected buildings; they convey no sense whatsoever that they're all part of a single city. I'm also struck by the fact that none of the players, tall as they are, seem quite as tall as they're listed in the program, which mythifies them by magnifying them. Staying away from stars, I ask Bill Cartwright, a backup center, whatever happened to Rod Williams, who played with Cartwright at the University of San Francisco nearly twenty years ago and was the best player I ever played against in high school. Cartwright says "Hot Rod" was just too damn slow. I ask Byron Houston, a reserve forward, about the *Death Gate* cycle, a seven-volume science-fiction series of which he is reportedly a devoted fan, and he declines to discuss with me the books' appeal. In the Sonics' media guide, Kendall Gill, the Sonics' shooting-guard, lists "playing in the Illinois high-school state tournament" as one of the two highlights of his life. Since the new documentary film *Hoop Dreams* is about the high-school careers of two basketball players from the south side of Chicago, I ask him if he'd be willing to watch a tape of the movie I've obtained from the distributor, then do a brief interview about his impressions of the film. What's fascinating to me about how Gill says no is that he says,

"Sure," but his eyes communicate, unmissably, *No, of course not, you must be kidding, never, not in a million years.* I think I'm trying to be friendly, to treat them as People rather than as Athletes, but what I'm really trying to do, I realize later, is neuter them, make them slow students in the back of my class, put them on equal or lesser footing.

On leave from the professoriat, I'm "covering" (pretending to cover?) the Sonics' '94–'95 season for the *Seattle Weekly;* a column or two a month is all that's expected of me. I love basketball a lot, have played the game my whole life, have been a fan my whole life, and this gig is an opportunity, I hope, to see brilliance up close. When I make my way from the locker room up to the press-row dinner buffet, I convey to my new colleagues my surprise at how chilly the atmosphere in the locker room is, how guarded the players are.

"Wait till they come back from a 1-and-4 road trip in the middle of February," says Glenn Nelson, the Sonics beat writer for the *Seattle Times.*

Rich Myhre, of the *Everett Herald,* instructs me, "You've got to get in and get out with specific questions."

"Otherwise they get suspicious," someone else says. "They think you're trying to steal plays."

"Apparently you're not supposed to just hang out there," I say. "You can't—"

Steve Kelley, a sports columnist for the *Seattle Times,* says, "The goal becomes just to get out of there and have them not tear your head off."

"I couldn't believe how confrontational it was," I say. "Still, for me it was fun."

"Well," they all say in unison, "you're new."

The Seattle Coliseum is being renovated, so all Sonics home games this season are being played an hour south at the Tacoma Dome—an antiseptic igloo, a terrible building for basketball. Barry Ackerley, a billboard magnate who is the owner of the Sonics and several TV and radio stations, including the Sonics' "flagship station," KJR Sports Radio 950 AM, can't abide the criticism he receives from sportswriters, so as punishment we're sequestered in a crow's nest less than twenty rows from the top of the stadium. The court, at the other end of a pair of binoculars, is barely a rumor. I'm nevertheless giddy to be here, getting stat sheets shoved under my nose every twenty minutes, and if my fellow sportswriters laugh a little at my puppy-dog enthusiasm, I find their Ring Lardner imitations awfully quaint. I've never been able to stand Kendall Gill's air of debonair elegance, and I tell Glenn Nelson how much I liked his recent story in which he wrote that Gill "decided," after three days, that he had a bad back.

Nelson insists he has no idea what I'm talking about and looks at me like I'm nuts. "I forget about a piece the minute I write it," he says.

It's a flat, listless game. Utah, playing its second game in two nights, appears tired. The Sonics shoot miserably. During halftime the Bud Light Daredevils perform gymnastic stunts so that when we drink beer we'll understand that we're doing something adventurous and risky. The Sonics overcome a 10-point deficit by making twice as many free throws as the Jazz. In the last few seconds of the game, with Seattle up by 7, Gary Payton, the Sonics' point-guard, is way ahead of everybody else on a breakaway. Instead of laying the ball in himself for an easy two, he throws it between his legs to Gill, who tries a needlessly difficult reverse dunk, which clangs off the rim. An Israeli journalist is sitting next to me in the press box; if I understand him correctly, he's the West Coast correspondent for an Israeli newspaper and his column this month is called "Hi, Seattle." He is absolutely apoplectic over this play by Payton: "It is not professional. It is not done. It could lose the game." He's right, of course, but isn't it obvious that Gary will do almost anything to make himself feel something in this anhedonic auditorium? This is what I adore about him.

At the post-game press conference with Sonics coach George Karl, I'm amazed at the timorous obviousness/obliviousness of the reporters' questions. A TV reporter says, "You knew tonight would be a tough game, didn't you?"

Another reporter asks, "Were you nervous?"

The crucial shots of the game were three 3-pointers by Seattle's reserve center Sam Perkins, and someone says, "Sam's threes were big, weren't they?"

I try to go to the head of the class by asking something at least fairly specific: "Did you consciously try to call quicker timeouts tonight than you did last year?" Last year it drove me crazy how long Karl would wait before calling a timeout when the other team was on a roll.

"Conscientiously?" Karl says. "No, not conscientiously."

Later, Karl says, "Anytime you play Utah, I call it a smart game. You're going up against Stockton [the only white superstar in the NBA], who makes great decisions all the time."

During the press conference, a young black man stands just outside the ring of reporters, leaning against a wall where I've placed my brief-case on the floor (I want both hands free to write notes and hold a microphone). His hand is just a few inches from my briefcase. At one point I find myself checking over my shoulder to make sure my briefcase is still there. At the end of the press conference he goes up and greets Karl, who gives him a hug, and then I feel, oh, just a little bit worse.

Just outside the Jazz locker room, a solidly built black man pushing an aluminum walker introduces himself to Stockton.

"You probably don't remember me, do you?" the man says.

"No," Stockton says.

"When we were seniors at Gonzaga [University, in Spokane], I was playing football and broke my neck and you played in a benefit game for me. I was really honored that you would do that and that's why I came here tonight to see you."

Stockton understands what he has heard to be a tribute rather than an expression of gratitude, so rather than say, "You're welcome," he says, "Thank you." After a pause, he adds, "It's good to see you're doing good."

"I'm doing better," the man says. "You didn't remember me at first, did you?"

"No, I was struggling a little there at first," Stockton says.

"But you remember now?" the man says eagerly.

"I do," Stockton says. "That goes back a long ways."

"Twelve years."

They pose together, briefly, for a photo.

When I come home, flush with all this new semi-insider gossip, my wife, Laurie, startles me by saying that during the first couple of months of my sabbatical, when I was home all the time, there had been "no energy in the house" and how grateful she is that I'm finally doing some-thing "purposeful" in public. One can forget this or disguise it or pretend it isn't so, but really the sexiest thing a husband can do is go out and return with news of the world.

. . .

11.6.94—On the phone, Mike Kahn, the Sonics beat writer for the *Tacoma News Tribune*, is entertaining me with a long, rambling monologue about the limitless megalomania of professional athletes, until I commit the faux pas of asking whether he thinks "racial payback of some kind" is a factor in the contempt with which Kahn says most NBA players treat sportswriters, e.g., blowing off interview appointments a dozen times in a row. Just a little too abruptly, it seems to me, he says no.

11.7.94—In its NBA Preview issue, *Sports Illustrated* writes, "The Seattle SuperSonic marketing department, apparently taking its cue from the trash-talking denizens of that team's locker room, is offering four customized ticket packages. Each features at least one game against a marquee rival of the Sonics, the NBA's most impudent team. Fans can take their pick from the 'Scottie Who?' plan; the 'Get Your Tickets Before Every Jerk in Portland Does' plan; the 'If I See Another Thing with Shaq on It, I'm Gonna Barf' plan; and the ever-popular 'Barkley Sucks' plan."

I take a curious pride in *Sports Illustrated*'s calling the Sonics the "NBA's most impudent team," because the ruling ethos of Seattle is forlorn apology for the animal impulses. According to a political talk-show host, "Seattle is almost an entirely different market than the rest of the country. There's a very polite approach here. In other cities, callers get much more acerbic. People here are civilized. You don't have to be abrasive or rude or say things in a boisterous, loud way to make your point." A cheerleader at the University of Washington named Robb Weller, who is now a game-show host, is credited with having started the Wave. In his review of *Cat on a Hot Tin Roof*, the drama critic for the *Seattle Post-Intelligencer* explained that he left at intermission because he can't waste his time anymore on theater that glamorizes dysfunctional families and alcoholism. When I castigated a carpenter for using the phrase "Jew me down," he returned later that evening to beg my forgiveness, and the next week he mailed me a mea culpa and a rebate. An editorial in the *Post-Intelligencer* argued that the authors of a *Harvard Law Review* parody of a murdered law professor's work should have been severely disciplined, and concluded: "The First Amendment simply cannot extend to expression which diminishes another's self-esteem." Kenny G. is from Seattle. "Louie, Louie" is often on the verge of being named the state song. When the *Seattle Times* published a front-page photograph of Kurt Cobain's dead body after his suicide, the executive editor wrote an interminable column about how the picture was not in fact sensationalistic (it wasn't). Seattleites use their seat belts more, return lost wallets more often, and recycle their trash more than people in any other city. Once a year, for twenty-four hours, thousands of people gather in the Kingdome to visualize world peace. In one of her weekly columns in the *Seattle Times*, psychologist Jennifer James explained that "women used to be attracted to big men because they could bring home meat and defend us against marauders," but "women are less likely to be battered by small partners," so she encouraged her readers to "reverse the current genetic trend and save the universe" by marrying "thoughtful little people." When people don't give money to beggars, they frequently say, "Sorry— no change today." When a restaurant closed, it put a sign in the window that said, "After twenty years of service to the community, we regret to inform our customers that we will be closed indefinitely"—twenty years of *service*. The most recent Republican (losing) candidate for mayor was a man who claims to have invented the happy face....

And what I love about the Supes, of course, is that they are not like this at all. So what does that make them? What does that make me in relation to them?

Speaking to reporters after practice, Karl says, "I bet I'm out of here [the NBA] in a few years, coaching somewhere else: college, back in Europe, maybe the CBA [the Continental Basketball Association, the NBA's minor league, in which Karl once coached]." A few days ago he said, "Coaches used to get rewards out of teaching, building the team, understanding character, and developing leadership. Now it doesn't seem like the little things of basketball are that important to many people. They're very important to coaches. We know the keys to success, but players don't understand them, and they don't want to hear about them. Discipline, commitment, trust—all those great words. They seem to have lost a little glory to the player. The players are so individualistic. The idea of a team isn't even in their thought process. They look at the team as their servant. The individuality factor is in our game because of money. A player's day is like a businessman's now: practice from ten to twelve, a meeting with a stockbroker at one, a meeting with TNT at two, dinner with his TV show host at four. It's made coaching into managing, and the best managers aren't coaches. Coaches are teachers and leaders." Before the season had begun, he had defined what the season is going to be about: all those great words.

Tonight, on *Seinfeld*, George says, "You know, if it's not about sports, I find it very hard to concentrate."

Jerry says, "You're not very bright, are you?"

George says, "No, I'm not. I would like to be. But I'm not."

Though I laugh, this stings: I used to read Proust, and now the crucial texts for me appear to be almost exclusively box scores and the accompanying articles.

11.8.94—In a packet of promotional material I receive about *Hoop Dreams*, the press release says: "Basketball has, over the past fifteen years, become America's most high-profile (and profitable) sport. Once culturally invisible, the NBA has become one of the decade's top international marketing successes, with this year's finals telecast in over one hundred nations around the world. The game has consciously made an effort to embrace the high-powered aggressive stylings of the 'street' game as played in America's inner cities, promoting the dominating, in-your-face approach of superstars like Michael Jordan and Charles Barkley." The press release trumpets the fact that these two realms—marketing success, the street game—exist in happy symbiosis; the movie demonstrates over and over that they don't. At the end of *Hoop Dreams,* William Gates, one of the two players whom the film has followed, says goodbye to his dictatorial high-school coach: "[At Marquette University] I'm going into communications, so when you start asking for a donation, I'll know the right way to turn you down."

On my way to a doctor's appointment, the East African cabbie says the most popular sport in East Africa is basketball. On my way back, the Israeli cabbie says the most popular sport in Israel is basketball.

.   .   .

On KJR, sports-talk radio nearly twenty-four hours a day and as such an
endlessly interesting essay on the rough patch of weather we white males
understand ourselves to be going through right now, a caller named
Keith, from Everett, says, "I know sometimes we all have a tendency to
overstatisticize; I don't know if that's a word or not, but—"

Mike Gastineau, sports talk-show host, says, "It should be. I kinda like
it. It sounds like: 'I went to the doctor and he needed to statisticize me.'"

Keith: "You just be sure to remind him to use a glove when he does
that, okay, Gas Man?"

Gas Man: "I hear you."

The Sonics' small-forward Detlef Schrempf's new tattoo is a 3" x 3" design
over his heart: an eagle, a lake, a forest, a sun, mountains. "Each symbol
stands for something," Schrempf explains. He was born and raised in Le-
verkusen, West Germany, though he attended high school in central
Washington and played college ball for the University of Washington. "It's
something I wanted to keep for the rest of my life. It shows some things
that I believe in. It has more to do with inner strength. If I do have some
doubt about certain things, I can look at myself and get the reassurance
of what I believe in." He also says, "I'm not a trash-talker. It's important
for us [the Sonics] not to have that label. Trash-talking can only hurt you.
It can never help you, with the referees, the crowd, anything. You can't
take away the vocal part of Gary [Payton]'s game. But there is a positive
way of doing it. Instead of directing it toward the opposing bench, he can
talk to himself or his teammates." Schrempf is such a Seattleite: *nature
is the one true source; impolite conversation is bad for you.*

The *San Diego Union-Tribune* reports that Shawn Kemp, the Sonics' star
power-forward, said—a month ago, at the time of his contract extension
and in reference to the trade that nearly sent him to Chicago in exchange
for Scottie Pippen—"We cleared the water under the table." What he
actually said was: "It was going to be hard for me to come in here and
worry about the trade and try to play ball. It's water underneath the
table. It's over with." In either case, it's not all that fascinating a statement, and the only reason the *San Diego Union-Tribune* is reprinting it

now, a month later, is to share a little unspoken joke with its readers regarding the fact that Shawn Kemp can't even keep his clichés straight: it's "cleared away the brush"; it's "water under the bridge"; it's "cards on the table."

11.9.94—At nine A.M., when, as instructed, I call the Sonics' director of media relations, Cheri White, to confirm my press credential for tonight's game against Sacramento, she informs me that "effective immediately," all reporters from "in-state weeklies"—a subset that includes, at most, half a dozen newspapers—will now be banned from the Sonics' locker room before and after games. Furthermore, there is no room for me in press row for tonight's game against the Sacramento Kings. Apparently, I erred by showing up in the locker room before and after the first game (the literary critic Roger Sale, who teaches with me in the English department at the University of Washington, had been covering the Sonics for the *Seattle Weekly* for the past twenty years and had never done this); the locker room is now said to be "too crowded." In September, I had approached the Sonics about spending the year with the team in order to write a book about them. My meeting with George Karl and Cheri White went well enough that they gave my project the go-ahead, but a week later someone higher up (Barry Ackerley? the general manager, Wally Walker?) said no, citing a need to "eliminate distractions." One of the reasons they felt a need to eliminate distractions was that a writer traveled with the team last year, when the Sonics imploded, and I now hear that his book on the '93–'94 season is being published this coming March. Hoping to get a galley copy, I call up the publisher, where a former student happens to be editing the book. I'm a little taken aback at how patronizing he is to me: he mentions titles of books about basketball I should read, professes his "admiration" for the region of the country in which I now happen to be living. What has *he* ever done, I wonder; what has he ever accomplished that he feels he can condescend to *me?*—which, of course, is exactly how athletes feel about sportswriters.

Standing in line at Safeway, I spot a *Sporting News 1994–95 Pro Basketball Yearbook* featuring Gary Payton on the cover. Inside is a long profile of Payton in which he says, regarding his tendency to talk trash, "I have to play that way. That's the way I grew up. That's what hypes me to play basketball. If I wasn't like that, I'd be another player just coming on the court. The emotion gets me hyper."

To the Safeway checker's question of "Paper or plastic?" the customer in front of me replies, "No thanks. I'm trying to save the forest." He then walks proudly out of the store, cradling nearly a dozen items in his arms. This sort of self-righteousness is commonplace here. It's gotten so bad that I find myself making it a point of perverse honor—in direct contradiction of local custom, and inevitably greeted with outright derision from my fellow pedestrians—to jaywalk if at all possible.

Which is why, in Seattle the Good, I so love Gary Payton. He's not really bad, he's only pretend-bad—I know that—but he allows me to fantasize about being bad. In "The Joy of Yap," an article about the Sonics that appeared in *Esquire* six months ago, Payton said, "I'm just the bad link in the whole thang. I'm the fucked-up crew. The mothers don't like me, but they gotta have me, man. I'm the Problem Child—that's what I am."

In the parking lot, when I punch the car alarm off, I inadvertently aim the remote directly at a black man with dreadlocks who is sitting in a car directly behind mine and looking right at me. As I leave the parking lot, he turns his thumb and index finger into a gun, winks, and shoots me in the head—which complicates things a little.

Adding Deputy District Attorney Christopher Darden to the prosecution team in the O.J. Simpson case, LA District Attorney Gil Garcetti acknowledges, "could very easily backfire. There could be a juror who says, 'Are you just bringing him on just because he's black?' The answer is obviously no." I'm struck by the fact that in all matters of human communication, when someone makes a point of announcing that something isn't so, it often means that it in fact is so; in matters of human communication relating to race, when someone makes a point of announcing that something isn't so, it means almost without exception that it in fact is so. It's Garcetti's repetition of the word *just*—"Are you just bringing him on just because he's black?"—that gives the game away.

• • •

For the Sacramento game I buy from Ticketmaster the best seat available, which is about fifty yards closer to the court than the press box is. An hour and a half before the game, Karl, wearing sweats, scrimmages with his second-string players. He's laughing and happy, throwing elbows, shoving, fouling. Walking back to the locker room, he's besieged by a dozen black kids seeking autographs, and their initial excitement quickly dissipates as the frightened—harried?—joylessness on his face keeps them at a remove. The kids say nothing as he signs. Karl says nothing as he signs.

Nearly all the head coaches are white; nearly all the refs are white; nearly all the fans are white; nearly all the reporters are white; nearly all the broadcasters are white (except for former players, who serve as "color commentators"); nearly all the owners are white; nearly all the players are black. Unable to find my seat, I approach an official-looking young black man, whom I believe to be the usher. He levels me with a look and says, "I'm not no usher."

Before the game starts, I look through my binoculars at the fans in the front few rows: the women dress Catch Me–Fuck Me; beauty doesn't get to be with beauty: beauty marries money; paper covers rock.

When the players come onto the court for their pre-game warmups, the music on the PA system changes abruptly from Garth Brooks to Snoop Doggy Dogg (Payton's rap god).

Bobby Hurley, Sacramento's 6', 160-pound backup point-guard, the only white player on the Kings, was nearly killed in a car crash last year; after an enormous amount of rehab, he's now nearly completely recovered. Hundreds of articles have been written about his return from the near dead, and tonight he receives a loud ovation when he enters the game. He doesn't play many minutes and he plays without distinction, quickly committing a couple of turnovers, making a couple of good passes, hitting a shot or two. To my eyes, his teammates diss him a little; he's a cute mascot sitting at the end of the bench.

Payton gets his first technical foul in the first quarter when, after knocking over the Kings' Mitch Richmond, he stands over Richmond and briefly stares at him. In the third quarter, during a jump ball, Payton seems to taunt a Kings player, and since this is his second technical foul of the game, he's ejected. Kemp escorts him off the floor; on his way to the locker room, Payton kicks over a chair.

The Sonics are worse than any team I've ever seen at making good ball-fakes. When Gill fakes a pass or Kemp fakes a shot, my daughter, Natalie—one and a half—wouldn't fall for the fake. When backup point-guard Nate McMillan passes to someone, he always makes sure to look directly at him. The Sonics seem to feel that pretending to do something and then not doing it is sort of an unmanly thing to do.

Almost without exception, the Sonics are extraordinary athletes with relatively limited basketball skills. This is the kind of player Karl loves to have on his team—"greyhounds," he calls them—but then he complains that they don't play good fundamental basketball. The Sonics have no half-court offense, no outside shooters, no "go-to guy" (a player to rely upon in crucial situations). "My philosophy is simple," Karl recently explained. "Play harder and more intense and more aggressive for forty-eight minutes than any other team in the NBA. To do that, you need defensive principles and depth of talent. It's a hell of a philosophy. It's a fun philosophy."

The Sonics are one of the two or three deepest teams in the league. Tonight they almost do wear out Sacramento, as they wore out Utah in the first game, but Karl loves to make the game about "rotation," and as a result of his perpetual substitutions, the Sonics have no rhythm on the court. The Kings, by contrast, are in sync, are in a groove, are much more energetic, have "younger legs," are having a blast out there; Sacramento wins.

In the parking lot after the game, directly in front of me, a black girl and a fifty-year-old white man bump into each other. The man says, "Excuse me." The girl says, "I hope so."

11.10.94—After practice, Payton, speaking to reporters, claims that he was thrown out of the game last night for speaking to one of his own teammates: "The refs have got to understand who we're talking to. They're gonna try to make an example out of us. We're the known ones—me, Dennis Rodman, Charles [Barkley]; we're all gonna be focal points. Every ref is gonna say, 'We got Payton tonight; watch out for this, watch out for that.' They can call what they want to call; I'm not going to stop what I'm doing [talking trash]. That's my ballgame." Shortly after Payton was drafted by the Sonics in 1990, he told a Seattle reporter, "My brother and father were always telling me not to back down to anybody. That's where I got my verbal game, because I always had to talk to the older guys and prove myself to them." Last year, he said, "If someone says something to me, I'm going to yap. If something happens, and I feel like I'm going to talk, I'm just going to talk."

Karl says, "I don't think there's any question that there's a group of five or six players who probably have been laid out very strongly. Gary and I talked about it before the first game. The NBA doesn't want taunting to be abused or cause problems."

Rod Thorn, vice president of operations for the NBA, says, "We don't want taunting. If you're going to taunt somebody, you're going to get a technical foul. If you get another, you'll be kicked out of the game. When you embarrass or disrespect another player, it could lead to altercations. It's also a terrible image to all the kids out there who watch the game and try to emulate our athletes."

New York Knicks shooting-guard John Starks is quoted in the *Seattle Times* as saying: "I'm not worried about taunting rules because I don't taunt to nobody." This line, like Kemp's "water under the table" line, is unremarkable except for its odd locution ("taunt to"); otherwise, it, like Kemp's, wouldn't have appeared in print. In other words, under our breath, we're snickering a little at Starks, at Kemp—*good-naturedly, though!*

In a hurry at the supermarket, I go careening around an aisle with my shopping cart, and when I nearly bump into a checker stocking shelves, he says, with a completely straight face and expression, "Sorry." Is this Northwest irony? If so, it's dry as dirt.

Riding home on the bus with my groceries, I notice two punky kids standing in the gutter, waiting for the light to change in their favor. Instead of just continuing past them—he has plenty of room to drive by—the bus driver makes a particular point of braking, opening his window, informing them that he has the green light, and then driving on.

Four blocks from my house, I'm holding my bag of groceries, standing a foot from the curb, waiting for the light to change. Although the light is with her, the driver screeches to a halt, virtually commanding me—via an exaggerated hand gesture—to cross in front of her. The gesture conveys so much: she's never in a rush, she has no will, no ego; if my self-discipline is that poor, if my needs are that pressing, she'll help me out. I refuse to go. Instead, I practically scream at her until she eases the car forward, "What are you waiting for? *You* have the green light. Just go!"

Seattle's passive-aggressiveness intrigues as well as aggravates me; it is a kind of daily riddle.

11.11.94—Payton just won't let the topic die down. On the *Gary Payton Show,* broadcast live Monday and Friday mornings at 7:35 on KJR, he says, "You know, that first technical wasn't even necessary. Me and Mitch [Richmond of Sacramento] is real tight. When I looked at Mitch, he was holding his chest, so I asked was he all right and the ref went and called a tech, thinking like I was talkin' to him and it wasn't like that." I love the extremely plosive way Payton always says "that," and I'm curious where this sound comes from, what it alludes to, why it is so mysterious and resonant to me.

In her review in the *New York Times* of a book about Clarence Thomas' confirmation hearings, Margo Jefferson writes, "Henry Terry, who had been one year behind Thomas at Yale Law School, recalled that Mr. Thomas could sound dignified in the courtroom but 'profane, scatological, and graphic' with his pals. 'That's my boy,' said Mr. Terry when Anita Hill offered her testimony. 'That's him talking.'...How much of our public life must play hostage to private grudges? On the day he was confirmed, the forty-three-year-old Mr. Thomas told friends he planned to spend the next forty-three years of his life on the Supreme Court because it would take that long to get even. That's our boy." This review is completely about itself—the ethnic identity of the reviewer (Margo Jefferson is black) and the timing of the review (until now, until right now, until today, or so it seems, the word wouldn't have appeared in print in this context, carrying in its train as it does so much blood of American history).

·   ·   ·

In regard to coaching pro players when he served as an assistant coach for Dream Team II, the group of NBA All-Stars that won the gold medal in the World Games in Toronto this summer, Providence College coach Pete Gillen says, "It's like, 'Larry Johnson, will you kindly think about rising and getting a rebound?' I don't want to get him mad. He might buy Providence [College] and fire me." The players are de facto owners; the coaches are de facto slaves; it's the history of the country turned upside down.

A fan named Murray posts this message to the Sonics newsgroup on the Web: "I was in Magnolia Hi-Fi yesterday in Bellevue [an affluent Seattle suburb] and saw Gary Payton. Just for the hell of it I had to ask him if anyone said he looked like Gary Payton. He said they say it all the time. Couldn't help but laugh."

In *USA Today* the trading-card company Skybox runs a full-page ad with the headline "Make the Trade of a Lifetime." In the 18" x 6" photograph, Shaquille O'Neal is thoroughly bug-eyed, and his tongue is sticking all the way out; he looks exactly like a toad. They couldn't have found a picture of him looking more inhuman if they had painted it themselves. The rest of the ad reads: "Send us your NBA Hoops Foil Wrappers along with a little cash, and we'll give you a limited-edition Shaquille O'Neal press sheet. Here's your chance to make the trade of a lifetime. A few measly wrappers for the ultimate rapper, Shaquille O'Neal. (He's not too shabby a ballplayer, either.) A limited-edition, 100-card, uncut press sheet featuring Shaquille O'Neal at his rim-rattlin', shot-blockin' best. This larger-than-life tribute to Shaq..." It's a tough shtick he's signed on for; larger than life, he's also lesser than life: he's Superman, but he's also a toad. The coupon says, "Yes, this is a limited, one-time only, never-be-seen-again offer. No, you can't buy this press sheet anywhere else. Yes, this is a must-have, suitable-for-framing addition to your collection. No, you can't dunk as hard as Shaquille O'Neal." Which you find unforgivable, and for which the only known cure is: "Yes, please send me my limited-edition Shaquille O'Neal press sheet. I have included a check or money order for $15.50 (this includes shipping and handling) along with my 10 1994 NBA Hoops Series I foil wrappers."

· · ·

Cheri White, the Sonics' PR director, denies my request for a press credential to the Seattle-Phoenix game: "The press box is full." Someone in
the Sonics newsgroup is selling two tickets for tonight's game, so I grab
them. My neighbor Richard, a librarian at the University of Washington,
and I go together. He complains incessantly about the price of the ticket
(the only player he'd pay to see is Michael Jordan, who, conveniently, is
retired at the time), about the "skankiness" of the cheerleaders, about
the lack of basketball knowledge displayed by the people sitting around
us, about the wall-to-wall music, about the incessant promotional activities, about everything, but especially about the Sonics. Shawn Kemp
commits too many turnovers; Vincent Askew dribbles the ball too much;
Sarunas Marciulionis, who is Lithuanian and in his first year as a Sonic,
is a defensive liability; Sam Perkins is too slow: all of Richard's observa-
tions are inarguable, but his saying so turns me into a fierce Supes
defender. Richard, who plays pickup basketball three times a week at the
Y, believes he can shoot better than anyone out there, and the text
through which he filters all of the action on the floor is an article in
Sports Illustrated, which he's recently read, which he's actually brought
with him, and which—during the break between the first and second
quarters—he insists I read.

The first paragraph says: "Step back in time for a moment, back to the
NBA of the late 60's. In your mind's eye you can see Jerry West going up
for a jump shot with picture-perfect form. Now it's the 70's, and there's
Rick Barry coming off a pick. Move forward to the 80's, and there's Larry
Bird casually tossing in three-pointers. Listen closely and you can almost
hear the constant flick, flick, flick of the net as these players send the ball
through the hoop. . . . It's become increasingly clear that the NBA has
entered the Dunk Ages, an era when jamming the ball through the net is
far more glamorous than tossing it in from long distance. And while dunking is being elevated, outside shooting is becoming, if not a lost art, at
least a fading one." Well, this is getting interesting, I think: the equation
of the dunk with darkness; the apotheosizing of Jerry West, Rick Barry,
and Larry Bird—probably the three best white players in NBA history.

"Why do you think that is?" I ask. "Why do you think players don't
shoot as well as they used to?"

Richard goes into a bizarre shucking-and-jiving routine: "Well, when you go to play ball in the *ghet*-to, you gots to throw it *down*, not shoot it." At halftime, the black man sitting directly in front of us gets up and doesn't return for the second half. I'm half-tempted to run after him and explain that Richard's sentiments aren't my own, but I decide against. At the beginning of the second half, I focus my binoculars on press row, and contrary to Cheri White's claim, it's nowhere near full.

Two of the new rule-changes—disallowing "hand-checking" (the player guarding the ball is no longer allowed to dig his hand into the ball handler's waist or back) and moving the three-point line twenty-one inches closer to the basket—help the Sonics and Suns tie an NBA record for combined number of three-point attempts. Phoenix, playing without its two best players, Charles Barkley and Kevin Johnson, spaces the court better, passes better, and is ahead for most of the evening; Seattle's superior defense just does manage to wear down the outmanned Suns.

After the game, driving home with Richard, I hear Marques Johnson, a former NBA star who is now the Sonics' color commentator, say on the radio: "It seems Gary Payton must have gotten the message from his ejection Wednesday [against Sacramento], because he demonstrated exemplary behavior out there tonight." Johnson, new to the Sonics' broadcast team this year, is making clear that he thinks the NBA rules are just fine and should be followed, i.e., he doesn't want Richard to hate him too much.

When I get home, Laurie asks why I didn't say anything to Richard when he went into his shucking-and-jiving routine, and I don't have an answer.

11.12.94—I pose these questions to Murray in the Sonics newsgroup: "When you said to Gary Payton that he looked like Gary Payton, did he know you were joking? Was it you who couldn't help but laugh or he? Did anything else happen? What was he buying? As you can tell, I'm a huge GP fan."

At the ferry terminal, going to my in-laws' for dinner on Bainbridge Island, I watch a black teenager—wearing Air Jordans and a Nike cap— sell copies of the *Seattle Times* to the cars in line. Suddenly, a Doberman barks ferociously at him from the back of a Jeep Cherokee. Air Jordan freezes. The owner doesn't get out of the Jeep but calms the dog down, smiling through the window and waving to the kid, telling him not to be scared, everything's okay. Air Jordan changes lanes. It simply would have been a different moment had the newspaper vendor not been black. The flushed embarrassment between the two people wouldn't have included what is to me the unasked but virtually audible question: whom had or hadn't the Doberman been trained to attack? Is this my own racist assumption, though, or am I just reporting what's there? I honestly don't know, which is what confuses and disturbs me.

11.13.94—Murray, from the Sonics newsgroup, replies, "I'm pretty sure Payton knew I was joking. Not sure what he bought because I didn't really want to bother him. I figure he didn't want someone asking him a bunch of questions and he didn't seem too talkative. He was there with a girlfriend (or is he married?)."

Cheri White grants me permission to sit in press row for the game tonight between the Sonics and Clippers. Why, I haven't the faintest; the mystery continues. There's something undeniably erotic to me about the way *ma chérie* teases and tortures and sometimes rewards. Driving to the game, I listen to *Sonics Rewind* on KJR—the week in review. I hear George Karl protest some more the NBA's stricter enforcement of its rules against trash-talking, then say, "But I'm not going to be a sociologist about it," which is an interesting way to both be and not be a sociologist about it. What I want him to say is, *The new rules are saying, "Stop your singing out there in the fields."*

When I arrive at my designated seat in press row for the Sonics-Clippers game, a guy from a radio station is sitting in the seat that has been assigned to me. Much more peremptorily than I ever would have before (I can't help it: I get off on being even the most microscopic part of athletic officialdom), I tell him, "This is my seat," and when he moves over but takes the folding chair with him, I tell him to return the chair, and he obeys. I feel the cheap thrill of dominion.

I find it impossible not to watch Gary Payton; my binoculars are always trained on him. Payton's the only player wearing black shoelaces.

He has a shaved head, a thin moustache, a goatee, and an inordinately long, muscular neck, like a brachiosaurus. (In his freshman year at Oregon State, when a University of Oregon male cheerleader called him "Hookhead," Payton took the gum out of his mouth and threw it at him, hitting him in the face.) He wears long baggy shorts and gold earrings. He has a luminous smile, even when he's faking it, and sharp cheekbones; according to Laurie, he's "very handsome, obviously."

In the second quarter, Karl calls out, "Get up, get up," urging his players to pressure the ball at the top of the key. A couple of players move to do this until Payton shouts, "No, no, no," and they all go back to where they were.

A group of young women strut around during halftime. They're not groupies, precisely, or at least most of them aren't, but the explicitness with which they place their wares on display—the self-conscious packaging of their own bodies—is startling to me. The women, showing off their bodies, with dollar signs in their eyes; the players, showing off their bodies, with dollar signs in their eyes: this level of explicitness about bodies and money is weirdly exciting to me. When I get home and mention this to Laurie, she says that I just never spent any time in singles bars; apparently, that's how everyone there dresses.

So, too, during timeouts, there isn't anything else to do, so though I feel somewhat guilty about doing this, I inevitably find myself locking my binoculars on the Sonics Dance Team. To be a pure body like this, to be looked at this way, to be adored and reviled for being so young, so physical, so unabashedly a body...

Toward the end of the fourth quarter, newcomer benchwarmer Byron Houston finally enters the game. I'm listening to the game on a Walkman from press row. Dave Harshman, who replaces Marques Johnson as color commentator for about a dozen low-profile games and is a former Sonics assistant coach, says, "We need a nickname for Byron. We don't have one yet. We need to see him in action first, get a sense of his spirit, his rhythm."

Kevin Calabro, the Sonics' play-by-play broadcaster, says, "Our producer just gave us a nickname for him; we're not going to say it—nothing derogatory, mind you, but we're not going to say it on the air."

Calabro and Harshman are laughing so hard they can't speak.

After a while, Harshman recovers enough to say, "Anatomically correct, though."

I'm dying to know what nickname they've come up with, and given all
the recent discussion in the media about Milwaukee Bucks rookie Glenn
"Big Dog" Robinson's contract negotiations, I have a mad moment,
blessedly brief, when I'm positive I know what it is: "Big Dong." Cf. the
Richard Pryor joke: "You ever heard? The niggers had the biggest dicks
in the world and they were trying to find a place where they could have
their contest, see. And they wasn't no freaks; they didn't want everybody
looking. So they were walking around, looking for a secret place. So they
were walking across the Golden Gate Bridge and the nigger sees that
water and it makes him want to piss, see. One said, 'Man, I got to take a
leak.' He pulled his thing out and was pissing. Other nigger pulled his
out and took a piss. And one nigger says, 'Goddamn, this water cold.'
Other nigger says, 'Yeah, and it's deep, too.'"

The Los Angeles Clippers are much the worst team in the league, but
for two-and-a-half quarters the Sonics can't pull away. As usual, the Sonics' bench strength—they regularly use ten players, whereas most other
teams usually use only seven or eight—wears down the opponent, and
Seattle winds up winning easily. Reserve small-forward Vincent Askew
scores a career-high twenty points. Since Askew plays the violin, he's
nicknamed the Fiddler—one would think his nickname might be the
Violinist, but that's simply not the way sports nicknames work—and
though fans continually beseech him to play the national anthem before
a game sometime, he always figures out a way to avoid doing this, which
I admire.

On the post-game show on the radio, a kid calls up and wants to know
Gary Payton's stats for the game.

"Is that all you care about—stats?" Calabro asks, pretending to be
irritated.

"Only Gary's," the kid squeaks, and *instantaneously* I get goose
bumps: what is it about Gary that moves me so much?

11.14.94—Over the next five nights the Sonics will be playing four games
in New Jersey, Boston, Milwaukee, and Indiana. Among players, journalists, and fans, much is made of the difficulty a West Coast team is likely

to experience on a trip "back East." Charles Barkley, who grew up in Alabama, played in Philadelphia for a few years, and for the last several years has played in Phoenix, recently quoted approvingly the former Boston Celtics star John Havlicek's observation that players in the West are "softer" than players in the East because Angelenos wake up to sunshine and Bostonians wake up to snowdrifts. It's amazing to me how thoroughly this myth persists throughout all levels of the culture. I grew up on the West Coast, spent most of my adult life on the East Coast, and now live again on the West Coast. I know people from all over, and most of them have moved around the country quite a lot, as have most professional athletes; none of the Sonics, for instance, is from the Northwest. I'm not in the habit of judging people according to their softness or toughness, but I've found that whether or not they shovel snow from their sidewalk bears no correlation whatsoever to their intestinal fortitude.

Laurie and I take Natalie for her first swimming lesson, which is not so much a lesson as a way for children, ages one to four, to get used to the water. A few minutes into the lesson, a little black girl cannonballs into the shallow end. Each child is supposed to be accompanied by a parent in the pool, and the girl is actually enrolled in the more advanced class that starts after this class, but the instructor spends virtually the entire half-hour playing with this girl rather than trying to teach any of the other children anything. Laurie and I smolder over the fact that the instructor didn't have the nerve to tell the girl to get out of the pool and wait until it was time for her lesson. Later, when I complain, I'm informed that the girl was accompanied by her grandmother, who can't swim; that the girl has been taking swim lessons from this instructor since she was an infant and was so happy to see the teacher—whom she hadn't seen for six months—that she jumped in the pool; that the instructor decided to let her stay rather than risk creating an argument. I feel like a shmuck for having said anything.

A former graduate student of mine is working as "content editor" and liaison between Microsoft and the NBA for a series of CD-ROMs about the NBA. So far he says his instructions from the NBA have been: "Drop

Dennis Rodman from the list of one hundred best players. No images of players fighting. No mentions of drug addiction. No backboard smashing in the product. No gangster aesthetic."

I respond to Murray in the Sonics newsgroup: "Payton's married, or at least he was engaged to be married a year or so ago; they have two kids. What impressions if any did you have of the woman he was with?"

Happy day! O happy day! I walk across the street when the light is red. Two teenage girls on the other side of the street follow suit, and as they pass me, they look at me with the purest expressions of gratitude and delight: *hey, this is fun; down we slide the slippery slope of moral ambiguity; we're killing our parents next...*

11.15.94—A plumber installs a new hot-water heater, and while he's wheeling the old one out to his truck, I ask him what he does with it. He says, "Take it back to the shop. These black guys come by for scrap metal. Every now and then I tip them a little something. I saw them today at Burger King, so I bought them each a ninety-nine-cent Whopper."

A woman calls KJR to complain that she brought six children—it's unclear if all six children are hers—to a Sonics promotional event to get Shawn Kemp's autograph. He is the "children's hero, he is their role model," but Kemp shows up late and leaves early, and the kids go home without an autograph and in tears. She says that all the children now hate Shawn Kemp and wish the Sonics had traded him to Chicago for Scottie Pippen.

Murray replies to me: "I only saw her later (she was with him when he was at the counter). I talked to him in the TV section while he was waiting for a clerk. Kind of funny that at first I thought it was a guy—the hair, I guess (I think they call it a fade). Not really my type."

Due to health problems arising from a nearly fatal car accident, George Raveling, the second black man ever to become head coach of a major-college basketball team (at Washington State University twenty years ago), resigns from his job as head coach at the University of Southern

California. In an article about his resignation, he's quoted as having once said: "Where I grew up, we used to steal things that began with 'A'—a television, a radio, a watch." Another article describes him as being "known for his vivaciousness." I've always liked George Raveling, not least because when he was coaching at the University of Iowa in the late '80s, my first novel, *Heroes*—which is about a white sportswriter's vicarious relationship with a white college basketball player whose goal in life is to become black—was published in paperback, and the owner of a bookstore in Iowa City told me that Raveling loved the book; whenever he visited the store, he'd always buy at least one copy.

I went to graduate school in Iowa City, at the Iowa Writers' Workshop, where the most fanatical thing I did, other than write *Heroes,* was attend University of Iowa basketball games. My closest friend at Iowa, Daniel, liked to talk about how, throughout his childhood, whenever he'd hear his parents screaming at each other in the next room, he'd just stare at the Knicks game on the little black-and-white TV at the edge of his bed and wonder what it would be like to be Walt Frazier. In the spring of 1980, when Iowa beat Georgetown to qualify for the Final Four tournament, Daniel and I jumped up and down and cried and hugged each other in a way we wouldn't have dreamed of doing otherwise. A famous writer would come to town to give a reading on the same night as, say, the Iowa-Indiana game, and it wouldn't even occur to us to worry about which event to attend. One of the happiest moments of my life occurred when Daniel, and several other people from the Writers' Workshop, came to the gym to play basketball. I was already on the court: out on the wing on a fast break, I caught the ball, reverse-spun on William Mayfield, who started at forward for the Iowa basketball team, and beat him to the hoop. (Was he dogging it? Who knows? I don't want to know.) Daniel and the other graduate students went absolutely nuts; they all kept saying, "You don't even look like a basketball player!" Glasses, love handles, etc.

That same year Leonard Michaels gave a guest workshop, discussing my (autobiographical) short story, which was about playing on an otherwise all-black junior high school basketball team, and Daniel's (autobiographical) short story, which was about getting held up by a group of black teenagers in a subway car. Michaels explained that racism consists precisely of the impulse to generalize, which in his opinion both of our stories, in their different ways, did. He then asked, "What's this thing going on here, anyway, between Jewish men and black men?" Mock-naive, as if he were unaware that the question itself was a generalization...

"You could, you know," Laurie points out, "just obey the traffic laws. Is that even a possibility? I mean, it's kind of a simple solution, don't you think?"

When I'm out and about with Laurie and Natalie, I wait for the green light and cross at the crosswalk, but when I'm walking around by myself, I find it literally impossible not to violate the rules of the road.

On TV I watch the Sonics lose to the Nets in New Jersey. Payton plays only twenty-eight minutes before fouling out, so he's fouled out or been thrown out of two of the five games so far—the two they've lost.

After the game, former Sonic Benoit Benjamin, who had a good game with thirteen points and nine rebounds and whom Karl used to call "lazy," says about Karl: "He'll never win nothing. He's a loser and always will be. I watched them on TV in the playoffs against Denver and I laughed and laughed. I don't like him. He has personal vendettas on players for no reason." Karl does seems to have a weird need for a new villain each season: World B. Free in Cleveland; Joe Barry Carroll in San Francisco (Karl ripped the door off Carroll's locker after he said he didn't think the Warriors could beat the Lakers); Benjamin, Derrick McKey, Dana Barros different years in Seattle.

On the post-game show, Karl tells Calabro: "I'll be honest with you, Kevin." When most people say, "I'll be honest with you," it means they're lying, but in Karl's case it actually means, I think, he's telling the truth. "Since Grg [assistant coach Tim Grgurich] left, our concentration and mental intensity has not been bad, but not at the level we need to play at. I've told all the guys, you know, a key to our basketball team is defense, and a key to our basketball team is intensity. And everybody goes, 'Well, Coach, all coaches say that.' That's not true. I coached a team at Golden State where intensity was not a part of our personality. But this team, for it to play at its top-notch quality, has got to have an attitude. We don't have a bad attitude, but we don't have the big-time attitude that we had last year. I think it's a combination of a lot of stuff—a long training camp, Grg leaving, the rule-changes messing with us a little bit. We don't know how aggressively we can play. We've got a long season ahead; we just gotta figure it out."

The first four home games I felt exceedingly disconnected from the game. Was it the drive to Tacoma, the sterility of the Tacoma Dome, the terrible view afforded from the nosebleed section of press row, their uninspired play? Just watching the games was more fun last year, when the players were holograms to me and my identification was total. My (very brief, very partial) peek behind the curtain this year has eliminated that for me. I want to get my basketball jones back. I want the Supes to convey something amazing to me again. I'm now watching the games with a notepad and a pen in my hand; I can't get truly into it this year; I can't root for them the way I did last year. I thought it was my own failure to connect, but no, I realize with relief when I hear Karl's comments on the post-game show, my distance is their distance: *it's their fault.*

They were—they are—feeling it, too. They're still not over the psychic wound that was last year's collapse: after winning more games than any other team in the regular season, the Sonics became the first number-one seed in NBA history to be eliminated in the first round of the playoffs by the number-eight seed, the Denver Nuggets. Over the last six months there has been too much talk about players who were traded (Dana Barros, Michael Cage, Ricky Pierce) or nearly traded (Kemp, Gill); too much talk about three front-office departures: Bob Whitsitt, Tim Grgurich, and Bob Kloppenburg. Whitsitt, '93–'94 NBA Executive of the Year, left to become general manager of the Portland Trailblazers. Grgurich, who served as buffer between the players and Karl, left to become head coach at the University of Nevada at Las Vegas. Assistant coach Kloppenburg, who coordinated the defense—too assertively for Karl's liking—got kicked upstairs. The Sonics seem self-conscious to me now in the way a couple does that has broken up but gets back together: unable to feel much anymore after they've talked the fucking thing to death.

Suddenly I'm crazy about George Karl, because he saw what was there and said it.

2

EVERYONE ELSE IS THEY

11.16.94—Or so I feel until I bump up against the implications of such sentiments in the form of a *New York Daily News* column by Mitch Lawrence about the Sonics-Nets game, which a friend faxes me and which seems racially coded: "Karl, a very good coach, goes against the conventional thinking by refusing to establish a go-to player on offense. The result is that there are games like last night when the Sonics take bad shots, have no flow, and play like a 36-win team. As if those aren't enough potentially fatal flaws for one team, the Sonics are built around three talents (Shawn Kemp, Gary Payton, and Kendall Gill) who rival the nuttiest Nets in the knucklehead department. Kemp's low-post game is based solely on athleticism. When it comes to actual basketball moves, it is strictly primitive. Payton talks tough to everyone but has to learn that passing for an assist goes a lot farther than trashing an opponent. Gill is a great talent who thinks he is a great player. The critical difference is often lost on him. Nice troika."

My friend Philip e-mails me: "Are you familiar with the UC Berkeley sociologist Harry Edwards? He has talked about how the white world has turned from the old view ('Black man is subhuman; he can't play with me') to the new view ('Black man is superman; I can't play with him').

Either way, Edwards says, we refuse to see the black man as a man, as a simple human being. Either way, we can't even begin to handle him as an equal." Speaking of which: when I'm jogging around my neighborhood—Wallingford, a lily-white, New-Agey district of Seattle—I often slow to a snail's pace and really pick it up only when a black motorist drives by, because I don't want him to think I'm some boring white guy with no get-up-and-go.

On the tube: Boston 120, Seattle 93. The Sonics shoot only 38 percent from the floor and are outrebounded 55–40. The entire Sonics starting team has only one steal (usually their forte). After the game, Karl tells reporters, "Other than after the Denver loss, I haven't felt like this during my time in Seattle."

Hosting the post-game show, Mike Gastineau—who prides himself on being the Voice of Reason, who in fact is usually quite reasonable, and whose hyper-rationality sometimes drives me crazy in the same way that Laurie's does in its indefatigable allegiance to the empirically verifiable—with uncharacteristic hyperbole calls the game against Boston "the most disappointing defeat in the George Karl era. I realize they're only six games into the season, but I think that loss against Denver last year has taken a tremendous lot of confidence out of this team. That was as big a professional embarrassment you as a professional athlete could have had—losing to Denver the way they did [after being ahead 2–0 in a best-of-five series, the Sonics began squabbling with each other and lost the next three games], and it may take them a while to get over it."

11.17.94—In the *Seattle Times*, Glenn Nelson writes: "Lacking the three-point shooting every other team seems to have, they [the Sonics] have tried, as they have in the past, to rely on defense. Yet, with the ban on outside contact [the ban on hand-checking], their defense has lacked aggression and is no longer a catalyst of their offense. It's a vicious cycle. Seattle defenders now seem gun-shy because they're wary of foul trouble. The rules probably aren't totally accountable for the Sonic malaise, but they've had an undeniable effect. No Sonic has been more affected than Payton, who typically has used his ballhawking to stoke every other part of their game. Add the crackdown against trash-talking to the hand-checking rules, and the league essentially has legislated Gary Payton out of the game."

The subhead on the *Esquire* article six months ago was: "Cover your ears. Hide your women. And be prepared to get trash-talked to death. The SuperSonics are coming to your town, and they're gonna bust a move on your sorry ass."

What is being legislated against is being sold is what we fear is what we love—is that clear?

After practice on an off day in Indianapolis, Nate McMillan, the team's co-captain, tells a reporter, "There's no communication, no talking amongst each other. It's like we have nothing to say. No matter how much talent we got, if we don't play together and have fun, you've got a major problem."

Schrempf says, "We don't move the ball, don't set picks, don't run the play, don't take good shots, don't rotate the way we're supposed to on defense."

Payton says, "We come out every night and we're down 30. Every fuckin' night. I don't know what I'm supposed to be doin' with this team. When I go out every night, I'm not happy. I'm not happy with myself. I have to get myself straight first. I'm going to find a solution." Payton, unlike other players, is almost always willing to point the finger at himself.

I e-mail Philip: "Did you take a class with Harry Edwards at Berkeley?"

One of the surprises to me of adulthood is how important money is—the degree to which feelings, in a marriage, flow through money. Feeling guilty that I'm going to be gone so many nights over the next six months at Sonics' "home" games forty miles away in Tacoma, I spend too much money on Laurie's birthday, e.g., buying her a Coach bag. She feels appreciated; she gets dressed up; she looks great; we go out to dinner; we make love, though that's not quite the right term—it's more like fucking: a rough physicality that I realize later is my attempt to imitate the athletes I spend so much time watching and thinking about.

·   ·   ·

11.18.94—How to explain the general tendency of Seattle motorists to refuse to pull over for ambulance, fire, and police sirens? In larger cities, there's never any room, so no one even pretends to try to get out of the way; here, the traffic is only occasionally that congested, and yet cars rarely edge to the right curb, let alone stop. I'm ecstatic about this weird contradiction of the Northwest's polite humanitarianism, until Laurie comes up with a simple and convincing explanation: everybody has the music in their cars cranked so loud that they can't hear the sirens.

Before their game against the Indiana Pacers in Indianapolis, the Sonics hold a players-only meeting at which they discuss the importance of maintaining better communication with each other on the floor. Payton and Kemp each meet separately with Karl. In general, the team plays better than it did against New Jersey or Boston, showing more life and enthusiasm, but again shoots poorly and again loses.

"We're all right," Payton says afterward. "We made changes."

"If we had the effort the first two games of the trip we had tonight, we probably would have won one, maybe two of them," Karl says. "The team you saw play tonight is going to win a lot of games."

It's gotten so bad that we're relieved they even came close.

On the post-game show, Marques Johnson asks Karl, "You took Shawn [Kemp] out when he committed his fifth foul with about three-and-a-half minutes left and didn't put him back in. Did you feel he was pressing a little bit tonight? He had some turnovers down the stretch in pretty key moments." Kemp is from Elkhart, Indiana; he always seems to try too hard against the Pacers. As a result, the Sonics usually struggle against Indiana.

Karl answers, "Oh, I'm not going to talk about why I do certain things, you know." Karl resents being quizzed by Johnson, who played in the NBA for thirteen seasons, averaged more than twenty points a game, and was a five-time All-Star, but who has never coached. "That's, I think, a little bit of a family situation with the team." ("Family," in Karl's lexicon, is virtually synonymous with "internal squabbling": *you won't be privy to our internal squabbles.*) "We got to get some discipline to our game in clutch situations."

So, despite protestations to the contrary, Karl winds up (obliquely) answering Johnson's question; he inevitably answers almost every question. As his wife, Cathy, says, "He doesn't know how to duck a question; it's just not part of his character," which makes him likable but vulnerable, needy. He's a bad bluffer, a weak politician; he craves approval, and it shows.

On the post-game call-in show, Doug, from Tacoma, says, "This team, when it looks to George Karl, doesn't give him too much respect. Whenever they talk about him, they think of him as sort of a nuisance, not as their coach who's trying to help him. I've noticed that." Is Doug right? I find that I'm constantly monitoring my reactions to Karl, namely, is any too thoroughgoing identification with Karl—and antipathy toward the players—(poorly) disguised racism? Karl is five years older than I am and considerably stouter, more easily and directly moved by the music of Crosby, Stills, Nash & Young; still, the easiest, the laziest, the grumpiest thing in the world to do is to agree with him. What I'm interested in is my capacity to identify with Gary Payton, since it's more difficult and, in a sense (the sense that romance is by definition difficult), romantic.

So much of what I admire about Payton is the indivisibility for him of playing and talking, of life and language. He doesn't see them in binary opposition, whereas I tend to, due, I think, to my lifelong stutter (considerably mitigated as an adult, but certainly still a significant stigma to me). "In Oakland, the players were on you," he said a few years ago. "The refs were on you. The stands were on you. You had to talk back or you were a sissy; you'd get run out of the league." His high-school coach, Fred Noel, pressed the point even further: "The Oakland Athletic League is really intense because it's a community thing. Guys living in the same neighborhood are playing for different schools, so there's a lot of taunting back and forth, a lot of putting my reputation against your reputation. There's a lot more at stake. In Oakland, talking is at least as important as playing the game."

I call and ask KSTW for a tape of Payton's two-minute interview of an opposing player on *SST: Sonics Show Time,* a half-hour TV show that I missed last Saturday. I say I want to do a piece for the *Weekly* on Gary Payton's language, and the production assistant I speak to says, "Is this going to be a positive piece?"

"Positive?" I say. "It's going to be a love letter."

· · ·

Somebody who calls himself Weebday posts to the Sonics newsgroup: "Being on the East Coast now, I don't get to see much of the Sonics anymore, but from what I read, it seems like they've slipped a notch from last year. How is that guy who got hired to baby-sit Kemp doing?" Virtually every NBA team has a white coach and (out of three assistant coaches) one black assistant coach, who acts as mediator between players and coach. Paul, my friend and former graduate student, calls these black assistant coaches "lawn jockeys." The Sonics' new black assistant coach, Dwane Casey, "who got hired to baby-sit Kemp," recruited Kemp to the University of Kentucky for the brief time Kemp was there before leaving.

Louis replies to Weebday: "Regarding Casey baby-sitting Kemp, that has yet to be determined. I don't think he or any other Sonics need to be treated like babies. If your only source of info about the Sonics is ESPN or some East Coast newspaper, that is all you will hear. You will probably also hear that they are still fighting, that Karl is going to be fired, and Payton, Kemp, and Gill are going to be traded for Nick Van Exel. Be careful what you hear from these sources; they are seldom correct." East is to West as white is to black; the former, understanding itself to be civilization, views the latter as a vast wilderness.

Philip e-mails back to me: "Yes, I took Edwards' sociology class at Berkeley. That's where he made that point (about subhuman, superhuman). The class, though, was a joke; he laments how schools coddle athletes and then teaches a class an eight-year-old could ace." Does Philip hear how condescending he's being to Edwards, and how closely related this is to the "subhuman/superhuman" idea he just mentioned? I can't tell.

A black teenager in a blue Camaro careens through Wallingford at fifty miles an hour—double the speed limit. Two moms, watching their kids at Wallingford Park, scream at him, "Slow down!" He flips them off and guns it through a stop sign.

11.19.94—Returning to last year's more aggressive offensive schemes and finally adjusting to this year's defensive rule-changes, the Sonics shoot a season-high 56 percent from the field and make 19 steals. Final score: Seattle 120, Milwaukee 96. Payton scores 25 points, most of them against the Bucks' younger, smaller point-guard, Lee Mayberry, and in the post-game interview Marques Johnson runs endless riffs on the metaphor "you took Mayberry to school": e.g., you not only took him to school, you tortured him during recess; you not only tortured him during recess, you ate him for lunch; etc. One of the tensions of the interview is that Johnson is trying to get Payton to acknowledge that he completely dominated Mayberry, which Payton won't do, because it's part of the athletic ethos to be mock-humble after you've dismantled the opposition. Johnson knows this, of course; he's just teasing Payton. What's even more interesting is the way that Johnson, in his first month as the Sonics' color commentator, has calculated precisely how much "blackness" to display: just enough to draw out Payton a little and let us—the overwhelmingly white audience back home in Seattle—feel the lure of the lingo but not so much that we feel intimidated, alienated, whiter than white.

Payton tells Johnson: "We went into a meeting yesterday and what we said we had to do was make the game more fun. So I decided in the hotel I got to come out more aspirited for the team to get into a groove. What we did was we passed the ball, got it to open guys, we wasn't selfish, we wasn't trying to play against five or six people, we did a great job, and once that happens our team is gonna click."

"We wasn't trying to play against five or six people" means that each Sonic wasn't trying to take the ball and do everything himself against the opposition, but the other team couldn't have more than five people on the floor, so what could "six people" possibly refer to? Payton often manages to leave open to interpretation some little enigma like this.

11.20.94—"Last week I was walking back to the office from the bank downtown when I came to stop beside a woman waiting for a light to change," Jerry Large writes in his column in the *Seattle Times* today. "She glanced at me, then took her purse off her shoulder and wrapped the strap tightly around her one hand. We went a couple of blocks at the same pace. She seemed to be sneaking more frequent looks my way, so I figured she was getting nervous and considered taking another route. I don't want to make someone nervous, and this kind of thing happens all the time, so I've gotten into the habit of walking a little faster or turning a block before I want to, but I was feeling perverse, so I kept walking. It's a free country. After about three blocks, she took one last look at me and ran across a street against the light. I hadn't even said boo. And she was a lot bigger than me. People, it's not me who's scary, it's those other black folk."

A few years ago, Laurie and I were walking around downtown Seattle late at night, when a black man and black woman jumped out from behind a bush. Laurie visibly recoiled, and the man immediately accused her of being afraid of black men. "No," she said, "I'm afraid of people jumping out from behind bushes," and we resumed our separate journeys.

11.21.94—Weary of wrangling with the Sonics every game for press credentials (it doesn't help that I've yet to write word one about the Sonics for the *Weekly*), denied access before and after every game to all members of the team (ditto), and exiled to the top tier of a press row that is already an eternity away from the action (ditto), I decide to stand up on my hind legs and bark. I buy a pair of season tickets from a coffee salesman who, dropping off the tickets, pulls up in a tan Mercedes and informs me that he just came from meeting with the owner's son, Ted Ackerley, to discuss the decor of the suite he and some of his friends are buying next year for $120,000 when the Sonics return to a refurbished Seattle Coliseum. The seats I'm buying are twelve rows up from the floor; he paid $4,800 and is charging me $3,500—about $45 for each ticket for the thirty-seven remaining regular-season home games. Borrowing the money on my credit card, I am, as they say (as my English department comrades would say), "invested": I worry that the Sonics are going to be lousy this year; that they already are lousy this year; that no one is going to want to go with me all the way to Tacoma for the games; that I've backed a loser and therefore am a loser; that so far from writing the chronicle of a championship, I'm keeping tabs on a journey to the end of night. I imagine running out the door and begging the coffee salesman to give me my money back, but looking out the window, I see that his tan Mercedes is long gone. When Laurie comes home from work, I convolutedly explain to her why I felt I had to buy the tickets, but I can't help knocking five hundred dollars off the sale price.

•   •   •

I drive seventy miles south to Olympia to give a lecture at Evergreen
State College. After the lecture, I catch up with my former graduate
student who is now teaching there, and for some reason, quite surprisingly and suddenly, the conversation turns intimate. She tells me over
and over how frustrated she is that she's not writing, which she blames
on the fact that she married a "companion," a fellow "artist," when she
could have married one of the yupsters who were courting her in LA
(she's stunning). She's married to a friend, she says, and now wants—she
puts it in caps—A HUSBAND. What is this—flirtation? game theory?
bloodletting? I'm not sure, but one thing I seem to be homing in on
about early-middle-age is everyone's quiet astonishment that *this is my
life, this is actually it, this is the warp-and-woof I've knitted,* and you can
kill everything with regret.

When I get back home from Olympia, both Laurie and Natalie are
already asleep. I'm restless, so I rent *The Program* from a video store
around the corner. *The Program* is an almost unimaginably bad movie
about the various medical, familial, and ethical obstacles surmounted by
the stars of a college football team. However, there's a very interesting
moment for me toward the very end of the movie, when Eastern State
University is playing its archrival, and I realize that the only reason I'm
rooting for ESU rather than the other guys is that for the previous hour
and a half I've been watching ESU players' life-stories. This realization
should have been self-evident and yet I feel like I finally understand why
we root for our team rather than their team: we've gotten to know these
guys; we know their hobbies, their personalities, their speech patterns,
little details about their families and favorite restaurants. Cf. Rudyard
Kipling: "All the people like us are We, / And everyone else is They."
Whenever I watch a Sonics game on TV with my former student Paul, he
seems to go out of his way to compliment good plays by the other team,
and I always want to ask him: is it a conscious effort on your part to not
succumb to jingoistic cheering, or are you constitutionally incapable of
the monomania required? I admire his equanimity, but I can't even pretend to emulate it, which is to say: ersatz though I know the cure to be
and unable to say exactly what the disease is, I want the Supes to cure me.

•   •   •

11.22.94—On the front page of the Metro section of the *Post-Intelligencer* is a color photograph of a beautiful blonde woman kissing her husband, a handsome black man, as he steps ashore after a three-month tour of duty with the Coast Guard. Although both have their eyes closed, what I feel, looking at their lips about to touch, is the almost unbearable heat on both of their parts of longing for his/her opposite: for three months both were trapped within themselves, and for each of them this otherness, this strangeness, this difference is screaming to the surface *right now*.

I can't find anyone to go with me to tonight's game against New Jersey. At the last minute, Paul says he can go, so I pick him up in the University District and off we head to Tacoma. Driving south on I-5 to the game, I'm struck by the exceedingly odd habit so many people here have of nodding at you as they pass by. What is the derivation of this smiley-face cheerfulness? I don't know, but it ain't me, it ain't mine, and I ain't participating in it. Out of principle, I simply refuse to nod back, which, disappointingly, doesn't ever seem to unnerve them: if I want to be a sourpuss, that's my loss.

All the way down to Tacoma we talk about the crying jags Paul and his girlfriend have been having as they're trying to break up.

Although I received a Sonics media guide when I was masquerading as a journalist, I've already managed to lose it, so the first thing I do when I get to the Tacoma Dome is stand in line to get another one—which my season tickets entitle me to—at the Sonics Fan Information Booth. When I hand the woman behind the counter a cardboard card that I received along with my season tickets, she gives me the media guide. A black kid standing nearby witnesses this transaction and asks me, "Are those free?" Paul and I are in a hurry to get to our seats before the game starts, so I shake my head in a curt no, unintentionally suggesting colossal conspiracies he'll never understand, leaving him to ask the woman behind the counter why I received a media guide without paying any money while he, for the nth time, gets fucked over.

I'm relieved to find that our seats are as good as Mr. Coffee assured me they were: they really are only a dozen rows above the floor, behind the visitors' bench, parallel to the free-throw line on the north side of the court. You can't quite hear what players are saying, but almost; you're close enough to the court that you feel connected, in some visceral way, to the unfolding action. I love our seats and, stupidly, I want Paul to be impressed, which he is.

Kemp and New Jersey's Derrick Coleman are remarkably deferential to each other, talking, laughing, kidding each other, helping each other up, barely playing defense against each other. They played together in Toronto this summer on Dream Team II. Fans want to think it's us against them (Seattle vs. New Jersey, say) and that the players on "our" team are in cahoots with us, in some difficult-to-define way—difficult to define, since their contempt for us is so manifest. One of the things I've felt at the games so far is how bound together the five Sonics on the floor are with the five players on the floor for the other team, like boxers, and how the opposition is really the noise of everything else—coaches, refs, cameras, commercials, mascots, especially fans. The players are the ones sharing the jokes together at the foul line. Fans always want to ask Player X what he was saying out there on the court to Player Y. Player X always deflects the question, since it is, in a sense, a rude question. It's tantamount to asking lovers the content of their pillow talk: *it's our cama-raderie, not yours.*

Coleman's head is shaved completely bald, which in his case exaggerates his fiendish persona. (Since I have so little hair left, I cut my hair like that now, too, shaving it down to almost nothing, and when I walk around with my big black coat and sunglasses and my shaved head, I imagine maybe I look a little like a bad guy, and in narcoleptic Wallingford it passes, it passes.) Paul and I wonder who started the whole trend of bald black athletes—Kareem Abdul-Jabbar, Michael Jordan? We're pretty sure it's unrelated to swimmers shaving their heads in order to be more aerodynamic, and only by default (the pendulum swing of fashion) does it seem to undo Afros of the '60s and '70s. I say that cutting your hair off is often the prelude to doing something antisocial and scary (cf. Travis Bickle), and Paul agrees that it carries the unmistakable sign of imminent danger. As with the word *boy* or *nigger* or *queer* or Nazism's inverted pink triangle, a bald head transfigures someone else's stigma (prisoner? patient? soldier? slave?) into an insignia of cool badness.

Detlef Schrempf is spending the entire game complaining to officials, as he so often does. There's a certain justification to his whininess, since the call rarely goes his way; referees seem prejudiced against most white players, and particularly antipathetic toward foreign players. Fans love to say about white players, "He's good for a white guy," as a way to intensify our imaginary identification with black skin. (The cover of a popular birthday card reads, "Happy birthday to a great basketball player…" and inside the punch line is, "…for a white guy." *You're physical…but you're not only physical.*) Schrempf is married to a woman who is half-black, and he speaks in a fascinating blend of German accent and black dialect. He's an excellent player—he was named to the All-Star team a couple of years ago, when he played for Indiana—but because he doesn't look particularly graceful, referees can never believe that he actually accomplished what he accomplished, so they frequently call him for traveling on offense and for fouling on defense. In him is gathered the reverb of a racist society cordoning off one arena in which the people it has oppressed will succeed. How much of this does he recognize? How does he feel about this? Cheri White will make certain I don't have a clue.

A man is sitting behind his wife rather than next to her—those are their assigned seats—but no one has been sitting in the seat next to her all game long, so with my usual tact, when she gets up at halftime to go to the bathroom, I ask him, "Why don't you guys sit together?"

"She might yell at me," he says.

Paul and I laugh: *Women.*

The ex-Sonic Benoit Benjamin is playing tonight for the Nets. During the break between the third and fourth quarters, the Sonics' mascot, Sasquatch (local parlance for the Abominable Snowman), puts on a jersey with the number 00 and "Big Ben" on the front and proceeds to jump off a trampoline, but rather than dunking a mini-basketball in dramatic fashion as he usually does, he drops the ball, bangs his head against the backboard, and gets dragged off the court. It's a witty if cruel send-up of Benjamin's clumsy play when he was a Sonic, and the crowd cheers ferociously. Benjamin makes the mistake of watching the skit, at the end of which he forces the most readable of all rictus smiles. I'm close enough to him that I can see his eyes, and it's painful.

One summer a few years ago, I saw Big Ben standing in the middle of Broadway Market, a shopping mall on trendy Capitol Hill. He was encircled by an entourage, to whom he was handing out bills of various denominations, but no one else came up to him; a relatively recognizable and famous professional athlete was just being ignored in public, which had an eerie, poignant, and even slightly ominous aspect. He was traded shortly afterward.

The most gorgeous play of the game tonight is a backdoor lob from Payton to Kemp. For just a millisecond, Payton and Kemp are the only people in the arena who know the ball is going to be there, and then it is there, and Shawn dunks it easily. One moment, Kemp is standing next to Coleman; the next, his hand—surprisingly ordinary-sized, when I study it with my binoculars—is twelve feet above the floor, tapping the ball through the rim. How do Shawn and Gary communicate to each other the exact timing? Who knows? Paul and I high-five each other, somewhat self-consciously, since on a local version of *Saturday Night Live* called *Almost Live* there's a frequent feature called "High-Fivin' White Guys."

Sometimes the entire game, as it does tonight, can sway back and forth between bad calls and what in basketball (much more so than in any other sport, because it is so mercurial and therefore the referees must make hundreds of calls in the course of a game) are known as make-up calls. It's virtually an unwritten rule in the NBA that if a referee makes a bad call against a team, he quickly attempts to rectify the situation by making yet another bad call—this time on purpose—to benefit the aggrieved team. And now of course the other team is angry about the second call, so a make-up call of the make-up call ensues, and the entire evening can be spent this way. Life, as you may have heard, is not like this: Paul and his girlfriend don't get to be happy all next week just because they've been crying their eyes out this week.

With a minute and a half remaining and the Sonics ahead by only 5 points, thousands of fans stampede for the exits. One sees this phenomenon occur in all sports and in all cities. What's the rush? To be a serious fan is to acknowledge that this is a major access in your life to grace and transcendence; exiting with a minute or two left, and the outcome of the game still in doubt, is an attempt by people to announce to themselves and everyone else that the rest of their lives are really quite important after all.

The Sonics wind up winning by 7. Despite still shooting poorly, the

Sonics play well together and feel like a team to me for the first time this year. I wind up screaming so much that by the end of the game I've lost my voice, which Paul is slightly appalled by but which I take to be a good sign: I feel like a fan again, finally.

11.23.94—One of the very first words Natalie said was *ball,* and she sometimes plays catch with me, but I can't escape the suspicion that she does so largely to humor me, as women humor men in so many other ways. She likes to see me, as a boy, happy, so she tosses the ball back and forth to me for a while.

Despite my renewed enthusiasm, I can't find anyone who wants to go with me to any of the immediately forthcoming games, and I'm panicky again about the money I've spent, so I decide to place an ad to sell one or both tickets to some of the games. "You'd be lucky to sell them at any price," a guy in the *Seattle Times* classified ad department informs me. "They had three thousand empty seats last night. You better put 'best offer.' This team really pisses me off. I mean, they really get me angry. They got a couple of clowns running the show, a couple of prima donnas. Kemp is wearing those ridiculous shoes of his." Shawn's new shoes are called Kamikaze Kemps, which *are* pretty ridiculous: green-and-black high-tops with a web-like design across the top and the sides. "Gary Payton likes to buy $50,000 watches." A couple of years ago, when Payton was robbed at gunpoint, one of the items he lost was an extraordinarily expensive gold watch. "A couple of clowns running the operation. They don't have the faintest idea why they won sixty-three games last year, not the faintest iota of an idea. This team needs a leader. Great sports town—who's everybody most excited about? The Husky women, for winning the NIT [the University of Washington women's basketball team won the National Invitational Tournament last night]. That's who they're most excited about. Unbelievable." *Everyone else is They.*

The Sonics, down by twenty points in the first half to the Utah Jazz at Salt Lake, actually come back to lead by a few points early in the fourth quarter but wind up losing. Utah's Jeff Hornacek scores 40 points on 8-for-8 shooting from 3-point range. The Sonics are the second-worst team in the league at giving up 3-pointers, because Karl loves to double-team the ball, even if John Stockton, the best passer in the NBA, is dribbling it. On the post-game show, in response to Calabro's request that he compare Stockton and Kenny Anderson (the overheralded New Jersey Nets point-guard, who played poorly against the Sonics last night), Karl says, "The difference between John Stockton and Kenny Anderson is that if you gave John Stockton fifty basketball decisions, he'd probably pass the ball fifty times. Whereas Kenny Anderson needs to get some shots up. He needs to score to feel comfortable in the game."

Karl adores Stockton, but then so does everybody. Even Payton, at the end of every game against Utah (including tonight), makes a point of shaking Stockton's hand, a ritual he observes with absolutely no one else in the league. Since they play the same position, they guard each other, and Payton has called him "the best player I've ever played against in the pros. He plays defense, he's tricky, can handle the ball and pass, and makes the big shots. He's not real quick, but he's real smart." Which delights me, for some reason—the reason being that Stockton is white, 6'1", 175 pounds, and has brown hair: the player I can most easily imagine being. Perhaps Payton is only fattening Stockton up for the kill, but his regard actually seems quite genuine. Stockton is six years older than Payton, who, when he finds it deserved, maintains an anomalously old-fashioned respect for his "elders."

I think of Payton's veneration of Stockton as being related, in an odd way, to the veneration in which Payton holds his father. "I love my father to death," he once said, completely unselfconsciously, on national television. Al Payton likes to tell this anecdote about Gary: "He was giving his [high-school] art teacher some problems. He wanted to be like the rest of the bullies around here [Oakland], wouldn't do what the guy said. He got an 'F,' and I went up there and wanted to know why. The teacher told me what had gone down, and I told him that the next time Gary gave him any trouble, to give me a call. I gave him my number, and then he gave me a call and I went down there. Gary was acting up with all his buddies in the back. I told him, 'I'm going to show you you aren't any big man.' I got his little butt and spanked him. From then on, whenever he did something wrong, he would holler, 'Please don't call my daddy, please don't call my daddy.' I think he might have gotten hooked up like some of the rest, but I gave every teacher my number. I told them if they called, I would leave the restaurant and go. I caught him cutting once, driving my car, and I got after him pretty good. From then on, he did what he had to do." G. Payton respects or wants to respect or pretends to respect the hierarchical verities. This is part of what makes him so interesting to me, why I spend so much time thinking about him: his baffling mixture of being very cool and very square.

11.24.94—Robert Parish, a former Boston Celtic playing this year with Charlotte—asked by reporters what he meant in a *Boston Globe* article last week that quoted him as saying, "Boston is a white town; they like white heroes"—replies, "I said this town is a white town that appreciates their white players. It caters to their white heroes. It has nothing to do with race. I don't want to get into that racial thing. It's not about race. It's just a fact." What interests me is not what Parish says, which is a bromide—working-class Irish Catholics don't embrace black athletes—but that he feels compelled to pretend to undo what he's saying even as he's saying it, thus enacting the weird code in which this discussion almost always gets encrypted.

Not always, though. Faye Resnick, the author of *Nicole Brown Simpson: The Private Diary of a Life Interrupted,* says she received a letter that concluded with this postscript: "If possible, please testify and really make the 'Big Boys' sweat and let us get that animal put away forever."

My father comes up from San Francisco to visit for a few days for Thanksgiving. It's startling to me the degree to which the things I do that drive Laurie crazy are the same things that—the first day, the first hour he's here—I in turn am bothered by when my father does them, e.g., leaving the bathroom a water-logged disaster area. Does everyone find this true in their relations with their parents? I'm lashing out at my peasant stock, I suppose, but I'm also situating myself on an evolutionary scale: I'm not as "civilized" as Laurie (with her blonde hair and good manners), but I'm more "civilized" than my father (with his dirty sweater and Brooklyn accent).

After Thanksgiving dinner with my father and Laurie and Natalie and my sister and her husband, by myself in the kitchen for a moment, I go on a brief, intense crying jag rather similar to the ones Paul described to me a couple of days ago. I'm thinking about my friend Deborah, who died in the crash of US Air flight 700 in Pittsburgh a year ago. I didn't know her that well—she was a college classmate with whom I occasionally corresponded—and I hadn't been affected by her death very much until now, but suddenly I'm racked with grief and feeling the most sentimental thing I've ever experienced on Thanksgiving: actual thanksgiving, gratitude for my life. I'm alive and, to my astonishment, I'm not alone.

11.25.94—My father, Laurie, and I take Natalie to the Seattle Aquarium, and while we're walking around with her, pushing her in the stroller or carrying her, several people give us a beatific look that I hate because it conveys: *your child's cute and you're cute in her company and aren't we parents special and wonderful?* I resent what seem to me the kitschy assumptions behind this look—*you know what I'm feeling; I know what you're feeling; what we're feeling is so simple that it can be reduced to a moony smile.* On the rare occasions that I get this look from a black person, I smile back, which I never do when a white person gives me the secret-conspiracy-of-parents face. Why do I do this?

A plaque at the aquarium reads: "Symbiosis means living together. Several types of symbiotic relationships exist. When only one animal benefits, the relationship is called parasitism. In a second symbiotic relationship called mutualism, both partners benefit equally. Commensalism, which means 'eating from the same table,' is yet another symbiotic relationship. Commensal animals are frequently found together but seldom interact."

The first game of the "Texas Two-Step" is in San Antonio tonight; the second game is tomorrow night in Houston. My father and I watch the Sonics beat the Spurs on TV. The game has a rhythm that is as lulling and predictable as waves: the Sonics go way out in front, the Spurs expend all their energy coming back, and then the Sonics go way ahead again to put the game out of reach. I'm proud of the fact that they played well "for" my father, as if this somehow reflected well upon me (intellectually, I know it doesn't, but emotionally I can't help feeling this is somehow the case; one of the things he regularly compliments me on when we talk on the phone is how well the Sonics are playing).

At the end of the game, McMillan high-fives everyone as they come off the floor. It's a bit corny, but someone has to do something to try to get everyone to feel as if they're part of a team—who else but Nate, the team's co-captain and good Negro? (Why can this phrase not be used anymore unless swathed in irony? Because, like "white trash," its meaning derives from the racist assumption that "bad Negro," or "black trash," would be redundant.)

Schrempf and Vinny Askew give each other chest-bumps. Sam Perkins tells the media, "We were tired of coming out and not playing. We were moving the ball and sharing it." My insanely giddy overreaction is: *in a second symbiotic relationship called mutualism, both partners benefit equally.*

Gill plays well, scoring 17 on 7-for-12 shooting from the field, but before, during, and after the game, there are rumors of a Gill-for-Rodman trade. *Do it,* I think, *pull the trigger, move Gill,* and I realize why I've never liked him: he's not secure enough with himself to just be a nice guy, as McMillan is, and he's not cool enough to be "the bad link in the whole thang," as Payton is; instead, he adopts a pose of aloof arrogance that is meant to seem tough but is completely unconvincing and really just makes him seem irritable. In other words, he reminds me too much of myself.

11.26.94—While my father, Laurie, Natalie, and I go out to dinner, the Seattle-Houston game is being televised from Houston, so I tape it, and when we get home and everyone goes to sleep, I try to watch it but find I can't. A sports event takes place entirely inside a very brief temporal frame; the moment the frame is broken, the artificiality of the event—its utter inconsequentiality—overwhelms it. Which is why Seattle football fans get so upset that the ABC affiliate here is the only station in the country that broadcasts *Monday Night Football* on a one-hour tape delay: the fact that the game is not unfolding in real time makes a mockery of everybody's fandom.

So I fast-forward through the game. The Sonics bench doesn't seem very involved in the action, which is a good indication that the team isn't cohesive (there goes my giddy optimism), but ancient Bill Cartwright, acquired to do a good job defending Hakeem Olajuwon, does a good job defending Hakeem Olajuwon. By the end of the game there seems to be at least some esprit de corps, and the Sonics beat the defending-champion Rockets by 4. I'm eager to hear whether Karl and Calabro and Johnson think the win could be a crucial morale builder for the Sonics, but the tape runs out before the post-game show begins.

11.28.94—After feuding the first month of the season with Don Nelson, the coach of the Golden State Warriors, Chris Webber has been traded to the Washington Bullets, who are coached by Jim Lynam. Webber says, "The players and coaches in the league know what kind of person I am. They know I'm willing to listen to instruction. I'm not going to try to prove to anyone that I'm a good person. I'm not going to make sure I have my ear right next to Coach Lynam's mouth when he tells me something just so you guys [in the media] will see it. I'm going to be myself, and the kind of person I am will become evident."

Lanny Van Emman, one of the assistant coaches at Oregon State when Payton was there, said, shortly after Payton graduated, "I remember during practices, Ralph [Miller, the head coach] used to huddle us all together and all the kids would be looking at Ralph, except Gary. I'd say to Ralph, 'That darn Payton wasn't even paying attention to you!' About the third time I said it, Ralph said to me, 'You watch; he heard everything I said. He'll run the play better than those who were pretending to listen to me.' And you know what? Ralph was right."

I'll execute the directive, but I'm not going to kiss your ass.

The Sonics are back in town from their three-game road trip. I go to the Seattle-Indiana game with Neal, my physical therapist (I have a chronically bad back). Neal is South African, a former gymnast, and a Sonics season-ticket holder for the last dozen years. I'm interested in his perspective on the Taboo Topic, so as he drives us down I-5 to Tacoma, I ask him: why do black players dominate the NBA?

He says, "It's the most curious thing, isn't it, that in the United States, where there are two hundred and fifty million people and there are maybe twenty-five million blacks, virtually all of our sports entertainment is by black athletes? From a young, black, ghetto-raised kid's perspective, the NBA is a reasonable career goal. He's got a reasonable shot at the NBA, he thinks, which is a delusion, of course. A black kid might be working to make the NBA from the time he's six, whereas my kid Sam said to me yesterday, 'I want to be in the NBA.' I said, 'Well, in that case, you better start practicing. There are people out there your age who can shoot hoops.' 'Okay,' he says, so we go to the park and shoot hoops, and he comes back and says, 'That's really hard to make those baskets.' Black kids believe they can make it in the NBA, because they have black athletes as role models."

I say, "You're saying there are more black players in the NBA because there are more black players in the NBA."

Neal laughs and says, "In last year's World Championships in Stuttgart, Chinese women dominated middle-distance events, the 1500 and 3K and 10K. They showed no evidence of steroid use and no evidence of blood doping and no evidence of other stimulant dosing. The questions everybody asked were: who are these women, where did these women come from, and how could they dominate so completely? You have a billion people, from whom are selected the very best middle-distance athletes; these athletes are selected not just on the basis of their capacity to run fast but also on the basis of their physiology—their ratio of one muscle type to another, their oxygen-holding capacity, and their VO_2 max."

VO_2 max? As required, I look lost.

"The amount of oxygen your blood can transport and your muscles can use," Neal explains. "They train these women with really intelligent training techniques at high altitudes for endurance purposes, and they bring them down for world-class competition and these athletes dominate. In the 3K at Stuttgart, the Chinese women went 1–2–3, against what was obviously world-class competition, and all three of them broke the world record. So, in the U.S., when you have the very best junior-high athletes being selected to represent their high schools and then the very best of the high-school athletes being selected to represent colleges and then the very best college athletes being selected to play in the NBA, what you have is a selection process quite similar to what the Chinese women athletes go through. Eventually those thirty new players who enter the NBA each year are phenomenal athletes."

This argument carries a certain suasion for me, but then a few minutes later Neal says, to my astonishment, "In America, I find race to be an aberrant issue, I really do. Granted, there was slavery two hundred years ago, but I also know black physicians, black writers, and black professionals of all kinds—people who have succeeded in spite of the fact that they were identified as a racial minority where stigmas are still attached. If you're black and have a certain amount of self-esteem, you can make it in whatever field you choose."

"Well, that's the trick," I say, "developing self-esteem in a society in which—"

"You can," he says. He's on a roll; it's as if he isn't talking to me anymore. "And you can get to the very top of that field. In spite of the racism you might have experienced, you can make it to the top of your field, whatever it happens to be. Therefore, from my point of view, to say, 'Well, we underwent the trauma of slavery, therefore we're underprivileged, underclass,' it's kind of a cop-out."

In one case, Neal is saying environment creates performance, and in the other case, he's saying it's immaterial. I tell him it can't be both everything and nothing. Neal then asks if I have any close black friends. I say no and he says that means I'm racist. I say that's ridiculous, and in what at first sounds like a bit of a non sequitur, he says, "When I was only about eleven years old, I knew that what was going on in South Africa was completely wrong, I just knew it. I remember when I was fourteen in a geography class we had to choose a place where we would like to live and write about it. I made an emotional commitment to myself that I was going to live in Canada. I had researched Vancouver, BC. You wouldn't believe how ostracized I was for wanting to leave. People would call me *kafferboetie*—nigger-lover. If you wanted to leave the country, you were basically considered a traitor, for not supporting the government."

So, as it always is in conversations like these, the ostensible topic—Chinese women in Stuttgart—isn't the real topic; the real topic, as always, is How Guilty Do You Feel Compared to How Guilty I Feel?

At the beginning of the game, a Sonics employee escorts a little girl to the center of the floor to sing the national anthem and snaps a picture of her. The same man accompanies fans on and off the floor for various activities and promotions—free-throw shooting contests, etc. He's black, bald, tall, has huge shoulders, a huge neck, and looks rather like Larry Smith (the former Golden State Warrior who is now an assistant coach on the Houston Rockets and whose main job appears to be to escort Vernon Maxwell off the court whenever he gets ejected). He doesn't depress everyone by being a boring corporate dweeb; on the other hand, he wears horn-rim glasses and fuzzy sweaters, so he reads as "smart nice dad." How calculated is all this on the Sonics' part? Is it racist on my part to analyze him in this way? The effectiveness of the mixed metaphor (basketball, business, family) is dependent upon no one having the temerity to point out the operational terms of the mixed metaphor. I want to bounce my theory about the huggable Sonics employee off Neal, but neither of us has built up enough scar tissue, so I keep it to myself.

Everyone understands that the cheerleaders pretend to be there to exhort the players and that they're really there for fans' erotic delectation. What I'd never noticed before is that when the visiting team is being introduced, the Sonics cheerleaders make a show of being uninterested to the point of being inaccessible. They're not even on the floor; they're hidden away somewhere beneath the bleachers. When the Sonics are being introduced, the cheerleaders—frantic with jittery excitement, as if the Sonics individually and collectively possessed incalculable sexual allure—run out onto the floor and form two lines, which each member of the Sonics' starting lineup then parts as he runs out to midcourt before high-fiving that earth-monster Sasquatch. The Sonics thereby accrue fertility to their side and the opposition doesn't, which is why the home team always wears white uniforms and the visiting team always wears dark uniforms.

I seem to focus increasingly on G. Payton, take notes only on G. Payton: "Behind-the-back pass—really nice." "GP fakes—fantastic fake." "Going into the lane: GP breaks the opposite of how anyone else would break." Five minutes after writing these words down, I have difficulty deciphering what they say or mean, but I seem to need to constantly try to translate Gary's actions into words, make him somehow understandable to me, make him mine.

It's such a palpable feeling when the Supes are playing well, as they are tonight: *they aren't worrying the details.* They're in total sync: chemistry, tenacity, and flow. I remind myself that this is a useful approach to life in general, which reminder, of course, constitutes precisely the paralytic self-consciousness that guarantees worrying the details.

With four minutes left in the game, Karl puts Gill in for garbage time, offering him meaningless minutes in pseudo-deference to his demand for increased playing time. Gill, who truly does seem to become more effective the more he plays, has been dissatisfied all season with the number of minutes Karl uses him (around thirty minutes a game). Unhappy with his playing time last season as well, Gill asked to be traded over the summer. Nothing happened. So he attempted to get written into his contract the guarantee of a certain amount of playing time a night; Karl said he'd quit before he guaranteed anybody minutes.

The Sonics overwhelm the Pacers—their third consecutive victory; they're now 8-and-5 for the year, a game and a half behind first-place Phoenix in the Pacific Division of the Western Conference. Payton has a great game. "Everything starts with me," he says afterward. "So I felt that I had to be more aggressive. If my team is in a drought, I'm going to do something to get them out of it. When I start scoring early, teams start looking at me, saying, 'We've got to stop Gary.' Then they start crowding me and I'm able to kick the ball for assists." Neal and I are listening to this on the car radio as we're driving home; weirdly, pathetically, amazingly, predictably, our mutual delight in Gary Payton thaws what ice remains between us.

Payton could easily have surpassed his career high for most points in a game (32), but he sat out the entire fourth quarter and settled for 28, along with 7 assists. Asked why he didn't attempt to record a new career high in points, he says he doesn't care about stuff like that and wanted the other guys (e.g., Gill) to get more playing time. I believe him and admire what appears to be his honest lack of interest in individual stats, which coexists, of course, with an almost limitless ego. In high school, even though I wasn't very good, I never didn't have a taxi meter running in my head to keep track of exactly how many points I'd scored each game.

The Sonics' center, Ervin Johnson (nicknamed "Tragic" by local wags to distinguish him from Earvin "Magic" Johnson), plays well for once—14 rebounds, 2 blocks. "Ervin's a player," Karl says. "I know not everybody believes this, but he's going to be fine." The very qualification says more than the praise. Ervin Johnson is not fine and is never going to be fine: he's a born-again Christian who is much too nice to ever develop the necessary cruelty to be a great athlete (if he elbows someone by accident, he apologizes).

Asked whether this was the Sonics' best game of the year, Karl replies, "It's probably the first time we really felt comfortable on the court. It helps when we shoot the ball as well as we did, and defensively we were solid all night long. I like what we're doing. We have a much more serious nature. But I like our win over Houston more because that was a big-time basketball game. It might not have been as pretty as this one, or as polished as this one, but it was a real serious game, and we found answers against a very tough team in a very tough building."

This is a rhetorical strategy many NBA coaches have learned from New York Knicks coach Pat Riley, who learned it from his psychologist-wife: no matter how well your team plays, always suggest room for improvement. In Karl's lexicon, *pretty* don't equal *serious. Ugly* is a compliment. *Cute* is a put-down. *Asshole* is laudatory.

11.29.94—This afternoon, on the *George Karl Show,* Karl tries to deflect discussion of a possible Gill-for-Rodman trade, but then the host, Brian Wheeler, asks, "To be very blunt: do you want Dennis Rodman on your basketball team?"

Karl replies, "I'd love to have him on my basketball team, but I don't know if I want him to be a part of my basketball family." Regarding Gill's requests to be traded, Karl says, "Those requests are not something we like. They're not something you can work out immediately. He's not totally happy under the circumstances, and we understand that. We may not be totally happy with the money we're paying him."

After the *George Karl Show* is over, the outgoing obese talk-show host, Brian Wheeler, says to the incoming rotund talk-show host, Mike Gastineau, "You smell nice. You going somewhere afterward?"

Gastineau, who is five times quicker on the uptake than Wheeler, says, "People usually buy me a drink before saying that, sailor; what kind of comment is that, Wheels?"

You just be sure to remind him to use a glove when he does that, okay, Gas Man? It would be impossible to overstate the degree to which

sports-talk radio is shadowed by the homosexual panic implicit in the fact
that it consists almost entirely of a bunch of out-of-shape white men sitting around talking about black men's buff bodies. I constantly wonder
why all the KJR sports-talk hosts are so fat, and I have three theories:
they have great faces for radio; like opera singers, they gain weight on
purpose to give their voice resonance; or they're just guys who spend all
day watching sports, eating pizza, and drinking beer.

I have to do some errands, so I listen to the *Mike Gastineau Show* on
my Walkman, and the entire show is devoted to the pros and cons of
trading Kendall Gill. The board, as they say, lights up: everyone wants to
groove on George, rag on Gill, and I have to ask myself what is it about
this roundtable discussion that is making me so happy. Part of it is that
the discussion, despite all rumors about sports-talk radio to the contrary,
is on this particular afternoon astonishingly nuanced and intelligent; Gas
Man is good at keeping callers away from easy invective. Part of it is that
I despise Gill's who-gives-a-shit insouciance, and it does my heart good
to see him come a cropper. But in our insistence that Gill must be traded
by yesterday, if not sooner, it is above all the sheer pleasure of moving a
human body around as if it were a battleship in a game of war.

An old crone wags her finger at me not for jaywalking but for placing
one foot off the curb while she drives past, and my first and only thought
is: *this is why I love the Sonics.*

At the market, primarily, I think, just to see what will happen, I bring
too many items into the 12-items-or-less line. I look at the checker with
a quizzical look, as if to ask, "Do you mind?" Rather than say, "No can
do," or "Don't worry about it," he checks me out but counts aloud each
item one by one. "Seventeen," he practically shouts, and I'm grateful
only that he didn't switch on his microphone and broadcast the infrac-
tion store-wide.

Posting to the Sonics newsgroup, Tom writes: "My 16-year-old stepson
lives and breathes basketball. I have never really been that interested but
that's another story. For his Christmas present I would like to take him
to a Sonics game sometime before the 18th of next month. I am looking
for a pair of tickets for a game against a fairly decent opponent. You

would probably know better than I, but he says that Houston is doing well, others?! He had the opportunity to see the exhibition in Spokane against I think it was Oakland or SF. And he still talks about it. (We live in Spokane.) I would like to get a pair of tickets for he and I that would be considered good or at least decent tickets. He got to sit on the floor next to the announcers' table at the exhibition so I am competing with that memory. He is a good kid, a B student at Valley Christian School in Spokane. I have never really done anything for him which could be considered 'cool.' (I am not cool!!) Obviously I do not want to be 'scalped' but am willing to pay the value of the tickets. Since we have to travel from Spokane to attend, our resources are limited. If you have tickets you will not be using or for some reason are willing to sell, please reply." For white guys, for millions of white guys including myself who are not cool!!, watching basketball is one last chance if not to be cool at least to get in contact with cool.

11.30.94—Karl, by way of apology, says, "I apologize for the smart-aleck comment I made yesterday about Kendall Gill. It was immature. I'm sorry this is going to serve as a distraction." Still, he says, "I stand behind my comments. My commentary on the radio was a generalization over the last four or five months of conversations between Wally Walker [the Sonics' new general manager], Arn Tellem [Gill's agent], me, and Kendall. It wasn't anything that's happened in the last few days. It's my job to coach the team. The way I'm going to coach is to play the guys who play hard and play well, and who have good attitudes. I've told everybody that I'm not into managing attitudes this year. If he doesn't do it my way, I'm going to sit him, and I'll even go to the point of hurting him"—Karl's famous sadism.

In response to my classified ad in the paper, a guy named Nick keeps calling me and guilting me with his life story: he's divorced and wants to get back in good graces with his sons by taking them to some "marquee matchups." One of his sons is a big Dennis Rodman fan; Nick thinks maybe he could take one boy to a Spurs game tonight and the other boy to a Rockets game down the road. I'm tempted to sell him the tickets, but he offers me only about half their face value, and I want to go to the game tonight myself—to see what suppressed antagonisms I can detect between Gill and Karl. Also, I don't entirely believe Nick's story, or so I tell myself, feeling bad, driving to the game in five-o'clock traffic. When I get to the Tacoma Dome, I approach five scalpers, all of whom are young black men; I sell the other ticket for $30 (I don't say fifty words to the stranger who sits next to me all game, though I'm itching to ask him how much he paid for the ticket).

Despite the Gill-Karl impasse, the Sonics play particularly well and beat San Antonio by a comfortable margin. Running around the court in Purity-symbol white low-tops (how much Karl must hate these sneakers), Gill projects even more than usual the attitude of a prima donna tennis player: a gifted, delicate guy flying solo. Working hard but not that hard, constantly avoiding physical contact with both his teammates and opponents, he values nothing so much as the appearance of being in consummate control of his own perfect body.

12.1.94—E-mail from Paul: "Recently returned from an anesthetizing weekend in Port Townsend—how do the locals do it? Nothing but antique stores and gray beaches and lazy breakfasts. So cut off from the world. As we were driving out of the parking lot at Fort Warden, I said to Janice, 'Christ, if I don't see a black man soon, I'm gonna scream.' We were stalled before a crowd of middle-aged WASPs, filing into the zeppelin-like hangar/auditorium to see something billed as the 'New Chautauqua' when something like full apprehension of the town's beatnik elitism began to dawn on me, and just at that moment, like an invocation, an AFRICAN-AMERICAN couple with a picnic basket emerged from a weathered Winnebago and joined the fray—the only blacks we saw all weekend." Black men, and how we expect them somehow to redeem our pale white lives…

3

PROOF OF MY
OWN RACISM

12.2.94—A woman named Mary has agreed to buy three pairs of tickets to games later in the season, and through phone messages back and forth we've agreed to meet outside the Tacoma Dome before the game tomorrow tonight, since she lives near the T-Dome. I call her to ask how we'll recognize each other, and she says, "Well, my name is Mary." She'll be wearing a name tag? "I'll be wearing a blue blouse. I have short hair. I'm black; my husband's white; my kids are real light. Anything distinctive about you?"

"I-I-I'm six feet," I stammer. "I-I-I have brown hair. I'll be wearing a black coat. I'll be with an older guy with white hair."

Maybe—maybe—she's telling me her husband's white and her kids are real light because they'll be accompanying her, but my overriding sense is that she's hedging her bets on the assumption that I'm racist.

12.3.94—The Milwaukee Bucks are in town for a game against the Sonics tonight, so this morning's *Post-Intelligencer* revisits the contract negotiations from a month or two ago between Bucks owner (and recently re-elected U.S. senator) Herb Kohl and star rookie Glenn Robinson.

Robinson wound up agreeing to a $70 million contract, but when Robinson was seeking $109 million for thirteen years, Kohl said, "I was thinking of telling Mr. Robinson, 'I'll tell you what: I'll take your contract and you can have my franchise.'" This line was widely credited with helping him get re-elected.

The "older guy with white hair" I go to the game with is Roger Sale. Driving together down to Tacoma, he asks me what I've been working on for the *Weekly*. He's a little astonished, I think, that I still haven't written anything—for publication, anyway. After I give him a brief description of the journal I'm keeping, he tells me about moving to Seattle in the early '60s: his kids went to black schools, their family went to a black church, they made a lot of black friends, and he ran a federal poverty project on the University of Washington campus for a couple of years. I don't know where he's going with this until he pauses and then says, "That was always the way I wanted to do race in America. When I hear about blacks in the NBA as a subject, I want to weep or scream."

A moralist of the old school, Roger is strongly reminiscent to me of my mother, who is no longer alive and who made gestures and performed actions that invariably struck me as admirable but somehow difficult to emulate, and my father, who is eighty-four and who makes gestures and performs actions that invariably etc. My mother was the public information officer for one of the first desegregated school districts in California. One day the human relations consultant informed her that the revolution wouldn't occur until white families gave up their houses in the suburbs and moved into the ghetto. My mother tried for the better part of the evening to convince us to put our house up for sale. My father has held dozens of jobs, but perhaps the one he loved the most was director of the San Mateo poverty program during the late '60s. He filed complaints against landlords who would tell him an apartment was available and then fifteen minutes later tell a black man the same apartment was rented. Black men who couldn't find a place would stay with us. In junior high school, as soon as classes were over, I'd frequently take a bus crosstown, toss my backpack under my father's desk, and spend the rest of the afternoon playing basketball with black kids. I played in all seasons and instead of other sports. In seventh grade I developed a double-pump jump shot, which in seventh grade was almost unheard of. Rather than shooting on the way up, I tucked my knees, hung in the air a second, pin-wheeled the ball, then shot on the way down. My white friends hated my new move. It seemed tough, mannered, teenage, vaguely Negro. The more I shot like this the more my white friends disliked me, and the more they disliked me the more I shot like this.

Mary never shows and I wonder why not—did she think I was a racist?

Once we're in our seats, Roger makes it clear he's not up for a lot of chitchat; he's concentrating. He really focuses on the game, think-ing about patterns and combinations, as if he were watching a chess match. I used to watch basketball like this—I'm pretty sure I can still watch basketball like this—but I'm not interested in that aspect so much anymore.

On the other hand, I do feel one with the throng who have come to see Glenn "Big Dog" Robinson, the Bucks' $70 million rookie; come to see "Big Dog" and boo "Big Dog"; come to see what $70 million looks like or doesn't look like; come to see him fail, I think. In the first few minutes he blows a dunk, and we boo our $1.98 lungs out.

Dwane Casey, the Sonics' obligatory black assistant coach, is the only person Kemp seems to listen to during timeouts.

Jon Barry, the only white player on the Milwaukee roster, literally doesn't touch the ball in the six minutes he's on the floor, and the diss is so obvious he complains to his teammates, who blow him off. I try to point this out to Roger, who's uninterested.

Schrempf, going into one of his usual tantrums about a ref's call, gets even more upset when Kemp tries to calm him down.

The Sonics force 20 turnovers and shoot better than 50 percent from the field. The Bucks miss a 3-pointer at the buzzer that would have sent the game into overtime; Seattle wins. When the Sonics win now, I just feel relief (the season might turn out halfway interesting, I can get peo-ple to go with me to the games, I haven't completely wasted the $3,500 I spent, I'm not wasting my life) rather than joy. It's funny the way a pen and a notebook alter the equation. I find I'm not as unfettered in my affiliation as I once was. I'm more rational, disgusted by the endless analysis—on sports-talk radio, in the sports pages, among my friends—even as I'm addicted to it.

·　·　·

12.4.94—In the *New York Times Magazine* six prominent black men debate the question "Who Will Help the Black Man?" The cover is a photo of the back of the buzz-cut head of a black man who's wearing an enormous gold earring: slave?/soldier?/prisoner?/athlete? The film director John Singleton says, "Our children need assets like technology that will lead us into the next century. And they need to learn that it's cool to learn this technology. That it's cool to learn how to use a computer. Enough of basketball. It's about learning how to use this stuff." Which reminds me of the Arthur Ashe line: "We blacks spend too much time on the basketball court and not enough time in the library." These statements make me feel defensive and guilty; they incriminate my romance with the game, but—guess what?—the guilt passes.

Bill Curry, the Auburn University football coach, appearing on *Viewpoints* on ESPN radio, says, "When I came to coach at [the University of] Alabama [before coaching at Auburn], I spoke to a gentleman. He was an attorney, a learned man and very astute observer. He said, 'I want you to thoroughly understand what you've got yourself into, so you can see why there's such resistance to certain types of personalities.' I was from Atlanta, Georgia—a Georgia Tech graduate; there was a certain aura that went with that, not particularly popular with this mind-set. And this mind-set, he said, has literally sprung from Reconstruction, which surprised me. He talked about the emasculation of the southern male identity that came with the defeat of the South. And it didn't sound strange to me after he started talking, because having grown up in College Park, Georgia, I remember, growing up in the '40s and '50s, the worst thing you could be called was a Yankee. And we're talking about the twentieth century—the middle of the twentieth century. I remember people actually talking that way; I remember separate water fountains and separate seats on buses and stuff. To this day I don't understand how any of that could have happened, but nevertheless it did; this illogical hatred lodged itself in the breast of the southern male when the South was defeated, and then came Reconstruction with all that humiliation, and then on into various civil rights movements, with the State of Alabama being held up to international ridicule in the '50s and '60s, and the one saving grace—to the minds of a lot of people, people with very low self-esteem, especially the uneducated—was Crimson Tide football, because we could whip those Yankees, we could whip anybody, and Coach Bear Bryant is God, and that is the one thing that became utterly sacred."

Curry's tone is one of appalled amazement, but I once asked my father what he thought the obsession he and I have always had with the Los Angeles Dodgers was all about (he was born in Brooklyn and I was born in LA), and he wrote back, "For me, it comes out this way: I wanted the Dodgers to compensate for some of the unrealized goals in my career. What do they call that in Freudian terms—transfer, is that right? If I wasn't winning my battle to succeed in newspapering, union organizing, or whatever I turned to in my wholly unplanned, anarchic life, then my surrogates—the nine boys in blue—could win against the Giants, Pirates, et al. Farfetched? Maybe so. But I think it has some validity. In my case. Not in yours." Oh, no: not in my case, never in mine.

In *Pain and Passion: A Psychoanalyst Explores the World of S & M,* Robert Stoller says, "The major traumas and frustrations of early life are reproduced in the fantasies and behaviors that make up adult eroticism, but the story now ends happily. This time, we win. In other words, the adult erotic behavior *contains* the early trauma. The two fit: the details of the adult script tell what happened to the child." This seems to me true not only of sexual imagination but also of sports passion—why we become such devoted fans of the performances of strangers. For once, we hope, the breaks will go our way; we'll love our life now; this time we'll win.

Laurie and I and our friends Karen and Ross go see *Pulp Fiction,* which Laurie and Karen and Ross like a lot more than I do. To me, *Pulp Fiction* just comes down to Tarantino's getting to play the only white character in the history of the movies who is cool enough to say "nigger" to a black man and use it—mean it—as black vernacular.

A view that gets ratified for me when, browsing the Web for a while after we get home, I come across Will Self's interview of Martin Amis in the *Mississippi Review.* Amis says, "I think the greatest American export has really been one notion, and that is 'the cool.' That's an American idea; it's certainly not an English one."

Self says, "Perhaps Afro-American?"

Amis replies, "I think just American."

Self keeps coming: "But I think there is a very powerful synergy between black and white. The modern popular song is an elision between traditional English ballad form and the 4/4 rhythm of Africa. It's a great myth that soul is black music; it's black/white music. And maybe 'cool' is black/white as well?"

"Well, wherever it comes from, all Americans are capable of it, and the English aren't," Amis says, concluding the discussion of the topic, thereby trying to convey that cool doesn't explain itself.

12.5.94—In the *New Yorker,* Terrence Rafferty reviews the movie *Cobb,* about the legendary baseball player (and legendary ogre) Ty Cobb: "Probably no one who was entranced as a child by the romance of sports is ever entirely free of that admiration for skill and daring, that reverence for the most and the best. And lurking somewhere in our consciousness, perhaps, is the idea that a genius like Cobb is inherently monstrous, unnatural—that his achievement as a ballplayer is somehow inseparable from his horrible inadequacy as a human being. *Cobb* is a wonderful movie: it's a raucous, brazenly entertaining exploration of some uncommonly subtle ideas about the relationship between character and creativity." I've always accepted the separation between the person who lives and the artist who creates. Knowing that, say, Picasso was a monster has never tarnished for an instant my admiration for his art; if anything, I must say, it probably enhanced it. Whereas—perhaps because I haven't thought of myself as an athlete since I was a teenager—I seem to want to admire (as people) my sports heroes, who, in truth, are even less likely to be nice guys than artists are. To be a great athlete is, on some fundamental level, to be not so nice, it seems to me, and yet, bizarrely, I always find myself feeling a sense of disappointment when it's reported that Hoopster X, such a "team player," is being sued for failure to make child-support payments to his ex-girlfriend. I want athletes to be the simultaneous impossible: great warriors and lovable darlings.

Tomorrow night I'm going to the Sonics-Rockets game with Kristine, who's married to Joseph, a fellow scrivener in the English department. Although the Rockets' star, Hakeem Olajuwon, will not be playing, due to a wrist injury, Kristine is psyched, and when I call her to confirm our plans to take a boat—the *Victoria Clipper*—to the game tomorrow (it's supposed to snow and the roads are never plowed here during the rare snowstorm), Joseph answers the phone and says, "She's been running around wearing her Sonics shirt and dunking on the five-foot basket downstairs." Kristine gets on and, kiddingly, says, "Isn't he patronizing?" Well, that's the problem, I think: what adoration does not, by its very zeal, transfigure the other person into an icon, an object, a thing? That's what adoration is; who can live without that?

12.6.94—The reveling fans look at us askance, but on the boat ride down to Tacoma, Kristine, a graduate student in English, gives me her take on the new rules the NBA has implemented this year: "In football, they've got all these pads and they've got this helmet on; they don't even look like human beings anymore. In basketball, they're very clearly real men: you can see their faces, you can see their bodies, they're not distorted in any sense, and they're sweating. You can see their muscles, and they're up against each other, and that's become more and more prevalent in the last six years, culminating with the kind of play of the Knicks under Riley—where it's just, you know, bodies on bodies and it's totally erotic. I think basketball had become almost too threatening in terms of its homoeroticism. Last year it reached its maximum threatening point and the NBA had to react, had to do something to make the visual spectacle less threatening, and the only way to do that was to separate these bodies. So now we have the no-touching-on-the-back rule—no standing behind another man and touching; the no-hand-check rule; the no-taunting rule. They can't even talk to one another: it pulls relationship out of the game, which pulls sex out of it; it makes it much more five separate players playing five separate players, and those players are completely distanced from one another by the 3-point rule. That's the worst, since it encourages all five players to play out behind that line, instead of just one or two. Now all of them are trying to make those shots, and so no one is under the basket, where everyone converges.

"Having the game become more congested around the basket—why is that bad or ugly? They said it was the violence. I think it's because watching men we can identify touch each other in that kind of way, an emotional way, watching emotional black men touch each other like that, close up like that, with the cameras right there, and all this excitement about *scoring*, well, that's threatening and it gets labeled as bad. In American culture the most dangerous symbol, the most frightening symbol, for white people, is black men in love. The moment black men love each other, the United States is done for." Everything Kristine says seems to me clever and maybe even a little true, but I realize that all my friends and I are like Will Self: we're adamant about articulating coolness because we can't embody it.

When Kendall Gill's name is announced during pre-game introductions, he receives a huge ovation from the crowd. We want to like him. We want him to like us. We're cheering our own good hearts as much as we're cheering him. He hustles but plays terribly. Although Houston's Hakeem Olajuwan doesn't play, he looks regally elegant on the sideline, wearing gray slacks and a black shirt, signing autographs. Earlier in the day, Payton hurt his back, slipping on ice in his driveway. There is general concern that this accident might reprise an earlier problem; three years ago, he was diagnosed with a serious back ailment (making us virtually twins!). "If it ever kicks into something serious, I'm going to cry," Gary once said, with the perfect expression of mock-concern that marks exactly the difference between how he responds to his back problem (*who the fuck cares?*) and how I respond to mine (keening trepidation). During halftime, as the Bud Daredevils ride their motorcycles around the court, the public-address announcer says, "I guarantee you that one of these guys will risk his life in order to make sure you have a good time," which captures for me something essential about the sadness of the exchange between athlete and fan in spectator sports. Despite his backache, Payton has a great game, scoring 30 points; the Sonics win.

When I get home from the game, Laurie tells me that when Natalie was going to bed, she said, "I want to kiss Dada," and when Laurie said, "He won't be home till later," Natalie wailed inconsolably. I'm happy to hear I was missed, but I don't want my prestige to issue from absence—that whole story; I also want to be a presence (or, in Payton-speak, "a present," which is even better). A friend of mine told me that upon hearing about my Sonics journal, he assumed my primary motivation was to "escape paternity" (he's divorced). It is odd to me that my obsession with the Sonics began just after Natalie was conceived, as if, on the verge of becoming a completely domestic animal, I needed to locate warrior-selves to identify with and glorify.

Paul faxes me a column of Susie Bright's about Jimi Hendrix from a new magazine called *Future Sex:* "He was, as they say, a fuckin' genius....I idolize him not only as a revolutionary guitarist, but as a revolutionary.... Everyone who has read the Hendrix biographies knows about Jimi's huge sexual appetite, his big dick, and his black erotic presence in a white milieu....Of course, I'm practicing the ultimate Spectator's Choice, making my hero into me, believing that we shared a faith instead of a good beat we could dance to. Hendrix introduced me to the blues, to sex funk, and to divine cacophony. If I hadn't been 15 at the time, I could not have hung my political and erotic identity on his hook—but I was. I've fantasized about fucking many rock 'n' roll stars, but I've never again had the feeling I got with Hendrix that I could fuck the whole wide world. With Jimi you could love it and leave it: the two philosophies were not exclusive. He carved an axis bold as love and left me—and a lot of others—spinning in it forever." This is, to me, honest and embarrassing, and though my feelings about Payton aren't (consciously) sexual, I resolve (futilely) to tone down the GP genuflections.

12.8.94—On the *George Karl Show,* a caller asks about the progress of a rookie with the perfect name of Dontonio Wingfield. (Cf. Angela Davis: "I think we have an obsession with naming ourselves because for so much of our history we were named by someone else.") Karl replies, "Well, it's kind of unfortunate, because with a coach and a rookie in the NBA a lot of negativity tends to build up, and so he becomes sort of a whipping boy." He immediately corrects this. "A whipping post. But Dontonio is coming along." Karl's enlightened enough to know that he shouldn't say "whipping boy," but not so enlightened that the phrase didn't come, unbidden, from his mouth.

Laurie tries out on me the image of Karl as a besieged inner-city high-school teacher and we discuss it for a while before retracting it, since it's inaccurate, and its inaccuracy is racist: he's dealing with twelve of the three hundred most talented people in the world in their profession; then we realize that the retraction itself is racist, since certainly the inner-city high school teacher has talented students as well. In the sports world, this is what is known as painting yourself into a corner.

Maybe it's opened this way for a long time, but I suddenly notice that the *Mike Gastineau Show,* which airs from three to seven every weekday afternoon on KJR, opens with Kevin Calabro intoning mock-melodramatically: "From the John Wayne Bobbitt School of Broadcasting, the man with the wireless microphone. Uncut. Uncensored. The Voice of Reason: Mike Gastineau." *Do we have to make it any more explicit for you? Sports-talk radio is about one thing: helping our beleaguered sports-club members feel better about their beleaguered sports-club members.*

12.9.94—Last night in Sacramento, the Sonics lost to the lowly Kings. In the fourth quarter Karl removed Payton from the game and afterward explained the decision by saying, "I was tired of getting outworked." On the *Gary Payton Show* this morning, New York Vinnie—Vinnie Richichi, a KJR talk-show host whose shtick is perhaps somewhat overreliant upon the fact that he grew up in Queens—asks Payton for his response to Karl's comment.

Payton's only reply is: "I can't really dwell off this." Not "on this"; "off this." Where does he come up with these expressions? They remind me of intentionally misspelled words on small-business readerboards, which, by virtue of being "wrong," command people to pay closer attention.

Vinnie: "Were you relieved to be out of that game? Did you say, 'That's enough of this'?"

Payton says, "That's the decision of the coach; that's, you know, what he wanted to do. Things weren't, you know, going our way, so, you know, he pulled us and you can't have any problems with that." I finally recognize where his very plosive "that" comes from—Snoop Doggy Dogg's *Doggystyle* CD; it's an exact match—but all those "you know"s are equivalent to my stuttering in that they mean he's uncomfortable, they mean he's bullshitting.

·   ·   ·

I tape a Nike/Foot Action commercial that has been airing the last week or so, and while Laurie and Natalie are splashing away giddily in the bath, I watch the tape over and over. The scene is a shopping mall at Christmas time. A line forms, leading to Santa. The camera finds Dennis Rodman's navel, which features a belly ring and a tattoo. Two men run to get out of Rodman's way; one of them looks up at Rodman and gasps. An old lady blubbers when she sees Rodman, and her little dog lets out a yelp. As Rodman makes his way toward the front of the line, people continue to stare at him as if he were Satan. It's a joke, how scared we are of him (the expression on his face is a parody of nastiness) and people like him.

A little boy, sitting on Santa's lap, counts on his fingers as he recites his Xmas wish-list. A smiley elf, standing by Santa's side, frowns when he sees Rodman, who makes his way up the stairs to the platform on which Santa is sitting, then lifts Santa to his feet, knocking the boy aside. In a calm, low, intimidating voice, Rodman says, "Hey, Santa," then lifts Santa off the ground. The elf looks appalled. Rodman, looking very serious, says to Santa, "Here's my list: I want another championship, an MVP trophy—"

Santa says, "I have a list, too, Dennis." Rodman lets him down.

The elf, looking scared, moves closer to Santa.

Santa says solemnly, "You led the league in personal fouls..."

Rodman lifts his hands up: *so arrest me.* The elf, staring at Rodman, moves away from Santa a little.

Santa, looking like a displeased parent, stares at Rodman and continues his recitation of naughty things Rodman has done: "technicals...tripping...elbowing..." The elf smiles again, moving farther away from Santa. Santa, in a scolding tone: "...trash-talking..."

Rodman smiles and looks up, as if remembering a pleasant event.

Santa: "...coach-dissing...chin-chucking..."

The elf smiles and says, "Chin-chucking's cool." S. Claus, his left hand holding a list, slaps the elf upside the back of his head.

Santa, wearing an even more serious expression, finishes the list: "...punching." He lifts his eyes to meet Rodman's, daring him to deny any of the charges.

The music stops.

Rodman, with a possessed look in his eyes, says, "I also led the league in rebounds."

Santa moves his eyes from side to side, thinking carefully. He looks down to the elf. The elf looks back up to Santa and nods, which connotes: *what Dennis is saying is true and should be taken into consideration.*

Santa lifts his hat, contemplates the difficulty of moral choice in an indifferent cosmos, purses his lips, blinks his eyes, sighs. "All right," he says, "I'll give you the shoes."

Rodman, picking up Santa again by the front of his coat so his feet are a foot off the ground, smiles a wicked grin, and says, "Thanks, Santa."

Music starts up again in the background—percussion from some R&B song.

To me, much the most interesting character in the commercial is the elf. He is my surrogate. He's the one who gets seduced by Rodman; he's the one who thinks being an outlaw is so erotic. Because being bad is more interesting than being good. Even little children, especially little children, know this: Natalie is friends with two girls, sisters age two and three. The other day the older girl, Julia, ran away from her mother, for which she was reprimanded. The younger girl, Emily, asked why and was told that running away was bad. "I wanna do it," Emily said.

12.10.94—In LA the Sonics beat the Clippers in double overtime, and Kemp and Payton both score the most points they've ever scored in a single game, but the Sonics make an astounding number of mental mistakes: Kemp gets a taunting foul after dunking; Payton, all alone on a breakaway layup that would have sealed a victory in the fourth quarter, eases up and gets the shot blocked; Perkins misses two free throws that would have also iced the game; Schrempf gets called for a technical and then applauds the call, for which he gets a second technical and automatic ejection.

Afterward, on the post-game show with Calabro, Karl is apoplectic: "Our attitude—taunting and getting technicals—is absurd. We have an attitude of arrogance without the intensity of a champion. All we're doing is setting ourselves up to get screwed. It's not just one or two guys [this is Karl signaling that he's not only blaming Payton and Kemp]; it's basically all through the damn basketball team. We'll definitely work hard Monday and Tuesday and try to clean some stuff up, but I don't think there's much X's-and-O's to it. I would say 75–80 percent of our defensive possessions were pretty sound. It's the soft possessions and the goofy possessions and the lazy possessions that for some reason we want to put into our basketball game that we didn't have last season."

On the call-in show, a fan named Chris says, "I just want to talk about how much I'm loving George Karl right now for railing against his team, because I think that takes a lot of guts."

The host of the show, Brian Wheeler, says, "I mean, the good thing is that George is not going to let them feel good about this victory."

Chris says, "Well, I'm hoping he rubs their nose in it on Monday and Tuesday at practice; that's all I have to say." Chris hopes Coach Karl will rub their noses in their own shit in the vain hope they'll learn to behave.

Caller after caller agrees with Chris. It's difficult to convey how explicit the vibe on the radio is that Karl is Our Man in Havana. Watching the game on TV, I was also cursing the Sonics' miscues, but now—hearing my own sentiments amplified—I recoil.

And then William calls. He sounds nervous, as well he should be. "I want to say something from my heart. I'm very disillusioned and disappointed in George Karl. Not for the fact that the Sonics were reprimanded but the tearing down publicly of his team. A basketball team is viewed as a family, and you don't let the family get away with things that they need to deal with." William has heard what this year's central metaphor is. "George Karl could have shared with us how disappointed he was and how he'd like to see something better in certain areas, but to tear your family down publicly, to call your team totally immature on the radio—I was very disappointed. And my personal feeling is, I hope that George Karl does not talk about his family that way, if they disappoint him in certain endeavors."

Wheeler says, "Well, you're bringing two different things into it." *You're conflating the personal and the political, and if the NBA is about anything, it's about keeping these realms separate.*

"I don't think I am, sir."

"Well, I think you are."

"I don't think so."

William is black, I think, and the racial subtext is so close to the surface you can practically touch it (Wheeler can't ask William if he's black; this would be a serious violation of protocol). I, on the other hand, am dying for everything to get out in the open—it would be such a relief to be honest, for once—but it never does.

12.11.94—A friend in the English department is renting her house next term to a black novelist from the Bay Area. He's renting the house for four months, but he insists upon only paying for three months. They argue back and forth—she points out that she's losing money as it is on the sublet; he says the house is smaller than he thought it would be—and finally he just wears her down until she agrees. It's a popular contemporary reparation ritual: black people regaling guilty white liberals with transparent untruth just to see how much of it they'll buy. Stanley Crouch once told me with a straight face that the reason senators were cowed by Clarence Thomas was that they were afraid he would stand up and belt them, and I was too stupid to demur.

12.12.94—On the *Gary Payton Show*, when New York Vinnie asks Payton what he wants for Christmas, he replies that he doesn't need anything; he's got it all. Vinnie persists: "You don't even want a Clapper for Christmas? They have a security one now: you can clap three times, and it calls the police."

Payton says, "Oh no, I don't want that. I call the police myself. Whoever be in here with me, I play with 'em a little bit, whippin' 'em. They come in here: I get to play with 'em for a while."

I admire Gary Payton, the way the passenger admires the driver.

A caller asks him, "Why didn't you just slamdunk that ball when you were driving in for that layin? It was contested; why didn't you just slam it with two hands?"

Payton says, "Well, you don't know if somebody behind you or not." Suddenly he loses his patience entirely and says, "You don't understand. I didn't know he was behind me." Then he forgets he's on the radio: "And don't be doggin' my game, anyway. You eat shit and run around for 52 minutes—you ain't thinkin' about no dunkin'." Then he regains his composure a little bit. "He [Malik Sealy of the Clippers] just went and got it [made a great block of Payton's attempted layup]."

Vinnie asks a brilliant question: "Why didn't you take English in school instead of math?"

By which he means that one can go back and second-guess anything after the fact; hindsight is always 20/20. Payton gets it instantaneously and improves it instantaneously: "You gotta say, 'Why didn't you take Spanish instead of German?'" It's as if he's taking an SAT test and is pointing out that English and math are not part of the same subset but that Spanish and German are. He suddenly feels a pang of guilt, though, for completely blowing off the caller, so (yielding just a little, just enough) he says, "You don't know who behind you unless you gonna turn around to look at him, and if you do that, then he catch you."

Brian Wheeler opens the *George Karl Show* by playing a tape of his favorite riffs from Karl's post-game tirade after the Clippers game. Talking to Wheeler now, Karl says, "I still don't think we're playing with the dominating intensity that we need to play with, and I don't know what the reason is. I'm not going to sit here and say I know the reason; we're searching for it. I'm really kinda confused." I still like the fact that virtually alone among coaches, he acknowledges his own confusion. "I think I'm a liberal, open-minded person in most situations, okay? But I don't understand the advantages of all the emotional individuality and strutting of your stuff and the trash-talking. I'm going: 'Who wants to see this stuff? Who thinks this is cool? Because anybody who has played athletics doesn't think it's cool, and any coach or anybody into motivating knows it only helps the other team's motivation. Maybe I'm wrong. Maybe I'm just an old-timer and dorky disciplinarian who doesn't know anything about the game. 'Your individual ego is more important than the team'—that makes no sense to me. It's totally anti-sport: it's the accentuation of the individual, the glorification of the individual. The individual is glorified because of marketing, advertising, Reeboks, Nikes, and all that stuff. It's not why we play the game, and it's why my enthusiasm is deteriorating."

I love this whole peroration of Karl's about the glory of losing your ego but finding your soul in the larger purpose of a team. He's just trying to be positive; he believes we can all work together; he believes we can all get along. Who am I to say we can't?

12.13.94—Minnesota Timberwolves coach Bill Blair, after a loss, says about his temperamental star, "Isaiah Rider has got to grow up."

Rider, who grew up with Payton in Oakland, replies, "What does growing up have to do with basketball? It doesn't really go hand in hand. Growing up is a part of life, outside of basketball, when you're trying to take care of your responsibilities. Where does that come into play in the game? I don't understand that."

The tension between players and coaches in the NBA seems a reflection, in part, of the fact that middle-aged white men are acting as faux-father figures for young black men, the overwhelming majority of whom grew up without fathers. When asked what they're going to do with all the money from their first big contract, players frequently say, "Buy a new house for my mom."

On the first night of Chanukah, Laurie and I have another ridiculous debate as to whether Natalie's hair is blonde (WASP) or brown (Jewish). Laurie's hair is light brown or dirty-blonde, and when she was a child, it was quite blonde. She thinks Natalie's hair is blonde; she wants her to be a seraph. My hair is fairly dark brown, what little I have left of it, and my fantasy—who knows how I'll feel when she's sixteen?—is for Natalie to become a bad girl. Cf. James Baldwin: "When you call yourself white, you force me to call myself black."

After lighting the menorah, we open presents. My father has gotten for Natalie *The Lion King*, which we immediately plug in to watch while we eat traditional Chanukah dinner (pizza). It isn't that *The Lion King* is "racist"; what it is is fascinatingly nervous, balancing as it does Whoopi Goldberg as the lead hyena (who is very, very bad) with James Earl Jones as the wise lion patriarch (who is very, very good). Laurie thinks I'm playing Paranoid Detective, urges me to give it a rest.

Last year, a student of mine, a young black man, wrote a funny essay about how he procrastinated over everything, including writing the essay. It alluded, glancingly, to a racial slight he received when growing up as one of the few black people in a small rural town in eastern Washington. I kept pushing him to see procrastination as a metaphor for his reluctance to wrestle with the racism he had faced all his life, until he finally said, "Mr. Shields, I'm just a procrastinator. Not *everything* is about race."

·　　·　　·

12.14.94—Halfway through the first quarter of the Sonics-Suns game in Phoenix, the Sonics are behind, 18–4. They wind up committing 24 turnovers and getting called for 8 traveling violations. No Sonic starter shoots 50 percent from the field. Phoenix coasts. Afterward, Kemp says about the Suns, "They played a good game. They played well as a team. You have to take off your hats to them." *It's water underneath the table.*

Explaining why McMillan started instead of Gill and why he didn't directly inform Gill, who found out by looking at the blackboard, on which Karl wrote down the lineup, Karl says, "I had reasons for not personally informing him of the change. Professionally, it's not right to talk about. I thought it was time to give Nate an opportunity to start and lead us that way. Yes, Kendall's probably unhappy, but it's not a demotion. I just want to look at different things. I want more intensity, focus, and aggressiveness at the start of games. I've said that behind closed doors for two or three weeks. Now I'm saying it publicly."

It's tempting, of course, to characterize Karl as the self-described dorky disciplinarian with his quaint romance of the basketball pieties, but I must admit I agree with him about Gill, who tends to treat the first quarter of the game as a friendly feeling-out period to get reacquainted with the players on the other team. Gliding around the court, he seems perpetually bored by or bemused by, but in all cases beyond, the immediate proceedings. When he sits for long stretches on the bench, as he did tonight, he mopes and barely pays attention to the action on the floor.

Gill's response is: "I was surprised about being benched, but I can't be surprised anymore by what [Karl] does. I went through this last year. I know it's going to be like this all year long. I'll have to adjust. I just have to handle it. I know I've got a good job, and I love my family and God. I'm happy." This carries the unfortunate echo of something which Gill said when he was playing in Charlotte and which turned fans against him: "Sometimes, I say a prayer in the car. 'God, I'm twenty-four years old, driving this Mercedes-Benz down the street, working two hours a day, and getting paid like hell. Thank you, God.'" What bugs Karl about Gill bugs me: Gill isn't hungry for anything. Who likes anyone who isn't hungry?

•   •   •

12.15.94—Seattle is back in town for the first game of a four-game homestand (to the extent Tacoma is "home"). Natalie and Laurie and I all have colds, so I sell my $45 tickets for $30 apiece to a guy in the Sonics newsgroup and listen to the broadcast on the radio. "Hey," Laurie says, "this whole Sonics thing is paying off big-time!" The Sonics beat the Trailblazers; their record is now 13-and-7, tying them with Los Angeles for second place in the division.

Afterward, Gill says, "Whatever happens, I'm still going to play the same. I don't have any problems. I have no insecurities about myself." Which, as we all know, means: *I have lots of problems. I have innumerable insecurities about myself.*

Gill and Karl and I share at least this one tendency: we talk until we incriminate ourselves, then we talk some more.

12.16.94—On the *Gary Payton Show*, Payton comments on the Sonics' win over Portland: "Everybody's not perfect in this game. Some nights I might be there and some nights I might not be there, but I'm gonna try to be there every night, and if it doesn't happen, it just doesn't happen, but most of the nights I hope it will happen." Whenever Gary plays well, as he did last night against Portland (23 points, 9 assists), he lapses into a bit of aw-shucks pseudo-humility; still, in the midst of all the Gill-Karl posturing, the easy understanding he has of his own flawedness seems awfully refreshing.

12.17.94—I'm curious whatever happened to Mary ("I'm black; my husband's white; my kids are real light"). Did we get our signals crossed? Did she not show? Was she late? I phone her, and when I call at around eight P.M., she's bathing her kids and somewhat distracted, but she says, "Oh, I decided I couldn't do it. I couldn't afford to do it. I needed to buy Christmas presents for the kids."

To my surprise and despite myself, I say, "I totally understand, but couldn't you have done me the courtesy of calling to let me know?" Suddenly I'm Miss Manners. "Because people called, wanting tickets, and"—this is a slight exaggeration—"I had to turn them down because I thought you—"

She says, "No, that would be rude, and I would never be that rude";

she says she thought I was going to call her again to confirm, and when I didn't, she just assumed I had blown her off. Now she's dissembling, I think, and getting huffy. The conversation is built entirely upon dishonesty and mistrust, and she has exactly what she prophesied, proof of my racism, and I've delivered exactly what I knew I wouldn't deliver, that proof.

Laurie and I go together to the game against Orlando, to see Shaq et al. Laurie acts like we're out on a date, which I suppose we are, but there's a formality and a distance to how she acts with me, and so to how I act with her. Her otherness moves me: she acts enthusiastically within the event—cheering when asked to cheer, standing for the national anthem, etc.—whereas the only way I know to exist within a group is to alienate myself from it.

At the beginning of the game, Laurie asks me why the players, when they're introduced, are identified by where they attended college. *To make what's only corporeal somehow seem legitimately corporate (they attended college; now they have a niche in society and are pursuing careers).* Why do the Sonics Dance Team—the cheerleaders—keep changing outfits? she asks. *To keep pace with the blue movie running in every straight man's mind.*

Just before the start of the third quarter, the Sonics' mascot, Sasquatch, dressed up in red with number 32 on his back and the name "Shaqzilla" on his front, jumps through an enormous butcher-paper poster of Shaqzilla, attempts to dunk and misses, then clomps about clumsily like Godzilla. The players on both team look on, aghast? amazed? *are we really seeing what we're seeing?* It's all I can think about the rest of the game—what the players must feel when fans' true view of them as ridiculous beasts has been revealed, dramatized, celebrated— but when I ask Laurie what she thinks about Shaqzilla, she says she missed it; was it that bad?

The origin of this shtick appears to be a cartoon spot the Sonics run: three ad execs—suits, cigars, ponytails—strap a regular-looking Shaq to a Frankenstein bed and jolt him; suddenly Shaq is wearing a uniform with a dollar sign on the front and he has much bigger muscles and shoes. The announcer says, "Shaqzilla, born of the demonic minds of

Madison Avenue: once a player, now a monster! His hideous image thrust upon millions of children." In a deep, droning, monster voice, Shaqzilla says, "Where's my endorsement check?" He has fangs, yellow eyes, huge hoop earrings, very red skin tone. Karl says, "We gotta take him down." Shaqzilla knocks out three Sonics flying in formation— Kemp, Schrempf, and Perkins. Karl says, "The shoes: deflate the shoes." Sarunas Marciulionis of the Sonics zooms down and punches the basketball "pump" of Shaqzilla's shoes. Shaqzilla deflates and disappears like a balloon losing air; only the colossal shoes remain.

Orlando is tired at the end of a long West Coast road trip, and Seattle beats them by 40. Shaq is held in check surprisingly well by Bill Cartwright. Payton scores 31 points in 31 minutes (going 11-for-15 from the floor and 7-for-8 from the free-throw line), has 7 assists, 7 steals. Gill has a nice game as well, and when he comes to the bench with a few minutes to go, he gets a huge ovation. *Don't leave,* people seem to be saying; *stay here and stop complaining and we'll keep bathing you in love like this—how's that for a deal?*

Speaking to reporters after the game, Karl says about Payton, "He was fantastic. I don't know if I've ever seen him play better."

Dennis posts to the Sonics newsgroup: "Gill had a poor first half yet ended the night with 25. Keep him and play him, George! What a great game. Let's just hope they keep it up. If they do, look out!"

My insanely giddy overreaction is: *maybe we* can *all get along.* (Laurie and I do the wild thing till midnight.)

4

THE BEAUTIFUL AND
THE USEFUL

12.18.94—Paul's father is an art historian specializing in African art who, according to Paul, "fucking loves black people." He gives to Paul to give to me Walt Frazier and Ira Berkow's book *Rockin' Steady,* in which Frazier says: "I think I relate best to young kids. Like at Kutsher's camp, I'll call the kids chump. They call me chump back. I tell them how great I am. They say to me, Jerry West is best. Or Pistol Pete." Both of these players are white. "But we're just kidding. We get along good. Kids are real. You can't fool kids.... Adults, they're shaky. Adults ride with the winner. If you lose, you're a bum. But kids live and die with you. They make excuses for you." The line "You can't fool kids" reminds me of former Pistons coach Chuck Daly's remark that "you can fool everyone but kids, dogs, and NBA players," i.e., they're all so simple that nothing could possibly interfere with their radar. Later, Frazier says, "Cool is a quality admired in the black neighborhoods. Cool is a matter of self-preservation, of survival. It must go back to the slave days, when oftentimes all a black man had to defend himself with was his poise. If you'd show fear or anger, you'd suffer the consequences. Today, the guy respected in the ghetto is the guy who resists the urge to go off—who can handle himself in a crisis, who can talk his way out of a fight." I agree with Frazier's analysis, but in an odd sort of way I'm disappointed by it. I want him to be so cool that he doesn't need to offer such a gloss. How weird is that?

12.19.94—I receive a fax from Cheri White, which tells me when to call to request credentials for games, when are the most likely times to obtain interviews, when the locker room is open to reporters before and after games. The Sonics public relations staff will send me all press releases. They welcome me aboard, and they hope I'll enjoy writing about the Sonics. The organization has, inexplicably, changed its mind about me. I must have friends in high places. I'm already planning how to sell the rest of my tickets, what questions to ask Payton. I call *ma chérie* to confirm that I'm reading the communiqué correctly and she says, "Oh, sorry. That was just a form letter sent to all reporters. It must have been sent to you by mistake. Nothing has changed."

After practice, Karl says about Payton, "We're always going to have our arguments. We both have that kind of personality. But there's no one on this team that I talk more to than Gary Payton. I think what's happening is that I'm taking the game plan more directly to Gary. I think when Grgurich [the former Sonics assistant coach now coaching at UNLV] was here, there was more interplay there. Grg had that role. He was more the middleman."

My colleague Geoffrey, who teaches political science at the university, e-mails me: "I heard on the radio that the problem with the Sonics is that Grgurich is gone. He was the go-between between Karl and the players. Sorta like the 'driver' on the plantation, standing between the 'ole marster' and the slaves. HA!" I don't understand the function here of Geoffrey's "HA!" if it's not to distance himself from his own observation, to undo the (interesting, nerve-wracking) analogy he's making at the same time he's making it.

12.20.94—I want to spend the last night of Chanukah with Laurie and Natalie, so I don't go to the game tonight in Tacoma, but I can't even give the tickets away. No one wants to see the Sonics play the Clippers, let alone drive the hour each way to and from Tacoma. Returning to the team of their crimes a week ago, the Sonics are on their best behavior and demolish the Clips (I catch bits and pieces on the radio). A little déjà vu is nevertheless required just to keep everyone angry about something as Christmas approaches: after dunking on Charles Outlaw, Kemp stares at him and receives a technical foul. Even staring is now a no-no in the NBA.

Afterward, asked about getting a technical for "glaring," Shawn says, "It was a strange call. This time, I didn't say anything. I was just looking. I think I understand what the refs are trying to do, but I think they're protecting us too much. We're all adults, and I think they have to give us some leeway." Who's a boy? Who's a man? Who gets to decide?

12.21.94—While I'm standing on my back porch, separating newspapers and magazines and bottles into their proper recycling containers, a black man walks past the house and, in proper Seattle fashion, nods and smiles. I almost never acknowledge such greetings—my deepest dread is becoming a true Seattleite—but I don't want him to think that I'm being unfriendly or wary to him because he's black, so I nod and smile at him. Entering or exiting a store, I don't usually go wildly out of my way to hold the door open for the person behind me, but if the person is black, I never fail to; so, too, if the bus driver is black, I thank him—a Seattle custom—when I get off at my stop, whereas I would never think of doing this if the driver were white. Are black people conscious of how excruciatingly self-conscious white people have become in their every interaction with black people? Is this self-consciousness an improvement?

Maybe not, because I'm thinking of people in categories rather than as people, which is a famously dangerous thing to do. I once mentioned to Laurie that in my experience black people tend, as a rule, not to tip very much—*we've been, over time, charged enough.* Laurie, who waitressed her way through college, responded, "Well, your proud race tends not to tip very well, either."

"What do you mean—like, ladies who lunch?" I said, thinking Judaism is a religion, not a race.

"No," she said, "in general," at which point I understood as I hadn't before the problematics of generalization.

•   •   •

In my disguise as a *Seattle Weekly* reporter, I attend the Gary Payton Celebrity Shootout, a charity event in which fans pay money to play pool with the Sonics and a few Seahawks. Before the tournament begins, KJR nighttime talk-show host Kevin Wall asks Nate McMillan if he's much of a pool player, and McMillan answers, "Naw, I'm just Gary's boy." I feel certain that Nate's tweaking Wall. Sam Perkins recently walked out of an interview with Wall after he called Shaq an "800-pound gorilla"; Wall insisted he meant nothing by it. But then, in response to another question (about how wonderful it is that Gary has put together this event to benefit such charities as the Gary Payton Youth Scholarship Fund, the Boys and Girls Club, the Oakland Recreation Department, and CARE), McMillan says, "I just think Gary has grown up," which plays back into the boy-man rhetoric he just mocked.

As if they need introductions, Payton introduces the Sonics who are here (McMillan, Kemp, Schrempf, Gill, assistant coach Bob Weiss), and when he gets to Gill, he says, ostensibly to the crowd but clearly to Gill, "That stuff in the papers: let that go." It's a revelation to me—I feel it both instantly and constantly—the degree to which the other players defer to Payton, the degree to which it is completely his team, the degree to which he is the verbal and emotional motor of everything that matters. It's nothing very dramatic; it's just a given in the body language of everybody around him.

A sportswriter for the *Seattle Times*—Hugo Kugiya, who often covers the Sonics along with Glenn Nelson—has made a contribution to one of Payton's charities, thereby buying a game with Payton and the opportunity to write about it.

"Take the bag off. You know you already lost," Payton says, delivering the smack Kugiya and everyone else has come to hear. "If you lose, it's going to be a short article. It's a win—easy. It's over."

Payton breaks; the eleven ball goes in a corner pocket. "Uh-huh. There it is. There it go."

Payton misses, and Kugiya hits one in. "That's a great shot—for you," Gary says.

Payton misses but says, "I leave you with nothing. What you gonna do now?"

Five minutes later, when Payton and Kugiya each have only one ball left, Payton bets him ten pushups that Kugiya can't make his exceedingly difficult shot. Hugo doesn't want to look like a wimp, so he says all right, then—improbably—makes the shot.

"You got something to write about now," Payton says, but when Kugiya reminds him that he owes him ten pushups, Gary looks at him in near disbelief. "I ain't doin' no pushups," he says. The life drains out of Kugiya's face, because he just won but lost.

Before fans, Payton riffs on Kugiya, making fun of him. Later, talking to him about the charities and the kids, he is quite business-like. Payton is very comfortable about this role-playing; it's just part of who he is.

Payton plays pool left-handed. Gill also plays pool left-handed, signs a check left-handed. Schrempf signs an autograph left-handed. I immediately have three theories, all plausible: they're intentionally protecting their good hand (they're sensitive geniuses); I've uncovered the cause of the Sonics' shooting woes—half of them are shooting with the wrong hand (they're idiots); or professional athletes are so ambidextrous they can perform ordinary tasks with either hand (they're physical marvels). I'm curious to know which if any of my exoticizing theories is correct but never get around to asking.

Dozens of people have ponied up to play against Payton, and the next person is a blonde babe. "Uh-oh," Payton says. "That's gonna be a distraction."

She immediately starts trying to talk trash with him; this is apparently everyone's fantasy, to go one-on-one with Payton not so much on the court but in language. I can't even begin to convey how much I groove on this, how much I groove on the constant verbal tattoo Gary beats on everyone's head, how much in love I am with how cool he is, how smart he is on a second-by-second basis.

"Talk bad," Payton says, "talk bad. She talkin' bad to me."

Gill makes a shot over on the next table, and Payton tries to bring Gill out of his perpetual gloom by saying, "Black magic, baby boy!" Gill barely manages a half-smile. Payton turns back to his opponent and says to her, "Walk the dog. Walk the kitty cat." What are these—pool terms?

"You know that ain't goin' in," he teases her. "Do you want me to miss?" No. "I won't." Finishing her off. "See ya, wouldn't want to be ya" (drug-dealer lingo at the point of purchase). You can feel the pressure he feels to come up with these little riffs, to not let us down, to be as bad (but as nice!) to us as we hoped he'd be.

Sam Perkins shows up late with his customary sleepy expression and lackadaisical manner.

Payton asks him, gently but firmly, "What happened?"—*why are you late?*

Perkins says, "I got a haircut, man."

Payton persists: "Today at practice—why was you late?"

"I was just late."

"Was you up?"

"Yeah, I was up [i.e., awake]."

Perkins plays a desultory game against someone who has paid to play against him, and Gary says, "Come on, Sam. Get into it."

"I am into it," he says.

A businessman introduces himself to Gary by saying, "Gary, I don't want to be square [our collective nightmare: to be judged square by G. Payton], but…" And then I don't hear the rest of the conversation.

Payton needs a pen to sign a poster for someone, so his agent, Eric Goodwin, says to me, "Can I see your pen?" Overdoing it a little, I offer him a whole pocketful of possibilities and he grins at me: he's already got me figured out. I wise up at least a little. During another game, the cue ball bounces off Gary's table and I pick it up and hand it to him. He says, "Thanks," and I don't provide the unnecessary "You're welcome." He seems to like this, or so I imagine.

Payton beats another opponent, a more casual woman whom Payton seems more comfortable with than the foxy lady ironed into her jeans and blouse.

"I'm in trouble, Gary," she says.

"You certainly are," he says, which mocks standard male reassurance rhetoric and offers instead something better.

When the game's over, he says, "You shouldn'ta missed that shot."

"But it was fun," she comes back with.

He gives her a genuine smile and says, "That's it"—*what else could life possibly be about?*

She asks him if he'll sign his poster with "Thanks for letting me beat you." Very loudly and quite earnestly, he protests, "I ain't gonna say that." She looks a little down. (Later, when I catch up with her, I ask her what he signed, and she unrolls the poster, which says, "I lost—you beat me—Thanks—GP.")

Schrempf, walking past Payton, says, "Hey, don't embarrass us now." You can feel, in Schrempf's slight strain, the pressure Payton puts on people to match him taunt for taunt.

Channel 7 wants Gary to do a quick promo for the event and for the station: "Hey, Harry [Wappler, the Channel 7 weatherman], we got a break in the weather; how about a break for the kids?" Then, of course, Gary breaks on the billiards table. Even this corny line he somehow manages—how, I have no idea—to make sound droll and *his*.

Standing just inches away from Payton, I'm struck mainly by how young he looks; he looks much younger than my twenty-six-year-old graduate students. He has a gold earring in each ear, a *G* and a *P*. He has a little nodule on the back of his neck. He's wearing work boots and Karl Karin jeans. (Kemp is wearing a plaid shirt; he really is from Indiana.)

A pool shark shows up, carrying a little wooden case of cues, and runs the table on Payton, who says, "Huh. Now I've lost twice" (to the shark and to Kugiya).

It's almost pathological how endlessly the language flows from him; he can't stop talking, talking to himself, whispering, singing. (A former teammate once said Payton would stop talking "about two months after he was dead." Another former teammate said that after spending the afternoon at practice with Payton "you just want to go find a library or something, someplace totally silent.") A businessman gives him what the businessman considers a large check, so Gary does corporate-speak for as long as required. The moment that's over, he's talking to his childhood friends from Oakland in a language so mercurial and cryptic I rarely have even the slightest inkling what they're talking about, which is, of course, the point or at least part of the point. He seems to have at least five distinctly different idiomatic gears (homeboy, bon vivant, businessman, athlete, comedian), which, depending upon whom he's talking to (friends, teammates, fiancée, agent, fans), he changes every twenty seconds or so.

A guy with his wife in tow thanks Payton because "you didn't make me scrub when I did some work on your Porsche—that's a beautiful car. I gotta get a picture of you and me." This guy's obsequiousness, reminding us of our own, makes everyone cringe.

There's much discussion of the injustice of Payton being only the tenth-highest-ranked guard in the fans' All-Star balloting, and of rectifying this injustice by getting a lot of his friends together to punch his name on thousands of ballots. "I'm like hundredth," he pseudo-whines.

One of the friends whom Payton grew up with and whom he put through college, Trevor Pope, has dozens of ballots in his hand. Gary says, "Hey, man, you don't gotta do all that"—punch ballots for him.

Pope says, somewhat sadly, "I'm not."

Eric Goodwin introduces himself to me to find out why I'm taking so many notes and I say, "You're his agent, aren't you?"

"I just count the money," he says.

I feel the weird need to immediately establish my liberal bona fides by asking him what he thinks of the Sonics' commercials featuring Payton and Kemp as cartoon characters.

(In the Payton cartoon, Gary gets transformed out of his sweats and into a superhero's outfit, a white unitard. "The Glove"—Payton's nickname, in honor of the tight defense he plays—appears, in comic-book font, across his chest. Coming down the court, Phoenix's Kevin Johnson has the ball and Charles Barkley is behind him. Kevin Calabro does the play-by-play: "KJ and Barkley challenge the Glove." The Glove holds out his hand, emitting a yellow stream of light. Calabro: "The Glove steals the ball…" The ball is magnetically pulled away from KJ by this light stream. The ball moves across space. Calabro: "…his car keys, his cell phone…" The Glove glides up over other hands to dunk. Calabro: "…and hammers it down." Everybody in the crowd has a grin on their face.

(The Kemp cartoon begins with a little boy standing against a threatening sky. The announcer says, "Shawn Kemp: Rain Boy" [Kemp's nickname is "Rain Man"]. A white woman says, "He's just a child." The white man she's with says, "He's a man." The announcer resolves the paradox: "He's a man/child." Lightning strikes and the boy turns into Shawn Kemp and changes back again. "And he came and he grew," the announcer says, "and he fed on the rain." Big rain drops fall. Lightning charges between the two balls in Kemp's hands. Kemp says, "I like this place." A giant bull—i.e., a Chicago Bull—uses spikes to uproot the Space Needle. Surrounded by the rain coming down, Shawn clutches an electrically charged basketball and throws the ball through the air, knocking the head off the giant bull. A black man says, "Way to go, Rain Boy." Shawn says, "Yo, that's Rain Man." The sky clears.)

I say to Goodwin that I don't know what to do with these commercials: are they as naive, garishly patronizing, exoticizing, and demonizing as they appear to be; or are they actually quite self-aware, reflecting back to fans their own racism?

"You'd be surprised how unsophisticated people are," Goodwin says.

Proving him right: two different girls' names appear within minutes of each other on his beeper, and for some reason (white trying to sound black), I say, "You've got the whole crew—all these girls—calling you on your beeper."

"Unfortunately," he says, "that's not the case."

Trying to make amends, I ask him what he thinks about the Rodman-and-Santa commercial, and he says, "People are complaining that the spot says if you can do one thing well, you can get away with anything. Well, hey, that's capitalism. Look at Steve Howe, Roseanne, Drew Barrymore. Look at anyone."

The only fan in the building who's black is a kid about ten or so whose mother, the sex-bomb blonde, sells ads for a cable-television station and keeps pressing her business card into everyone's hands.

Payton mentions something to Goodwin about wanting to get shoes from Nike but that whenever he calls to get some, they're not available.

Goodwin says, "Excuse me, you don't have to deal with that anymore."

Someone comes up to Payton and says, "All you hear is 'Sign this, sign that.' You should start charging us."

Goodwin is wearing a sweatsuit and is black and very large, and fans keep mistaking him for a Seattle Seahawk. "I'm not a player," he keeps insisting with a certain exasperation. "I don't play." *I orchestrate play.*

"I'm so privileged to meet you," someone tells Payton.

"G., I'm leaving," Gill says to Payton.

Payton doesn't hear him, so Gary's fiancée, Monique James—who has known Gary since childhood, is a year or two older than he is, and looks like a thrillingly impossible combination of Rosie Perez and Sandra Bernhard—says, "Gary, Kendall's leaving."

"I'm out," Gill says.

"Thanks, baby boy," Payton says. "See you tomorrow."

Nice nickname: Gill's such a baby boy everyone has to treat him with kid gloves. Earlier, a fan said to him, "Hang in there, Kendall. We love you." And he just walked grimly past her. Granted, how is someone supposed to react to a total stranger's profession of support and love?

"We touched knees," someone says about herself and Monique. "That's my brush with greatness."

Monique mentions that if Payton gets named to the All-Star team, she wants to go to the All-Star game in Phoenix with him.

Payton says, "I'm not sure."

She pleads, "No. No. I want to go."

He turns away.

Several of Goodwin's clients—Payton, Jason Kidd, Cedric Ceballos, Isaiah Rider—are featured on *Basketball's Best Kept Secret*, a rap CD released last month. I've been trying to schedule an interview with Payton about his single on the CD, "Livin' Legal and Large," and Goodwin says Payton would be interested in such an interview, which contradicts what *ma chérie* had told me.

The NBA didn't grant its license to the project, because it objected on moral grounds, Goodwin tells me. "I told Gary no gin, no Stoli, no bongs on his track, but this is getting ridiculous; it's becoming the Roman Catholic Basketball League," he says.

Chubby white people are doing soul-shakes with their heroes; *at least they're trying*, I think, somewhat sentimentally.

A lady wants to pose with Gary for a picture and asks Payton's friend Trevor Pope to snap the photo. It's not an uncomplicated camera, and so she overexplains a bit the proper procedure.

Amazingly, and amazingly quickly, Payton forces the racial subtext out into the open: "Hey, Bubba, press the *red* button."

Pope and the woman blush, Payton grins, and Pope snaps the picture ASAP.

Former Sonic Slick Watts' son, Donald, a high-school phenom, is wearing a T-shirt that says *We Want Justice—Not Blood.*

I run out of paper in my notepad and write on my hand until I can find some more paper. Pope notices this and says, "You're writing on your hand."

All I can come up with is: "I'll survive."

He then observes how small my hands are, in particular my thumbs.

I'm very aware that we're both aware how we're not measuring up to Payton in the trash-talking department, and so our conversation stops. We have nothing more to say to each other than that neither of us is Gary Payton.

12.22.94—Driving to the Seattle-Dallas game tonight, Paul and I listen to a college radio station. People call up, telling loss-of-virginity stories. One woman says she had a horrible experience. The host asks, "How horrible was it?" She says, "Let me put it this way: rap was playing in the background." The host says, "Ouch." Paul and I take stupid pride in screwing the Sonics out of five bucks by using my old press pass and a bullshit explanation ("my colleague, a cameraman, has tonight's pass and he's waiting inside," etc.) to park in the press area. Rebellion of the White Negroes...

As we walk into the Tacoma Dome, Sonics staff hand us posters (All-Star promotions) of Payton dressed in western garb and pointing a pistol—"Fastest glove in the West." I get confused: are we being given gifts of the fear, or the fantasy, of a black planet?

The players walk out to center court for the start of the game. A drunk guy sitting behind Paul taps him on the shoulder and says, "There's a whole lotta meat out there on the floor, isn't there?"

Although Jason Kidd, the Mavericks' star rookie, is several years younger than Payton, they grew up playing together in Oakland and have a friendly rivalry. A handful of Payton's and Kidd's mutual friends are sitting together in the front row, and Payton can hardly make a play without going over and kibitzing with them about it. An endlessly iterated sports cliché goes: "He can talk the talk, but can he walk the walk?" Such a question would make absolutely no sense to Payton, for whom walking the walk is meaningless until it's been talked to death.

The Sonics play very casually all game long, then really turn it on at the end. With the score tied in the last ten seconds, Gill makes a steal and passes downcourt to Payton, who beats Kidd to the ball, then races to the basket for a layup just in time to beat the buzzer. The Sonics win. Afterward, Payton tells reporters, "He was going to have to run me over to get the ball, but he didn't want to do that, because he didn't want to put me on the free-throw line. I was just trying to keep it inbounds, and I knew he had the angle. I got hungry for the ball." This hunger is a lot of what everyone loves about him. "Playing hard," as George Karl likes to say, "is a talent."

The second the game's over, Payton (28 points, 8 assists) rushes over to gloat with the group of his and Kidd's friends sitting courtside. He hops up on a table and sits talking with them long after all the other fans have gone home.

As so many Sonics games seem to when they're facing lesser teams, the game started sluggishly; fans weren't engaged at all. Fan interest rose slowly but surely. It ended quite dramatically. There's much discussion on the post-game show about how the fans wouldn't let the players quit, and the pride the fans should take in this victory for cheering on the Sonics when they were down by several points late in the fourth quarter. Is this an utter delusion? Players insist upon how crucial a catalyst the crowd can be. Still, whenever the announcer commands us to "Get on your feet for your SuuuperSonics," I blanch: I can't deal quite so directly with the fact of our collective obeisance. Cf. Renata Adler: "We were talking about *No, No, Nanette.* I said I thought there was such a thing as an Angry Bravo—that those audiences who stand, and cheer, and roar, and seem altogether beside themselves at what they would instantly agree is at best an unimportant thing, are not really cheering *No, No, Nanette.* They are booing *Hair.* Or whatever else it is on stage that they hate and that seems to triumph. So they stand and roar. Every bravo is not so much a Yes to the frail occasion they have come to make a stand at, as a No, goddam it to everything else, a bravo of rage. And with that, they become, for what it's worth, a constituency that is political. When they find each other, and stand and roar like that, they want, they want to be reckoned with."

12.23.94—On the *Gary Payton Show,* a caller named Brian says, "Hey, what's up, G.?" He sounds very cool at first—very male, very down.

"Hey, how you doin'?" Gary says, responding warmly to how cool this guy sounds.

Brian says, "I'm all right." He's still cool through here, but then he says, "I was at the game last night and I was wondering, man, what the philosophy in the half-court offense is? It seems like late in the game last night everybody was—"

New York Vinnie jumps in, "Proust, isn't it?" Maybe Proust was a philosopher; maybe he wasn't. Vinnie knows he must punish Brian for referencing the intellect, because if being a sports fan is about any one thing, it's about men building a cathedral to their own bodies via other men's bodies.

Brian says, "What's that?" He has no idea what he's in for.

Michael Knight—the co-host with New York Vinnie of the morning show and a man who, as a reader of Paul Bowles, seems cheerfully out of his element in sports-talk radio; a man who, as a reader of Paul Bowles, knows that Proust wasn't a philosopher—says, "No, Kierkegaard." A dubious maneuver, since it puts him in Brian's geeky camp.

Gary gets it, laughs a mean laugh—what I've come to think of as his Snoop Doggy Dogg "not-that-lunatic-nigger-who-you-thought" laugh.

Brian, totally defeated by his devolution from hipster to nerd, from body that's down to mind that's lost in the clouds, dumbly persists, "What *is* the philosophy, Gary?"

Relatively gently, Gary blows him off: "We just gotta run the right play at the right time." *It's all instinct, you idiot.* "When we struggling, we need to get the ball inside, and I think Detlef and Shawn is a great thing to go to." On the off chance Gill is listening, Payton doesn't want him to pout, so he says, "If Kendall is hot, we gotta get him the ball. We don't really have a philosophy." *Which is for losers like you.* "We try to run the right play at the right time." *Life is simple, you idiot.* "If whoever has the weaker man on him, we try to go to that person." *Okay, I'll dish out a dollop of strategy, to let you down easily.*

Another caller says, "Hey, G., I heard Karl say a couple of days ago that it's kinda hard to keep focused with the holidays—getting ready for it and the parties and that. How much of that actually affects your ballplay?"

Gary says, "It doesn't affect mine at all. I mean, we had functions for the last two or three days; we got one tonight. It's just something that happens." This last sentence is a favorite locution of Payton's, and always refers to something negative, which betrays how he feels about all this holiday gaiety. "This is the time, being around Christmas and every-thing—you got to celebrate it. You can keep your mind focused on bas-ketball, too, but you gotta have fun, too." Not quite Ebeneezer Scrooge, but admirably close—a man after my own heart, feeling colonized as I do by the Xmas music and decorations and rituals that overrun my house every December. Last night, hanging ornaments on the tree, Laurie wanted me and Natalie to help. Natalie kept taking the ornaments down and taking them apart. I discouraged her from demolishing the orna-ments, but in my heart of hearts, I must admit, I was cheering her on.

12.24.94—Laurie usually lightens her hair, but today (Xmas eve) the hairdresser darkens it a little and it looks great and she asks me how I like it and I'm thinking, *Make it even blacker. Make it jet black.*

12.25.94—As I wash dishes before we go over to my sister-in-law's house for Christmas, I'm listening on the radio to *Sonics Rewind:* highlights of their recent wins over Orlando and Dallas. The moment Calabro describes Payton racing to get the ball and lay it in to beat Dallas in the last seconds, I get chills down my spine. I seem to be particularly sus-ceptible to these rapid flights of feeling when I'm knee-deep in the quo-tidian: *I'm not him. I'm really not him. I wish I were him. I love him—the phantasm of him—to death.*

I keep sneaking away from Xmas festivities at Laurie's sister's house on Bainbridge Island to watch the game. There's much talk that the Sonics will bury the past by beating Denver in Denver this afternoon and thus free themselves to move on, but as you may have heard, the past is not buried that easily. Gill and Schrempf play well and they each score 21 points, but overall the Sonics (especially Payton and Kemp) play miser-ably in exactly the same way they played miserably against the Nuggets in the playoffs last year, for instance, getting outrebounded by a margin of nearly 2-to-1. Shawn is in constant foul trouble, on silly fouls, and plays less than half the game. "You idiot," I shout at TV-Kemp when he gets in early foul trouble again. "Quit dogging it," I find myself screaming at TV-Payton when he seems to be "slacking up," as he would say. "Back to the fucking drawing board," I mutter at all of the Sonic TV-selves as they troop disconsolately off the court at game's end.

They're not only not over Denver; they don't have the faintest idea how to get over Denver.

12.26.94—I need the money—I'm going broke on the two-thirds salary I'm receiving on sabbatical—so I sell my seats when I get approval from the Sonics to watch the Sonics-Kings game tonight from press row, although it's still nearly the worst seat in the house and I know I won't be allowed to visit the locker room before or after the game. (I've stopped trying to figure out why or when they say yes or no, as perhaps they've given up trying to figure out if I'm ever going to write anything for the *Weekly*.) When I compliment Hugo Kugiya of the *Seattle Times* on his recent, gently satirical piece about the NBA's orchestration of Kemp's visit to the Renton Boys & Girls Club the week before Christmas, he blows me off. Was this some sort of faux pas? I think so; we're all probably supposed to be as competitive as the players. *Ma chérie* doesn't acknowledge me, either. Eating my spaghetti dinner in press row, I'm feeling a little paranoid.

Before the game, I get up and walk around and wind up watching the Sonics Dance Team doing warmups. Jumping and running in their black tights on gray concrete underneath the black stands, they look to me like enemy warriors in a futuristic movie.

Gill never joins everyone else in huddles during timeouts, never cheers when his teammates (especially his replacement, Marciulionis) are playing well, or if he does cheer, he does so in such a lackluster way that it's parodic. Most athletes are considerably more poker-faced than this; what's curious and, in a way, endearing about Gill is that he acts—tries to act—cool, and he's about as cool as I am.

As opposed to Payton. Olden Polynice, Payton's former Sonics teammate who's now a center on the Kings, pretends at one point that he's going to double-team Payton; Gary pulls the dribble back close to his own body and gives Polynice a funny look, as if to say: *please—what are you doing?*

But rather like Kemp. The Sonics come back onto the court after a timeout, and Sasquatch hands Shawn a mini-basketball, asking him to throw it into the stands, which he does. But he doesn't break a smile. I'd say either throw it and laugh about it a little, or don't throw it and keep your game face on. To throw it while maintaining your game face, though, just seems too weirdly conflicted.

Benchwarmer Byron Houston makes a bad play and Karl shoots him a look.

Gary scores only 16 points, but he puts the clamps on the Kings' Mitch Richmond and gets the Sonics playing more up-tempo. The Sonics win by 20.

Leaving the arena, I put on my coat, put on my headphones, walk past *ma chérie* without saying a word, take a quick right, and keep on walking out the door.

12.27.94—On the *Gary Payton Show,* Michael Knight says, "Now we have the new microphone under Gary Payton's bed in his home. Talk about intimacy." Doing the show, Michael and Vinnie are always "in studio"; Payton is almost always on the phone from home.

New York Vinnie says, "I would watch where I put that switch, Gary, because you turn that thing on at 7:15 this mornin' [twenty minutes before the show is scheduled to begin] and the *Gary Payton Show* is going to be the best-rated thing in the country." Cf. What Lanny Van Emman, the Oregon State assistant coach, said about Payton his senior year: "There's an awful lot of life in that young man's body."

"There'll be folks tuning in all over the place to figure out exactly what's going on at Gary's house," Michael says. Cf., for that matter, what David Bowie once said to Tina Turner at the Grammy Awards: "I feel like I'm standing next to the hottest spot in the universe."

"Yeah, exactly, man," says Vinnie.

Gary immediately empties out these attempts to glamorize his body: "All they're gonna hear is somebody sleeping."

Michael, weakly, chastened: "Well, that can be exciting, too."

Vinnie, too, finally gets it and changes topics: "Bring anything back for Christmas? Anything you got for Christmas real ugly, real bad, something you don't want, something you don't have to return?" Vinnie's going to keep talking until Gary responds, and Gary's not going to say anything until Vinnie shuts up.

Payton: "Naw, you know my girl's sittin' right here, so I can't say that. Everything I got was real nice. I appreciate everything I got."

Vinnie says, "See you in line at Nordstrom's," i.e., returning things. Nordstrom is the quintessential Seattle department store with its no-questions-asked return policy; *we'll kindness you to death.*

Payton laughs his Snoop Doggy Dogg laugh. No comment.

Knight: "Remember, Gary, turn off that microphone under your bed now."

Vinnie: "No, Gary, leave it going."

Gary laughs his Snoop Doggy Dogg laugh again. No comment.

In *Esquire's* annual "Dubious Achievements" issue, Shaq is quoted as saying—in reply to someone asking whether he had visited the Parthenon during a trip to Greece—"I can't really remember the names of the clubs that we went to."

It's water underneath the table.

I don't taunt to nobody.

You have to take your hats off to them.

12.28.94—A commercial which I hear on the radio this morning, and which I hear constantly, begins with Gary saying: "Y'all ready? Check it." ("Y'all ready?" promising a down journey to come; "check it" being both rap-speak and hoops-speak.) "Okay. Come on. If I'm so annoying, if I'm so obnoxious, if I'm *so* arrogant, then how come everybody's trying to *dress* like me?" He breaks off to laugh and says, "Here I go"; the illusion is that we're getting the out-takes of the spot—the real, really down Gary Payton mocking the ad at the same time that he's performing it. "How come the Bon Marché's got a whole department of official NBA authorized Sonics sportswear by Champion and Starter? Including jerseys with my number on them? I mean, there's a whole bunch of people out there walkin' around in number 20 jerseys in all kinds of sizes. What's so annoying about that?" Payton laughs his Snoop Doggy Dogg laugh.

The official voice of reasonable civilization intrudes, confirming that what Gary said is indeed true: "Now, find the latest collection of official NBA teamwear from famous makers like Champion and Starter. Choose Sonics sweats and jackets, logo hats, jerseys, and warmups featuring your favorite NBA players and teams. It's all officially licensed apparel, and you'll find it in the Sports Forum at the Bon Marché—including the number 20 Gary Payton jersey, which happens to be very popular."

Payton, inevitably, gets the last word: "Hey, it's not easy being misunderstood, but looking good helps."

It's a complicated argument: *You're a teenager. You feel misunderstood—who doesn't? You dig Gary. Wear his jersey and then you, too, will look good, even though, like him, you're still a social misfit, which is what we think we like about him but what we know we don't like about you.*

The Philadelphia 76ers are in town for a game tonight; I sell my tickets again in order to sit in the press box. The last few days I've been talking with Jodi Silverman in the Sixers' media office to set up an interview with Dana Barros, a former Sonic who now plays for the Sixers and whose cut is the best thing on *Basketball's Best Kept Secret;* although he has a rather cherubic on-court persona (he's only 5'11"), his single "Check It" burns down the house. Back and forth I go with Silverman. The interview is all set up; "Dana's usually pretty good," Silverman assures me. I prepare my little list of questions to ask Dana—whether he has any control over pre-game music when the Sixers play at home, when he got interested in rap, what the relationship is if any for him between shooting and language (in graduate school, at the height of my basketball apex, I had the sudden revelation that the only two things I'd ever devoted myself completely to were writing sentences and shooting baskets), whether rap riffs are ever going through his head when he's playing, if it bugs him when bubblegum rock is blaring in his ears during a timeout. Barros, of course, never calls. In the NBA, as nowhere else in America, white people are utterly beholden to black people, and they're not about to let us off that easily; it is a kind of very mild payback for the last five hundred years.

Payton and Barros were rivals when they were both on the Sonics, since they played the same position; Gary doesn't greet Dana at the beginning of the game. Payton gets hit in the head with Barros' accidental elbow near center court, where the radio mikes are located, and on my headphones I can hear Gary say to the ref, "Don't be trippin'. I all right." (I admit it: I'm happy here, snug in my little perch, well fed with food from the Sonics, binoculars pressed to my eyes and headphones pressed to my ears.) Barros encroaches on the shooter's circle as Payton is about to shoot his first free throw. Payton gives Barros a funny look—*don't be encroaching on my free throws, little man.* When Dana is shooting free throws, Gary makes a point of talking to a ref or a teammate about some matter of suddenly pressing importance. Payton's shooting more long-range jumpers than usual tonight, as if to demonstrate to Barros—who's a much better shooter if a much less good all-around player than Payton—his newfound shooting touch.

In the third quarter, with the Sonics up by 20, Gary is all alone for a layup but instead tries a behind-the-back pass, which goes out of bounds. "Too fancy," declares Dave Harshman, Marques Johnson's occasional replacement on the radio. "Not a smart play. When you're ahead of the pack, don't throw it behind you." Harshman goes on and on about the stupidity and immorality of the play. "Detlef," he says, by contrast, "has come in and given a calming influence in there."

Payton questions every foul ever called against him. One of the referees, Bob Delaney—classic Irish cop—gets tired of listening to it and gives him a technical. Karl substitutes for Payton, and as Gary leaves the floor, he gives Delaney an utterly icy look, coming close to getting ejected, and Karl, in a crucial and expected show of solidarity, attempts to give Delaney a similar look, but it has the odd and unintended effect of expressing commiseration with the poor, embattled official.

The 76ers' coach, John Lucas, a former player and coke addict and now a drug counselor for many players, gets ejected, and as he walks off the court, shouting and waving his arms, he pulls down one of the straps on Perkins' jersey, making Perkins laugh. It simply couldn't have happened if both Lucas and Perkins weren't black; no one would have gotten that it was a joke, this pseudo-assault.

In the last few minutes, Payton feeds Gill for two soaring jams. Gary seems to be making a specific point of trying to bring Gill out of his funk. Forgetting that I'm in press row, I clap in appreciation of these plays, earning the disdain of my journalistic brethren: I've blown my cool; not that I ever was, but now I'm definitely no longer Ace Reporter.

I thought it must have been my imagination that the black usher and I seemed to be having a secret communication going all night long: how much we both love basketball, me with my binoculars and radio up here in nearly the worst seat in the house, him stomping his foot and clapping. But Schrempf makes a dumb outlet pass that gets intercepted for a dunk the other way, and the usher and I both simultaneously point to our heads (*idiot*, we're both thinking) and laugh; at the end of the game, when I walk down the stairs to leave, he says, "Good night, man."

Showing the Sonics they shouldn't have let him go, Barros scores 26 points (four 3-pointers), but Payton scores 23; Schrempf, 23; Gill, 25; and the Sonics win big. Their record is 18 and 8—two-and-a-half games behind Phoenix in the division.

Kevin Calabro is an uncommonly good basketball announcer, but occasionally—out of sheer perversity, it would seem—he tries to get down, and the result is always excruciating. Perkins has a radio show on KJR's sister station, KUBE-FM; on the post-game interview tonight, Calabro tries to draw him out by saying, "You'll be in your crib, spinnin' tunes. What are the hot tunes out there?" It's all Perkins can do to muster the following: "Listen to my radio show; KUBE is good for urban contemporary music." What would possess Calabro to fall into such a burlesque of black diction? I imagine he feels trapped sometimes in his own lingo, always speaking to players in his Indianapolis-bred language, always relating to the players in this false language of whiteness and sportsness; then, suddenly, of the moment, he's feeling loose or he's feeling some rapport and, out of a surge of empathy, he tries to jump the chasm and—the chasm yawns; the rope breaks; *what do you mean* we, *paleface?*

•   •   •

12.29.94—Laurie and I and Natalie are doing a jigsaw puzzle together, one of Natalie's favorite things to do. When she fits a piece into the puzzle, a portion of the puzzle depicts a net and she cries out exaggeratedly, "Oh no!" At first Laurie and I are baffled, but after a while we deduce that to Natalie, a net means basketball and basketball means Daddy crying out "Oh no!" at some snafu or other. Laurie is helpless with laughter.

The first game of a five-game Sonics road trip is against the Lakers tonight in LA. Payton has a terrible night, scoring only 8 points and missing two free throws with 55 seconds left that would have won it. Down by 6 points, with 4:25 left in the game, on a four-on-none breakaway when he could easily have scored himself, Gary sees Shawn trailing and underhands it off the glass for Shawn to grab and jam, but Kemp bangs the ball off the back of the rim and it goes flying off. Calabro says: "Oh no, oh no, I don't believe he did that. Oh, my goodness. I can't believe he did that."

The Sonics lose, 96–95.

After the game, Karl tells reporters, "I don't think one play is more important than your team's success. At any time." (Cf. Alexis de Tocqueville: "Democratic nations will habitually prefer the useful to the beautiful, and they will require that the beautiful be useful"; what Payton likes to call "putting a little style in our game" Karl calls "too stylish and too cute and too pretty.")

Payton says, "You can't worry about how Karl's going to react. I just went over and told him what I had to tell him. He was mad. He had a right to be mad. It was a wrong decision by me—my fault. I take the consequences." Who can't admire how dignified this is? Asked if, in a similar situation, he'd lob the ball off the glass again—it's a rhetorical question, really; the assumption is that Gary has learned his lesson and will become a good citizen—he says, "Maybe I would, and maybe I wouldn't." This is everything I love about him: he can stay straitjacketed only so long. "The problem wasn't the pass; it was the finish. If Shawn had finished the play, everybody would be hollering and cheering. The pass was there. I don't think that play made us lose the game." Asked what he was thinking on the play, Payton says, "Nothing. Just playing basketball.

The ball was right in his hand. It was just something that happened"—his shrugging fatalism that sneaks in whenever something bad happens.

Brian Wheeler, the host of the post-game call-in show, says, "During our highlight segment, you'll be able to hear and relive once again one of the bonehead plays of this or any other season."

Bob, from Renton, says, "I think the Sonics' problem really is they don't have guys with heart. All the guys care about is how they look when they dunk the ball. I mean, they don't care if they win or lose. It's how do you look when you make that dunk? I mean, that's their biggest problem."

Wheeler: "I don't know if it has anything to do with heart, though."

Bob: "What's it got to do with?"

Wheeler: "I think it has something to do with thinking."

So far they don't have a heart or a brain; they're two-thirds of the way to joining Dorothy.

Joe, from Seattle, calls to say, "They're kids out there playing, Brian. I mean, these guys are twenty-five, twenty-six-year-old kids out there playing. They're playing the game; we want them to have fun; every other day we talk about how we want them to enjoy the game, to have fun. That's the way they have fun." *And the way we have fun is to analyze how they have fun.*

12.30.94—Verbatim dialogue between two cashiers at the drugstore, a young black man and an elderly white man:

Black cashier: "Did you watch the game last night?"

White cashier: "Yeah. They lost. That's all that matters."

Black cashier: "No, that's not all that matters."

The white cashier busies himself with his next customer (me). The silence between the two cashiers is so fraught I'm seconds away from beseeching them toward some sort of rapprochement.

The conversation usually goes about like that. Sometimes, though, it's really lovely; sometimes it goes like this:

Posting to the Sonics newsgroup, Alan writes: "Last week I was headed into the post office at 23rd and Union when I saw these two guys walking across the parking lot; one of them looked like Gary Payton. I stood in the doorway for a minute, staring. It was him. I could go up and talk to him. I could go ask what it's like to be a premier point-guard in the NBA or what's up with that hand-checking rule or what's with that 3-point line or how many points did he have in only 3 quarters against Orlando? I could ask for his autograph. I could say it was for my nephews. But my hands were full of Christmas packages, and I didn't have a pen. I went into the post office. I wanted to tell someone, not just anyone, the perfect fan, a confidant who could understand the magnitude of the find. There was no one. (So I'm telling all you guys now.) I scanned the place for a pen I could steal. They were all attached to metal chains or behind the counter too near the clerk. The line was long—four days before Christmas. GP could be in Tacoma by now. I left the post office and looked around the parking lot. There was a small crowd of people at the opposite end of the strip mall. I thought about walking over. Then it occurred to me that I might be deluded; maybe GP didn't walk by and not only might not be over there—never was. Then it occurred to me that I was the only white guy around. I decided to drive by and check it out. I knew I had a pen in my car and I was pretty sure I had a ticket stub from the recent Houston game in my backpack. It was a barber shop or hair salon, and Gary was definitely in there. There was a swarm of people around him, mostly women, I think. And there were people standing around outside. I had my pen and ticket stub in my hand, but I could see there was nowhere to park. So forget it, I would just head to work.

"Halfway to work, I turned the car around, as if answering a dare. I mean fuck it, I'll just walk in and interrupt his haircut and start talking with him. It will be like one of those tennis-shoe commercials where David Robinson and Dennis Rodman are sitting around bullshitting. Except I'm not in the NBA. The crowd had dispersed. I walked in and the place was dead silent. I felt responsible for the silence. I looked around as if to ask someone's permission to be there. Gary Payton was in a chair a few feet away in the middle of his haircut. He didn't look my way. I found it difficult to speak. I said, 'Ah, Mr. Payton, I was wondering if I could get your autograph?' The guy cutting his hair smiled and took five. Gary signed the ticket stub without really looking at me, which kind of embarrassed me, so I looked away. We exchanged a glance when he handed me back the ticket stub. I said, 'Thank you' and 'Merry

Christmas.' He said, 'You're welcome' and 'You, too.' I read the signature as I walked out the door—'Gary Payton #20'—and looked back through the barber shop window before I was out of eye-shot. He watched me walk away. I gave the autograph to my nephews on Christmas Eve. Peace."

5

CONVERTING OUR SELF-
LOATHING TO HATRED

12.31.94—Last night I dreamt that I went to a game, but when I checked in at press row, I read in the press handout "Sonics Notes": "David Shields' brief, agonizing stay in press row has come to a merciful end." It was as if I had a huge desk there. I spent the entire game endlessly packing up all my stuff, but then—within the dream—I realized, *hey, this is just a dream. I should get out of here and go watch the game.*

New Year's Eve: Natalie is asleep by eight. Throwing caution to the wind, Laurie and I stay up until nearly eleven, playing Scrabble and eating Christmas cookies.

1.1.95—Paul e-mails me the rumor that in jail O.J. is reading Cormac McCarthy's *All the Pretty Horses.* The joke behind the rumor is that O.J. is reading a book that offers a theoretical "defense" of violence, i.e., man is a savage beast. The joke behind the joke behind the rumor is that O.J. is unlikely to be reading a theoretical anything.

• • •

1.2.95—Bill Russell lives in the Seattle area—Mercer Island, a fancy rural suburb—and while I'm out pushing Natalie in her stroller, I catch an unmistakable glimpse of the bearded wonder piloting his Rolls-Royce into the Wallingford Center parking lot, just a few blocks from my house. What's interesting to me is how instantaneously I know it's Bill Russell. I suppose the KELTIC6 license plate (he played for the Boston Celtics and wore number 6) didn't hurt, and how many people are riding around Seattle in green Rolls-Royces, let alone 6'9" black men? Still, I feel as if I knew it was Bill Russell even before I calculated these things, and to me it was the way he swerved into the left-hand-turn lane and scooted through the yellow light: the rhythm, the pace, the left-handed *lurchingness* were so eerily reminiscent of that left-handed hook shot that I had seen him take and make so many hundreds of times against my beloved Lakers. (I was born in LA and lived there till I was six; while growing up in San Francisco, going to college in Providence and graduate school in Iowa City, living and working and writing and teaching in New York City and upstate New York, I remained a Laker fan. Only after moving to Seattle in 1989 did my loyalty begin, year by year, to shift.)

Natalie—in her stroller—and I go flying across the street to try to talk to him, but by the time we get to the Wallingford Center, he's parked and gone inside. We can't find him anywhere, so I leave a note ("Please call if you'd be willing to talk," etc.) on his windshield and am amazed that I don't set off the car alarm and am not amazed that he never calls.

I still remember, when I was a kid, how strange and irritating I used to find it that when Russell was introduced at the beginning of games, he would never come trotting onto the floor, but instead would just walk slowly onto the court to join his teammates. Although, after he retired, Russell claimed that it was just one more way to conserve a little energy, I now see how beautiful a gesture it was in its dignified renunciation.

1.3.95—Sonic reserve Vince Askew, angry about a decrease in his playing time, refused to go back into the game against the Sixers a few nights ago; he received a one-game suspension. Today his agent, Ron Grinker, tells reporters, "Vinny and I accept the suspension and have decided not to contest it. George is the boss. He is the coach. He has the right to do

what he has to do." This is the point Laurie always makes, that someone
has to be in charge. On a practical level, it's true, I suppose, but it does
little to assist me in my need to maintain the illusion that I'm some sort
of potentially subversive individual and the Supes are my surrogate sub-
versives.

1.4.95—Natalie doesn't get to sleep until late, and when she does, Laurie and I turn on the Sonics-Cavaliers game toward the very end of the
game. The game's in Cleveland and many of the seats are empty, so I
immediately predict that it's a Sonics blowout and guess the score. When
a graphic gives the final score (Sonics 116, Cavs 85) and I'm off by only
a few points, Laurie's semi-impressed. The things I know...

It turns out that Payton has gone 14-for-14 from the floor, setting a
team record for consecutive field goals made without a miss and becoming one of only four players in the history of the NBA to have a perfect
shooting game with a minimum of 14 attempts. Afterward, he says, "I
wasn't even thinking about it, really. I knew I hadn't missed a shot, but I
didn't know I had taken 14 shots without missing. It's an experience, and
a struggle, not to miss a shot."

Karl says, "I bet you of his fourteen shots, he had ten layups. I'm not
saying I could have made them all. I couldn't have *gotten* them all." My
father apparently goes on and on about me all the time to everyone else,
but face-to-face he has trouble ever saying anything unqualifiedly com-
plimentary to me; if I send him something I've written, he usually brings
most of his attention to bear upon errata and typos. I asked him once if
he felt competitiveness was simply part of being father and son, and he
scoffed at the very notion of such a thing.

Karl is asked why he didn't leave Payton in to attempt to break Wilt
Chamberlain's record of 18-for-18, set twenty-eight years ago. He says,
"You lose the record if you miss a shot, right? I felt bad enough for them
[the Cleveland Cavaliers], letting him go back in and get the record."

Payton says, "I'll take it any way I can take it"—improving the cliché,
as always, by fucking it up; in 1990, upon being named College Player of
the Year by *Sports Illustrated,* he said, "Everything is going like clock-
wise."

•   •   •

1.5.95—Laurie tends to be very practical; I tend to be very impulsive. This plays itself out in, for instance, our different views of my bracelet watch, which clamps to my wrist and which has engendered more conversation with other human beings than anything I have ever done. Despite the fact that it appears at first glance like a piece is missing, it manages to stay on my wrist, at least most of the time, though it manages to fall off often enough that it drives Laurie crazy how much money I spend repairing this watch: "Why don't you just get a regular watch which will stay on your wrist and won't keep needing to be fixed?" She's right, but I have trouble giving up on this watch, which seems to function for me less as a timepiece than as an emblem of still-barely-breathing youth.

So many of Natalie's favorite books and movies—*The Cat in the Hat, Winnie the Pooh, Mary Poppins*—set utility against pleasure. The villain—the fish, Rabbit, George Banks—invariably defines himself in terms of humorless, obsessive practicality. A creature of *qué-será-será* sensuality—the Cat in the Hat, Tigger, Mary Poppins—enters, undoes, and revivifies this world of tedious efficiency. This is a way to flatter children's satirical view of their parents, and it also explains why for the last week nobody has stopped complaining about Gary's pass off glass to Shawn against the Lakers: it lays bare the underlying mythology of We're Serious People Who Turn to You for Relief and Release and Joy in the Toy Department of Life; *how dare you shove in our face that it's only a game?* In the melodrama of my own imagination, I am my own villain; the Sonics are my heroes.

Ron Shelton, promoting his movie *Cobb,* is doing dozens of press interviews, and while speaking to the *Seattle Times* film critic, he waxes enthusiastic about a new movie he has in mind: a true story about two boxers, "best friends for life," who wound up "beating each other's brains out" in a boxing match in Las Vegas. "Then they blew their meager earnings in the casino and drove home together to LA. It's a very simple story, as clean and compact as *The Last Detail,* and I can see Wesley Snipes and Larry Fishburne in it."

I hope he doesn't make the movie, because it's perfect just the way it is.

•   •   •

On the *George Karl Show,* host Brian Wheeler says, "We finally have an opportunity today to check in with a guy who should be pretty happy about this team, the head coach of the Seattle SuperSonics, George Karl." Karl says, "Coaches—happy? Come on." (Happiness is for the dumb brutes beating each other's brains out, then blowing their meager earnings in the casinos.) "It's a situation where we're all trying to go to the same goal. Sometimes we're not all on the same rope getting there, and I think the big key is to get back on the same rope. When we need each other's help, we can help each other and become more of a team, more of a mentally tougher team, and when we start losing our confidence, let's fight together, not fight individually."

A caller, on a cell phone, lobs one to Karl underhanded: "If I'm in a situation where I just don't want to go to work, I'm fired. But here's a guy [Vince Askew] who quite frankly is probably not as good a caliber as many of the people on the same floor as him, and he doesn't want to play. He's suspended for only one game—now what kind of message is that sending?" Fans always want to compare the NBA to their situation at work, but it's not the same, because nobody cares about their situation at work.

"Well," Karl replies, "it's a good question, and at times I can't deny it was very frustrating and it hurt me a lot to have it happen. But Vince doesn't have a family, and Christmas time is a time of the year that sometimes people can get depressed when they don't have some roots. They see that a lot of other players and a lot of other people have their families around. I'm just gonna give Vince the benefit of the doubt. It was a bad day. He made a bad decision. And so in a way Vince is now on a shorter rope." (There's the good rope of "The big key is to get back on the same rope;" then there's the bad rope of "Vince is on a shorter rope.") "Or a bigger hammer or whatever." Karl changes figures of speech because he hears how problematic it sounds to have a player on a short leash, and it's problematic precisely because of race, and all this passes through everyone's mind in the fraction of a second it takes Karl to correct himself, and none of this would ever be articulated or acknowledged in a million years.

Asked by a caller how he gets out of being depressed, Karl says, "My two ways of really getting out of depression is exercise and comedy."

After the *George Karl Show* is over, without being aware that I'm aping Karl's advice, I shoot baskets at my local playground for the first time in months and rent two Albert Brooks movies.

1.6.95—On the *Gary Payton Show,* New York Vinnie asks Payton: "Is Steve Scheffler [a white benchwarmer who has been injured for a while and who is religious and extremely conservative] on the trip with you?"

Payton: "Uh, no."

Vinnie: "Takes up too much room on the plane, right?"

Payton: "No, we just can't bring him. That's too much baggage for us." You can't tell whether "baggage" is meant literally or figuratively, which is, to me, a kind of genius.

Michael Knight says: "I saw in the paper last night, in Glenn Nelson's story in the *Times,* that George Karl showed the team a film of everyone not running and it sort of woke up everyone to the idea that you guys have to move more."

Payton: "Well, yeah, he gave us a tape that shows how we look when we're really moving compared to how different we look when we're just standing around. People will realize that we need to run for us to win ballgames." So Gary shows that he got the gist of the lecture, but then he shows, as he always does, the irrelevance of the lecture: "You know, we knew that from the git. Sometimes we get in a mood where we just watch people, which we should just go and play ourselves." For *which* he means *whereas,* but it's close enough; you get the point (and you also get something else). He seems to me near-phobic about making sure he doesn't say too many correct words consecutively.

Natalie, jumping up and down on her trampoline in the basement, informs me that she's "Shaw"—i.e., she can jump as high as Shawn Kemp. I raise my hand higher and higher, seeing if she can jump high enough to graze the top of her head against the palm of my hand. She really does have amazingly strong legs and is delirious with the feat of her jumping, as am I.

The Sonics beat the Bulls, 108–101, in Chicago. Payton scores only 14 points but has 13 assists. On the post-game show, a Sonics fan named

Phil says, "I've decided to personify Sam Perkins as a keel on a sailboat," i.e., he's a steadying influence. It fascinates me that Phil not only imagined turning a man into a piece of wood but felt compelled to share this information with us.

1.7.95—Driving home from work, a white female colleague in the English department picks up a black male hitchhiker in order to prove to herself that she's not racist. She tells the hitchhiker, "I picked you up to prove to myself I'm not racist."

The hitchhiker says, "You're a fool. I could have killed you."

1.9.95—On the *Gary Payton Show*, Vinnie asks Gary: "At the beginning of the season, I remember we talked when the team was kind of in the doldrums, and you said at one point that you'd rather have the slump at the beginning of the season and kinda hit your groove come January. Well, here we are, moving into the second week of January, and I don't think the team could be any more in the groove than it is right now"; they've won eight of their last ten games, and at 22-and-9 are in second place in the Pacific Division, two-and-a-half games behind the Suns. "Is this something that you guys were able to plan on happening or is this something that just happened?"

Payton says, "This is something that just happened."

What's the philosophy in the half-court offense, Gary?

We don't really have a philosophy.

For his 14-for-14 shooting against Cleveland last week, Payton is named NBA Player of the Week. Asked for his reaction, Gary says, "I just have to move on. This week, I could be a goat"—thus refusing to accord the honor the respect it's supposed to merit.

1.10.95—The Sonics play the Warriors in Oakland. Gill, furious that he isn't in the lineup for almost the entire first half and at the insult of being inserted for only the final two minutes, is talking to himself when he checks in at the scorer's table. His first two shots are 3-pointers—the first one an air ball, the second from about 25 feet away, which also badly misses. Karl is goading Gill, and Gill is goading Karl back.

In the second half, surprisingly, Gill plays and is effective. At one point Karl pulls Marciulionis from the game. As Marciulionis leaves the court, he flashes Karl a nasty look. Defending the substitution, Karl says to Marciulionis, "He's playing well, too," meaning Gill. I imagine Karl feels guilty for his shameful, shameless toying with Gill.

Perkins makes two free throws to send the game into overtime, then hits two 3-pointers in overtime to win it for the Sonics.

Afterward, Karl tells reporters, "It was my choice [not to start Gill]. He [Gill] didn't show up for practice. He was the last man in the rotation."

Gill tells reporters, "I'm happy we won the game, but I'm tired of dealing with this shit and George and his immature antics." *I'm the father; he's the son.*

Payton asks Gill, "What's up?"

Gill says, "Same old shit, different day."

Payton starts rapping without rhyming: "They call us the Glove / And we don't care / We're going to pick your pocket anyway." Despite his love of rap, he's an astonishingly uninspired rapper. His "Livin' Legal and Large" track is easily the most boring and square thing on *Basketball's Best Kept Secret;* he's livin' large (he's rich) but legally (he's not pushing). Its main themes—stay out of trouble ("Keep yo' eyes on the prize / if ya wanna rise"), find a job ("Gotta keep my game tight / or I could lose it all"), work hard at it ("Ya gotta strive and try / to be the best that you can be to survive"), and save your money ("I be walkin' to da' bank with a smile on my face / Have 'em sayin', 'Mr. Payton, have a nice day' / Yeah, and that's real")—wouldn't be out of place in *The Autobiography of Ben Franklin.*

1.11.95—My father, who is still the sports editor of a suburban weekly in the San Francisco Bay Area, sends me an article he's written about a star black football player named Daren Gordon who plays for the Bay Area high school I attended twenty years ago. My father writes that Gordon ran "through the opposing defense as though it were made of *papier-mâché.* In thirteen games this season, Daren gained nearly 1,600 yards to lead all rushers in the Pacific Athletic League. The 220-pound, 6'1" Daren played both offense and defense and also did the punting. He did everything except take tickets at the gate and operate the electronic scoreboard." Sometimes my father and I will have a twenty-minute phone conversation, and for nineteen minutes we'll talk, contentedly, about one of the teenage stars he's just seen play.

1.12.95—Rudy Washington, the head basketball coach at Drake University and one of the leaders of the Association of Black Basketball Coaches, says, "Every industry has its own lingo. The computer business has its own lingo. Banking has its own lingo. Trash-talking is the language of athletics; it's the language of the game." Last week, Margo Jefferson, reviewing the *Pulp Fiction* screenplay in the *New York Times*, wrote, "The words vibrate long after the screen has gone blank: despite all the blood and gore, the real thrill comes from Mr. Tarantino knowing how language crosses the boundaries between violence and contemplation." *Language* is what's most alive and dangerous—Gary Payton knows this; so, qua stutterer, qua writer, do I.

Kevin Wall, who hosts his own show on KJR from seven to ten P.M., has an opening section called "Sports Graffiti," in which fans call in with "one line and one line only." One caller says, "George Karl should go back to the CBA so he can coach all the scrubs there." Wall later refers to "the continuing saga of eternal torment known as Kendall Gill." The whole day has a sad, melancholy, unsympathetic feel to it for me: each of us is trapped in our own space helmet.

Case in point: Natalie is playing with her toys in the bathtub. I'm lying down in Laurie's and my bedroom, with the door three-quarters closed and the lights off. Natalie says to Laurie, "Dada—basketball, Dada—basketball." She thinks I'm watching the Sonics because whenever I watch basketball on TV, I have a tendency to close the door and kill the lights; it's a guilty enough pleasure that my impulse, apparently, is to hide it.

1.13.95—On the *Gary Payton Show,* Michael Knight says to Payton, "You had a good night [three days ago] against your nemesis Mitch Richmond."
    In a flat voice, Payton corrects him: "Tim Hardaway."
    Knight says, "I'm sorry."
    Payton says, "You asleep today?"

Knight says, "Must be. You do your show from bed. I do it from bed, too." To my ears, the subtext of this exchange is: *cut me some slack, Gary; I don't think all black men look alike.*

New York Vinnie tries to change the topic of conversation by mentioning the fact that they played overtime in their last game, the win over Golden State: "You don't get paid extra for that, do you, Gary? Because I know if we work overtime, we have to get paid a little extra. Do they slip a little extra in your envelope if you play in overtime?"

Payton is capable of the most subtle irony, but he tends not to get other people's jokes. At least he doesn't get this one (chooses not to get it? doesn't like it?): "No, they give us the same amount of money."

Vinnie tries again: "Next time you play overtime, I think you oughta ask for five, six, eight bucks extra for meal money."

Payton really doesn't like this. Very coldly, he says, "Yeah, I think I'm gonna ask for a little more than that, though."

Vinnie, amazingly, persists: "All right—ten bucks, okay?"

Silence. Gary doesn't dig it and I dig him for not digging it.

After winning four out of five on the road, the Sonics are back home, playing the Clippers tonight in Tacoma. Someone in the Sonics newsgroup offers me $25 for both tickets and I take it, gladly. My first article about the Sonics finally appeared this morning in the *Weekly*—an ode to Payton's pass off the backboard to Kemp: "The bored workers, trying to suck the boredom out of the game, were asking everyone else to elevate their games along with them," etc.—and I'm convinced that *ma chérie* is giving me the freeze-out in the press box tonight because she read it and found it just too weird for words.

With eight minutes left in the fourth quarter, Kemp grabs a loose ball and passes it to Gill, who throws it to Marciulionis, who throws it to Askew, who throws it back to Gill, who runs the length of the floor for a one-handed dunk, giving the Sonics a nine-point lead. Gill grabs both of Askew's hands, butts heads with Kemp, gets a hero's welcome back at the bench.

A fatal traffic accident on I-5 caused half the team to arrive just barely in time to play the game tonight, and after the victory, Gill says, "I was thinking, 'Man, if I'm the only one late, this is really going to be messed up for me.' I don't need this. I called the Tacoma Dome and reached Cheri White," who told him that other players were also late. "I asked her if Shawn was there and she said, 'No.' So I said, 'Okay, cool.' I didn't want to be the only one." Maybe it's just me: I must admit I find it difficult not to like someone as manifestly insecure as this.

Karl says, "Kendall ran well. He's one of the best if not the best running athlete on the team. And he rebounded aggressively. Those are two of the things where we think he can be a prime-time player."

Gill says, "I want to leave this stuff alone and come and play ball. I don't care what anybody says or thinks about me as long as I'm cool with my teammates. That's all I'm concerned about."

For the moment we can all, just barely, get along.

1.15.95—It's such an ugly, rainy night that not even the scalpers are out at the T-Dome; I have to eat the other ticket. During the game—against Portland—I look through the Sonics' media guide and wonder why Payton changed from jersey number 2 to jersey number 20 after his first year with the Sonics. I develop all sorts of elaborate theories until I ask the guy sitting next to me on press row, who informs me that Payton's favorite older sister wore number 20 on her softball jersey. Also, why does he never smile in team photos? How conscious is he of not making that concession? (I've always loved how Miles Davis would turn his back on the audience for enormous stretches of time, always been disappointed when musicians politely say thank you after a ferocious set.) I'm also struck by the fact that over the last few years, whoever the photographer was kept flooding in more and more light, trying to get the players' dark faces to come out clearly, until in 1993 he finally got it right, washing out the white faces.

In the last seconds of the game, with the Sonics comfortably ahead, Payton, all alone for a layup, stops and, with one hand, throws the ball straight off the backboard for Gill to grab and jam—a slightly more modest (only because slightly more slow-motion) version of the pass to Kemp a couple of weeks ago that caused such a ruckus. I take it as a fairly explicit *fuck you* to Karl: *it's my team, not yours*. I wonder if I'm just imagining this, but when I zero in on Karl with my binoculars, he looks stricken, despite the fact that they've just won.

Afterward, Gill, comparing getting a pass off the backboard to a straight lob pass, says, "Actually, it's easier when it's coming off the glass because you can see it. It wasn't meant as a backstab." Of course it was, and what intrigues is, again, the mixed message—the *fuck you* gesture combined with the claim that nothing of the kind was intended. In seventh grade, caught flipping off my shop teacher, I insisted I was just saluting him.

On *Second Quarter Report,* a TV special about the most recent month or so of the Sonics' season, Kevin Calabro says to Detlef Schrempf, "Thanks so much for joining us here at Hec Ed Pavilion [the gymnasium of the University of Washington, where Schrempf played college basketball after moving from Germany to Washington during his high-school years]." They shake hands.

Schrempf says, "Thank you."

Calabro says, "The old crib. The old turf."

At this point Schrempf appears to have no idea what Calabro is talking about, just says, "Yeah," then after a while seems to get what he means and smiles. It's difficult to tell exactly what Schrempf's thinking. Maybe this: two white guys get together, and so what does Calabro do?— he acts black; Calabro must figure, *Well, at least I'm blacker than the German; now I get to be black for a minute.* Race is the one thing that makes Calabro act foolish, as it does nearly every white man in America.

1.16.95—On the *Gary Payton Show,* New York Vinnie says, "All of a sudden you're gonna need Nate [McMillan] in the playoffs. And maybe he's wearing himself out a little more than he should at this point in the season."

Payton says, "Nah. He wants to play. He gotta stay playin'. We can't just let him sit out and rest, because he won't be on beat." Payton obviously loves the figure as much as we do, so he repeats it: "I think he has to come in and play just a little taste so that he can stay on beat. By playoff time, I know he'll be ready; that's forty-five more games from now. Get him a little rest. I think we shouldn't play him as much as we do right now, but let him get a little rested and by playoff time he'll be at full stride." This is one of my favorite things Payton has said so far this season, because he states one opinion, then states the completely opposite opinion, has them cancel each other out, and lets you choose.

Vinnie asks him if Vince Askew and Sarunas Marciulionis are the strongest guys on the team. Marciulionis is supposed to have amazingly strong hands; Askew has shoulders like a linebacker.

Payton says, "I think so. They're both real strong, because they both can get to the basket. Their upper bodies are extremely strong. And they know how to finish when they get to the basket. Them two are the strongest on our team."

Vinnie says, "Maybe we could go in the locker room and get them to arm-wrestle?"

Payton says, "Let's do that after the season." Which sounds, to me, slightly offended.

Knight says, "Ed Middleton [a referee with whom Gary quarreled during the Portland game] said he wants to arm-wrestle you."

Payton: "I don't want to arm-wrestle him." *Don't demonize me in the cartoon physical.*

Knight phrases the next question in a nicely neutral way: "The tension that seems to be mounting between coaches and players in the NBA— you think you understand it?"

Payton says, "Well, I understand it. A lot of players in this league wants to play, and coaches have to basically deal with it. I think Dan Issel [who resigned yesterday as the Denver Nuggets coach] just got a little tired of it. The way I hear it, people there are complainin' about a lot of things. And I think he got really tired of it and he wants to be living a life where he doesn't want to be in that predicament. It's almost like the same on our team. There's a lot of people on our team that wants to play, that needs time to produce, and Coach Karl has been trying to keep everybody happy, but it's not gonna happen. It's hard for a coach to deal with that, because players that he has have to play, and Coach is in a tough situation. He has to play 'em or deal with what they gonna do or what they gonna say." I would never have expected him to offer such an even-handed view of the matter, tilted even a little toward the coach. Payton always reverses expectation, always keeps you off guard.

Knight says, "We gotta be one of the toughest home teams in the world. The Sonics are 55-and-5 for the last sixty games played in Seattle [or Tacoma]. That makes it a lousy town to visit if you happen to be, for instance, the Cleveland Cavaliers [the Sonics' next opponent]."

Payton: "If you're looking forward to comin' here, don't look forward to it." Can he do no wrong?

Asked who's going to win the Super Bowl, San Diego or San Francisco, Payton doesn't even dignify the question with a response. San Francisco is heavily favored and Payton is from the Bay Area, so he's even more certain the 49ers will win. His hometown is Oakland, which he calls Oaktown; I grew up in San Mateo, a Peninsula suburb, which I call San Francisco. Sports passion is deeply, infamously territorial: *our city-state is better than yours, because our city-state's team beat yours.* I'm fully cognizant of how ludicrous this is, yet part of my adoration of Payton is bound up with what I contrive to think are our shared geographic roots. Also, his birthday is only one day (a crucial day—making him a Leo lion to my Cancer crab) and twelve years after mine.

Laurie is replacing the bathroom sink. She's trying to pry the old one loose. I lift the old one off, which she couldn't quite do. I've always liked Rocky Balboa's line about Adrienne: "She fills gaps." There are distressingly few gaps I fill for Laurie, since she's so handy, so seemingly self-sufficient. For once I feel, acutely, the pleasure of doing something physical that she can't do herself.

I recently had a dream in which Nicholson Baker (the author of *U and I,* a book about Baker's hero worship of John Updike) and I were riding along in a Honda Accord. Baker was driving. John Updike was driving ahead of us. Baker suddenly turned to me and said, "You realize, don't you, that Updike's driving a Mercedes?" What is this dream about—the anxiety of affluence? Two WASPs and a Jew? No. It's about mechanical aptitude.

Posting to the Sonics newsgroup, John writes: "Gary Payton is a cocky asshole. He is way overrated as far as I'm concerned. He has no jumper, is not the best clutch player, and thinks more 'me' instead of 'team.' The only way Gary Payton should attend an All-Star game is if he sweeps the floor." One way or another it comes out, it just does.

·   ·   ·

1.17.95—Paul and I go to the Sonics-Cavaliers game. He's flush, for some reason, so he not only pays for his ticket but treats for "dinner" at the T-Dome. In order to prevent an ultra-folksy rendition of the "Star Spangled Banner" from entering his bloodstream, Payton wraps his head in a towel.

Gary's shorts: why does he wear them so low? how do they stay on? where did that particular fashion statement start?

The two guys next to Paul keep up a running commentary on the game: "I coulda done that, I coulda done that, for a million dollars a year I wouldn'ta missed that." It pains everyone around us, because we've all at least thought these thoughts.

Whenever Gary throws a spectacular pass—especially a lob to Shawn—he always looks away as he throws it. Part of it is deception; part of it is that it makes the play look so much more stylish. I imagine it would take great discipline not to watch the pass, not to see what happens.

Despite having the flu, Payton goes 7 for 12 from the floor, scores 20 points, and has 5 assists. The Sonics win. They've now won seven in a row and are just two games out of first place.

After the game, Michael Cage, a former Sonic now playing for Cleveland, tortures the Sonics with effusive praise: "I think they can win an NBA championship this season. They certainly have the ingredients. Whether the chemistry holds up, that's totally up to them. They're keeping teams out of their half-court offense by doubling [double-teaming] with different people. They took us out of everything we wanted to do. The loss suffered in the playoffs to Denver will help this team more than hurt it. It will reignite the fire they used to have. Every team has in-house problems. If you're good at keeping problems at a certain level, you'll be successful. If not, they can be cancerous. George has his hands full."

This is too transparent: encouragement as curse. Later, when Karl is asked for his reaction to Cage's comments, he says he heard about them from his wife, i.e., he couldn't be bothered to read them himself. Which is also too transparent, and which reminds me of an occasion several years ago when a vituperative critic launched a lengthy assault upon a well-known writer's body of work. The writer, asked for his reaction, said life is too short to be bothered with such things and so his wife summarized the review for him. It amazes me when people say they're too busy to cause themselves internal bleeding, because my first thought is always: who's ever too busy for that?

1.18.95—Gas Man reads on the air a statement made by Derrick Coleman of the New Jersey Nets in reply to criticism about his play: "'Don't worry about Derrick. Derrick takes care of Derrick. Derrick goes out and gets the job done, night in and night out.' Holy smokes," Gas Man says. "How *do* you get your head through the door? How *do* you get your head through the door?" He says this with just the right inflection, the right spin: not so much angry as amazed, at some sort of odd impasse— how helplessly invested we are in their performance, how much their insouciance mocks our vehemence, how this is what rankles. As Gas Man himself said recently, "The moat between players and fans is ever increasing. We can't fathom what it's like to be them. There's only one reason they're paid the astronomical salaries they're paid, and that is: we're addicted to sports. We are addicted to sports."

Laurie and I and Natalie are shopping for shoes in the kids' shoe department at Nordstrom. A salesman shows a mother and her ten-year-old son a shoe. The kid says, "Don't you have the Shawn Kemp model [the Kamikaze Kemp]?" They don't; the kid cries us a river. I am as happy as I've been all season. I could stand here all night.

Making love with Laurie, I feel like I am—I imagine that I am—as tall, thin, and muscular as Gary Payton.

1.19.95—My university colleague Geoffrey sends me e-mail: "If I see Kemp fall on his face one more time this year on the baseline spin move, I'll, I'll, well, I don't know what I'll do, but it sure is exasperating."

I write back to Geoffrey: "Kemp is sort of amazing. He's been playing pro basketball for six years and he's accumulated a grand total of two moves and a shooting range of eleven feet."

Geoffrey writes back: "And do you notice that he now does a variety of 'struts' whenever he dunks, as if to say, ain't I the top? What a laugh."

We're ganging up on Shawn. We're taking him down a peg. He ain't the top. We're the top.

In Minneapolis, the Sonics beat the Timberwolves. Payton has a lousy offensive game, missing two easy layups, but he still has a great game defensively. The T-Wolves' point-guard, Winston Garland, says the Sonics "make a point-guard's night a living hell."

What I spend the whole game thinking about is why fans hate the T-Wolves' Christian Laettner so much. Part of it must be that name, even though he's not, so far as I know, a big God guy. His headband and long hair don't help; he looks at times like he's auditioning for a role in a movie about the Yippies. Plus, he's a Duke graduate and he wears this on his sleeve. What a crybaby he is—his incessant complaining to referees and coaches and fellow players. We come here to get out of ourselves, and he in his high-strung whiteness just takes us back into ourselves; we take all our self-loathing and convert it to hatred and send it Laettner's way, while we pour all our yearning to be other than we are into those other guys who look so different and act so differently from us and, in a way, but only in a way, we send our love in their direction.

6

HISTORY IS JUST
A RUMOR SOMEWHERE
OUT THERE

1.21.95—A teenage kid on the street has a T-shirt that says *Just Do Me*, which of course travesties Nike's slogan *Just Do It*. What does *Just Do It* mean exactly? It means: *don't think about it; don't offer excuses; don't rationalize your ineptitude; ambivalence is for pussies; the contemplative life is one long evasion; mine is not to reason why;* but also, clearly, *just fuck; don't offer bullshit reasons why you don't want to; if you do, you're just fleeing the physical life; the physical life is the only reality; only conscientious objectors retreat to the hospital waiting-room of the mind; black people will teach us how to fuck and how to exist in a purely physical realm.*

Twenty years ago—my freshman year of college—I put a quarter in a booth in a Times Square porn palace, and the curtain came up on a black man and black woman fucking. I thought the glass window was up but just unusually transparent; in fact, it wasn't up. During a break in the action, the woman reached over the four-foot partition and tried to swat me.

. . .

The Sonics beat the Mavericks, in Dallas; Payton scores 22 points and has 8 assists. Toward the end of the game, Marques Johnson says, "It would be a stretch to call [the Mavs'] Doug Smith a poor man's Karl Malone. He's more like a homeless person's Karl Malone." If Kevin Calabro had said this, it would seem offensive, but because Marques Johnson said it and he's black, somehow it's okay, it's funny. Even in ever-vigilant Seattle, nobody would have the effrontery to lecture Johnson about treating the homeless with respect; it would just seem too weird, too many wires pulling in too many different directions.

1.22.95—Last night I had a not-particularly-momentous dream in which Payton cuts backdoor, and I throw him a perfect pass. The play gets foiled somehow, although I'm not sure how; it's unclear.

1.23.95—John Stockton of the Utah Jazz is on the verge of breaking the NBA's all-time assists record. Jim Chones, a former player, talking to a reporter about Stockton, says, "He has to be the most unselfish athlete in any major sport. He always looks to pass first—to create—and shooting is second. How he does it, and why he does it, is a lost art. This is deep." David Benoit—who is Stockton's teammate and who, like Chones, is black—says, "You get the impression that he's not all that quick or strong, and he's not really flashy. I mean, his passes are usually straightforward, nothing behind his back, or between the legs, and rarely a no-look. I know that a lot of other point-guards in the league, especially black guys, have said, 'I can take that little white guy.' And then he makes dead meat out of them." A reporter asks Benoit, "Like who?" Benoit says, "Take your pick." I so love the line "Take your pick" that I reread the paragraph half a dozen times.

1.24.95—The Sonics are playing Denver in Tacoma tonight. The Nuggets' center, Dikembe Mutombo, is from Zaire, 7'1", and has the nickname "Mt. Mutombo." All afternoon, on KJR, fans going to the game are being urged to wear white in order to "white out Mt. Mutombo." I literally don't understand how the instigator of this scheme could be that oblivious to the implications.

At the beginning of the game, Mutombo offers his hand in a handshake and Payton just stares at it, saying something to make Mutombo laugh, finally slapping it. What did he say? I don't know; Paul and I have good seats, but they're not that good. There's still a huge concrete apron between us and the court. Paul loves talking about this apron, this distance between the fans and players; for him it's the symbol of the season, an effective implementation of Gas Man's "ever-increasing moat between players and fans."

Payton, as always, is the last person to walk onto the court to start the game, tucking in his shirt as the referee is about to toss the ball up for the center jump, still not focused until the very last moment, when the ball bounces to him and he snatches it out of the air. It's a funny ritual that conveys to me: *it's only a game, people; now watch me win it;* also: *I'll concentrate for the two-and-a-half hours the game takes but not a minute more.*

Tacoma tends not to remind too many people of Europe, but tonight, when I walk around at halftime, the T-Dome crowd reminds me of my few visits to Europe in this precise way: the striking number of relationships that appear to be nakedly transactional—well-heeled older men squiring around much, much younger women with cheekbones.

The Sonics are way ahead toward the end of the game. I tune in on my Walkman: Calabro asks Johnson, "What do you talk about in the huddle when you're down 20 points, 2 minutes to go, the game is over?" Johnson says, "The blonde in the third row." I train my binoculars on Calabro: he seems stumped (he knows how un-PC this is but isn't about to correct Marques), so he says nothing.

Coming out of the locker room for a post-game television interview, Payton is handed, as a sort of reward, a Sonics cap with the price tag still on it. The moment the red light comes on, he turns the cap sideways so it looks ridiculous and so the price tag is unmissable on the Sonics' pay-per-view telecast. No one's better at shoving the hidden (the "game" is a business) out into the open.

1.25.95—Walking around the neighborhood, I come across a little black kid—age seven? eight?—who is shooting at the portable hoop set up in his driveway. I ask him to throw me the ball, which he does, then I shoot and miss: air ball, not even close. I see him swallow hard; he seems to be worried what will happen next, whether I'm some sort of weirdo. I'd just wanted to create a little moment of basketball connection, but it's all gone flooey on us. "Thanks," I call, "bye." He's long gone, though, scooting into the house.

1.26.95—For tonight's Sonics-Jazz game in Tacoma, I get a little more for my tickets than I paid for them, so the evening's already pretty much of a success. While Calabro and Johnson are doing pay-per-view pre-game shtick, Payton walks into view, mugs, breaking the frame. He never stops talking during pre-game warmups. Gary and Askew do their usual hip-bump and high-five before Gary takes the court.

In the second quarter, Stockton hits Payton on the chin, drawing a little blood, but later when Payton fouls Stockton, he puts out his hand to help him up. Payton's exaggerated respect for Stockton still seems to me quite genuine. In the fourth quarter, Payton's 2-pointer is taken away when offensive goaltending is called on Shawn. Shawn looks to Gary for forgiveness. Gary only looks away.

Utah beats Seattle badly. As I make my way out of press row, I look over the shoulder of a reporter filing a story to deadline, and I read: "It was push come to shove. The Jazz destroyed the Sonics on the boards with an edge of..." Where does this language come from, I wonder; why is sportswriting so beholden to cliché? To testify, I think, to the irrelevance of language in the face of overwhelming physical force.

Afterward, a group of fans congregates outside the arena, waiting for the Jazz players to walk by on the way to their bus. Another fan walks up to the group that's waiting and says, "I've done that before—waited for them. You say hello. They just blow you off."

Payton walks out of the locker room with his head up, chin out, wearing black shoes, black slacks, black shirt, black jacket, black beret, black shades. The effect for me is Huey Newton, circa '68 (the year Payton was born). By contrast, Karl, talking to reporters, looks nearly teary-eyed.

1.27.95—On the *Gary Payton Show*, Payton says: "I think we trapped him [Stockton] a little bit too much [last night]. When we trapped, he was throwin' a lot of passes underneath the basket, and they [his team-

mates] were sittin' under there for dunks. We should have realized that
we was gettin' beat by the trap, by them rotatin' the ball and passin' the
ball. It was something that we should have called off, but we kept trap-
pin' and they kept passin' the ball underneath the basket for easy baskets." My sentiments exactly—it was the question I was waiting for all
the reporters to ask Karl at the press conference—but to my astonishment no one did, and for some reason (actually, I know the reason: I
didn't want to stutter) I felt too shy about asking.

An amazing moment then follows, which is the entire season so far for
me. Vinnie, whose accent is very broad, very New Yawk, very Queens,
very Italian, puts on a supernerdy "white guy" voice, saying, "What
exactly is this 'Living Legal and Large' thing?" (Vinnie consciously says
"Living" rather than "Livin'" to sound like a doofus.) "People ask me all
the time [here Vinnie goes into even more of a CPA's voice]: 'Does that
mean you're puttin' on weight or what, Gary?'" Vinnie is trying to convey to Gary that he knows what it means, but that some listeners need an
explanation, so could Gary please explain it for them?

Payton, totally straight, says, "Oh, no, see, you gotta come back to my
neighborhood to understand that."

Vinnie says, "Naw, I—" but they have to cut to commercial, and he's
crestfallen. He can't believe that Payton thought he was that square, and
yet at least he knows that it would be even more pathetic if he then
explained on the air that he knows what "livin' legal and large" means, so
he doesn't say any more, which leaves him—in Gary's eyes, in his sense
of Gary's eyes, in my sense of his sense of Gary's eyes—a hopeless dweeb.
As Martin Amis was trying to explain to Will Self, "Don't talk so much."

1.28.95—Laurie and I go together to the Lakers-Sonics game. Payton
talks to guys from NBC in the first row as he makes his way down the
court. During a timeout, he's talking to more media people in the front
row, and one of the referees, Bob Delaney—whom Gary has never gotten along with—comes over, ostensibly to see what he's talking about but
actually to irritate him, to qualify his pleasure. What is it that I want to
say about Payton's relationship to language? It's not just that he "likes to
talk smack," or that he's simply being clever or trying to psych out the
opposition. It's that he's trying to find the words, and if he can get com-

fortable with the words, he knows his game will follow. It's as if he knows the words come first; he's always working on the words. He seems to love language more than anything else, and he seems to understand that everything else—his game, his mood—flows out of getting the words right, not the other way around.

Although Payton scores 22 points and has 13 assists, LA wins in overtime. To Laurie, it makes the whole day a bit of a downer. I honestly don't feel that; I just like watching Gary do things. At one point during the game, he dove for a ball and knocked it off Nick Van Exel. Gary pointed in the direction of the Sonics' basket to indicate that it was the Sonics' ball, and I just liked the way he pointed (excited but somehow also mocking excitement).

1.29.95—Laurie and I watch the Super Bowl—or we watch ourselves watching the Super Bowl—and hang with Natalie. (Can we be self-conscious of our existence and still exist? Apparently so, though sometimes I wonder.) When each player is introduced and comes running out onto the field, Natalie runs from her room into the living room, imitating with stunning and hilarious accuracy their macho struts. After a few minutes the spectacle has given way to just another game, which is unbelievably boring, so Natalie and I go play in a nearby park. Climbing a metal-chain ladder, she knows exactly how high she can climb and still feel comfortable, at what exact point she's scared. Being a parent is, to me, an endless lesson in, among other things, Mind Knows Nothing—Body Knows Everything.

1.30.95—*Sports Illustrated* collects quotes from players and coaches concerning all the bad things players are doing this year.

Karl, for instance, says, "The vast majority of the players are very mature and disciplined. Unfortunately, the focus is on the minority of players who are anti-establishment and making the most noise." To the coaches, history is over or, at best, just a rumor somewhere out there, whereas to the players, history is about to begin in earnest.

Payton, for instance, says, "The players all have to stand up for themselves. Maybe it's more that way than it used to be, but it *should* be that way. A coach shouldn't talk to you as if you're something less than who you are. People all think this is about contracts and who's making how much money. It has nothing to do with that. This is about manhood. The respect of one man to another. If the coach doesn't respect you as a man, or treat you like a man, then you have to stand up for it whether you make the $150,000 minimum or $5 million."

In the NBA an enormous amount of money is given to a few hundred black men in order, it sometimes seems, to make up for a society's collective guilt, but it doesn't work. There will never be enough money stuffed into the wounds to stop the bleeding. White people revere and resent this concentration of triumphant blackness; black players, as if charged with the task of getting retribution for black people everywhere, act like the most pampered divas: *I will take absolutely no shit from you; the terms will be as follows…*

The Sonics play the Sixers in Philadelphia. Payton seems to spend half the game talking to media people in press row, scoring only 7 points in 39 minutes, but the Sonics still win. Sometimes I think he is a machine meant solely for the production of language, and basketball is just an odd gear left over from this other apparatus.

1.31.95—While Laurie and I are putting on Natalie's clothes to take her to day-care, Natalie cries crazily, complaining that the clothes are the wrong ones, this is the wrong color, that's too tight. She keeps saying, "Mine, mine, mine." Afterward I ask Laurie what she thinks Natalie meant by "mine," and Laurie says, "She meant, 'These limbs, these legs, these arms: they're mine. Don't do this to my body; it's my body.'"

I ask *ma chérie* to reconsider her decision to grant me a credential to only two games per month, "since seeing so few games makes it difficult for me to write a monthly article on the Sonics." She says she'll get back to me. My bad faith equals her bad faith, neither of which can ever get talked about.

After a Sonics practice in Orlando, Payton talks with Gill. Asked by reporters what they talked about, Gary says, "We were talking about where we were going golfing." I love this: he hates as much as I do the ever-expanding phenomenon of NBA players, especially superstars like Jordan and Barkley, golfing. On the other hand, this is only my (racist?) supposition; for all I know, Payton is an avid golfer, though this seems truly hard to imagine. My father recently wrote a column disputing a sociologist's claim that a "quiet revolution" has taken place in golf and that "the racist, sexist country-club stereotype is on the run." "I've been playing golf for ten years," my father wrote, "mostly at the San Mateo Municipal golf course. I've also played at Palo Alto and several other courses in San Francisco and Sunnyvale. In the time I've been playing at San Mateo Muni, I haven't seen ten African-American players, men or women." Tiger Woods recently said, "I'm Indian, black, Asian, and white. It's an injustice to all my heritages to just single me out as black. It's just unfair. I'm mostly Asian, but early on I've been labeled black. I can't figure it out." Tiger Woods can figure out but can't say that everyone wants to view him as black because golf is so unblack, which is why so many NBA players are drawn to the sport.

2.1.95—I call the Sonics and get Calabro's phone number on the road in Orlando. He leaves a message on my machine and says he isn't interested in talking. His voice is quite businesslike and impatient and harsh, and though it shouldn't, it comes as a revelation to me that his (antic, fun-loving) on-air persona is in fact a persona, it's just an act, a cartoon creation for fans to identify with. He's not like that at all.

2.2.95—The city attorney of Gainesville, Florida, recommends that a taxicab company's operating license be revoked for discouraging its drivers from picking up young black men at night. The manager of the company had told his cabbies, "Rule No. 1 is never pick up a young black male after dark, if the place they're calling from can't clearly be identified. Rule No. 2 is never pick up two black men under these conditions. Rule No. 3 is never pick up three black men under these conditions." Reading about this in the paper, I'm disgusted, but I must admit I also laugh a little, which further disgusts me.

In Orlando, the Sonics beat the Magic. Payton has a great game: 11-for-18 from the field, 7 assists, 26 points. After the game, Karl joyfully approaches Payton to shake his hand in congratulations; Payton offers a reluctant grip. Virtually all the power is his, and he loves to remind Karl of this fact. (When the day comes that black people are demanding all manner of recompense, we want to know, what exactly will that be?)

2.3.95—On the *Mike Gastineau Show,* caller after caller after caller begins by asking the Gas Man how he is. It's been established that Gastineau is feeling fine; this drives the Gas Man crazy and it drives me crazy. What drives me even crazier is a caller who goes on a much-heard tangent: the Sonics don't appear often enough on national television, and the rest of the country doesn't give Seattle any respect. He then says that people who went to Harvard, people from New York—network executives?—are always smarter; they always win. Gastineau says, "I've met a lot of idiots from both places," but the caller just doesn't get it: he needs to see himself as other and Seattle as *there;* he can't see himself as real and Seattle as *here.* Not exactly not my problem, either, truth be told.

A guy named Henry, an employee of the Elma Lanes Bowling Alley, has agreed to purchase a single ticket for six of the remaining games, but I realize I'm a snob and don't want to go to six games with an employee of the Elma Lanes Bowling Alley. I also realize I'm a coward, so rather than call him, I fax him the following fiction: "I'm the guy who was going to sell you a ticket to 6 Sonics games. However, the friend of mine I bought the tickets with—who thought he was going to get transferred—turns out to be staying in Seattle, after all. I feel I owe my friend his tickets back, so I'm afraid I have to cancel our agreement. My apologies."

The Spurs are coming to Seattle soon to play the Sonics, and a commercial that keeps running on KJR goes: "Come watch the Sonics contain the nut, Dennis Rodman." *Come watch bad craziness; come watch bad craziness get corralled.*

The Sonics are still on the road, though, for now. Against Atlanta, Payton makes an amazing pass—dropping the ball between his legs right to Vince Askew for a dunk, then, as he sometimes does, slapping himself (rather than a teammate, let alone a sub like Askew) on the chest when he makes a good play. G. Payton is utterly narcissistic, utterly self-referential, but (and?) somehow I adore whatever he does. Unlike every other Sonic, his personality is both mysterious and whole to me. The Sonics beat the Hawks. Payton goes 9-for-12 from the field, scores 22 points, and has 9 assists. "You the man, you the man, you the man," I hear myself chanting aloud at the end of the game to TV-GP, until I remember where this is from: the final scene of *Raging Bull,* in which Jake LaMotta speaks to himself in the mirror.

2.4.95—In "Slave Hair and African American Culture in the Eighteenth and Nineteenth Centuries," an article in the February issue of *Journal of Southern History,* Shane White and Graham White write, "Blacks were not supposed to be proud of their hair, as they or their ancestors had been in Africa; any suggestion that they were would have sharply challenged complacent white cultural assumptions. In this context, hair worn long and bushy, an arrangement that emphasized, even flaunted, its distinctive texture, may have been, in some cases, an affirmation of difference and even of defiance, an attempt to revalorize a biological characteristic that white racism had sought to devalue." Which is precisely how a shaved head now seems to function.

2.5.95—In Miami, the last game of a four-game road trip, the Supes dominate the Heat, 136–109. Afterward, the Miami coach, Kevin Loughery, says, "That's the best we've seen a team play against us all year. It's the best team I've seen this year." Kemp scores 26; Gill, 21; Schrempf, 18; but I'm like the little kid asking Calabro only for Gary's stats: 18 points for Payton. During the telecast from Miami, I notice that Marques Johnson uses a lot of clichés, but he always puts invisible quotes around them—e.g., "a force to be reckoned with." Although he has a nicely ironic distance from sports jargon, at least on the air he doesn't have a language that would replace it, which reminds me of how seriously a black Comp Lit professor I know takes academic jargon (even more seriously than the white comp lit professors I know, which is saying something). When for so long the loop declared you null and void, it's difficult to declare the loop null and void.

•   •   •

2.7.95—The Sonics lose to the Spurs, in Tacoma. Rodman gets 27 rebounds. Every Sonic except Gill has an off game. Just 14 points for Payton. I'm sick, so I don't go. Paul and his new girlfriend use my tickets. Afterward, Paul relates to me how, on the game's opening tip, the ball was tapped toward Rodman, but he was busy adjusting an earring and didn't want to be interrupted, so he just kind of batted the ball away in no particular direction.

2.9.95—At a charity roast, Billy Crystal says about Charles Barkley: "Charles and I have a lot in common. He once played with Julius Erving. I have two uncles named Julius and Irving." Jews, in the Jewish imagination, are jokes; black people like Julius Erving and Charles Barkley have wings.

I go to the Sonics-Bulls game with the husband of a woman who is a coworker of Laurie's. We don't have much to say to each other. Although I feel a little self-conscious about doing so, I take notes on Payton: GP rags Ron Harper; they pretend to be mad at each other; some fans sitting courtside think they're genuinely mad at each other, but they're not....Boredom is part of the season, part of every game—GP mixes moments of very deep boredom with moments of intense frenzy....GP gambles a lot on defense; sometimes he'll get a steal, but he also loses his man a lot....What makes him so good-looking is what makes most people good-looking: how sharply etched his features are—in particular, his jawline, his cheekbones; by comparison, my face feels vague....GP is always mugging for fans, other players, refs, coaches, himself....

During halftime, a Harlem Globetrotter comes running out to center court, spinning a ball on his finger as if he were a trained seal, though who am I to talk? Spinning a ball on my finger is the one basketball feat I can perform as well as anyone. The minstrelsy feels immediately wrong, ghastly, embarrassing to both him and ourselves. What saves and transforms the moment, though, is that when the Globetrotter pulls a kid out of the stands to engage in a little skit, he grabs a black kid. A white kid would have signaled that *nothing has changed in forty years; I'm still exclusively comic relief.* But by choosing a black kid, he forces us to recognize who's black, who used to be black, who's white, who used to be white, who's watching, who's performing: *he and I are just going to play some hoops together, have a little conversation here, we're talking to each other as much as or more than we're doing anything else, we're just hanging out really, and you can watch if you like, but we're not exactly performing for you—though of course we are.*

When San Antonio was in town, we came to see Dennis Rodman act like a nut and we were disappointed. With Chicago, we come to see Scottie Pippen throw chairs and we are disappointed again. We pretend we want them to be controlled and "classy," but really what we want them to do is misbehave, so we can equate their talent with inadequacy, reaffirming their deep otherness, their mad difference.

Perkins hits a 3-pointer to send the game into overtime, then makes two more 3-pointers in overtime to win the game. The Sonics beat the Jordan-less Bulls for the second time this year, finishing the first half of the season at 33-and-12, in second place, three-and-a-half games behind the Suns.

2.10.95—At one point in the game last night against the Bulls, the other Sonics congregated on one side of the floor to allow Gill to go one-on-one against Ron Harper. Gill faked right, went left, and beat Harper to the hoop for a dramatic left-handed dunk. Payton, who was sitting on the bench, teased Harper mercilessly. On the *Gary Payton Show* this morning, Vinnie asks Payton, "What were you saying to Ron Harper?"

Payton says, "I was just trying to have fun, make the game go a little bit faster." *It's our camaraderie, not yours.*

Michael Knight says, "Kendall came over, told Gary to quiet down."

Payton: "Kendall crossed him over and dunked on him afterward, so I just had to let him [Harper] know it was a great play."

Vinnie: "I think you used the word *ka-pow,* didn't you?"

Payton: "Uh, *ka-boom.*" The words that matter to him…

Vinnie: "Last night, in the overtime, Shawn came up behind you and had his arms around you for a long time, whispering something in your ear. I want to know what he said, and is your girlfriend jealous?" The bottomlessness of our interest in what they say and do; they are other and we are trying to understand them; they are our dream-selves and we want to become them.

Payton: "Well, that's between me and Shawn." *It's our camaraderie, not yours.* "Me and Shawn do that: we come and try to pump each other up. I hope his girlfriend *is* jealous." It's impossible to tell if Payton misunderstood and thought Vinnie was asking if *Shawn's* girlfriend was jealous, or if he understood perfectly and was rewiring Vinnie's voyeurism.

Geoffrey e-mails me a couple of lines from Stephen Fox's recently published book, *Big Leagues: Professional Baseball, Football, and Basketball in National Memory.* The book quotes Will Adams, a former slave, saying, "Our sports and dances was big sport for the white folks. They'd sit on the gallery and watch the niggers put it on brown." I love how "sports" becomes "big sport"; I love how easily Will Adams imagines it from the slave-owners' point of view: "They'd sit on the gallery and watch the niggers"; I don't love how long it took me to realize that *brown* means not "skin" but "ground."

At the All-Star Weekend Jam Session in Phoenix, Shaq says, "Look at us. We've got everything. Money. Security. Adulation. Happiness. We really do have everything." They have everything and they know they have everything and never lose an opportunity to remind us they have everything and we love them for it and we hate them for it and it is endless.

2.12.95—A commercial on TV for Champion athletic wear features a much put-upon locker room attendant cleaning up after a Chicago Bulls practice. The locker room attendant needs to be white, as the kid the Globetrotter dragged out of the stands had to be black: the hoopla of black hoops transcendence needs, first, to erase memory.

In the All-Star game, the Western Conference defeats the Eastern Conference. Payton scores only 6 points and makes only 3 of 10 shots from the floor, but he has 3 steals and 15 assists and is voted a close runner-up to Mitch Richmond as the MVP of the game. Afterward, Gary gets the game-ball autographed by most of the other All-Stars and hands this ball and his shoes to Michael Hirsch, a twelve-year-old kid who attended the game as a guest of the Make-A-Wish Foundation (a subset of Ackerley's empire) because he has bone cancer and his right leg is being amputated tomorrow. For some reason, when Payton does things like this, it doesn't seem saccharine or phony or PR-mad; his sentimental side slays me.

2.13.95—Houston Rockets guard Vernon Maxwell recently ran into the stands and punched a fan who was heckling him. On the *Gary Payton Show*, asked for his reaction to the incident, Payton says, "If the security guards aren't going to do anything, there's not much we can do. Our job is not to retaliate. To me, if a heckler is on me, I say something back. If it's racial, I react that way. If he says something about my mama, I'll say something about his mama. If I give it back to him, then he'll laugh most of the time. You've got to make it fun. I know Vernon was upset. I get upset sometimes, too. But we can't be going into the stands doing that. Racism has always been in the stands, and it always will. It's part of the deal when you get into this. They figure if they pay money for a ticket, they can say or do whatever they want. That shouldn't be the way it is. It just is. You have to let it go." His amazing equanimity.

When Charles Barkley was recently asked by a reporter whether "the problem of groupies in the NBA is as bad as people think it is," Barkley dismissed the question by replying facetiously, "That's why I hate white people." Tonight, on Ron Barr's *Sports By-Line* radio call-in show, which is based in San Francisco and syndicated nationally, Barr asks Reggie Theus, a former player who's black, his opinion about the brouhaha that has surrounded Barkley's comment.

Theus says, "Some of it is the media's fault. The media has allowed Charles to say things and make it very public and go ha ha ha."

Barr: "In other words, they usually take his quotes in a humorous way and then suddenly they decide to get upset when he does something they know he intends humorously. Maybe there was a slow news day or something. If the knife is going to cut, it's gotta cut both ways, in a sense."

Theus: "But it doesn't and you know that it doesn't and everybody listening knows that it doesn't." Exactly so. Because the NBA is myth-theater in which all the roles are reversed. "It's about: black people can call each other 'nigger,' but if a white person calls you 'nigger,' you have to face facts on that."

Barr: "It's confusing to whites that they can turn on *Def Comedy Jam* and hear one black person refer to another black person as a 'nigger' and yet that's offensive if it's used by a white person. That's confusing to a lot of white people."

Theus: "The difference is black people call each other 'nigga'; when a white person calls you something, they say 'nigger.' There's a difference."

Ron Barr is totally lost.

When I was in eighth grade I played basketball all the time with my friend Nicky Baxter, who was black. At the time, I had the annoying habit of adding -*er* to everyone's name whenever I addressed them: Doug-er, Steve-er, John-er, etc. Nicky and I were running down the hill to the hoop to play. I cried out to him, "Nick-er." I meant nothing evil—I only meant for him to pass me the ball—but his face registered: *oh, I see where things finally stand.*

7

AN AGONY OF
ENTHRALLDOM

2.14.95—An English department newsletter refers to some good news
pertaining to a black professor with the words "our own Carolyn Purdy,"
which Professor Purdy objects to as the phraseology of a slave-master. "I
don't belong to you," she tells the administrator who wrote the newsletter. When Carolyn Purdy was taught in graduate school to deconstruct
texts, no one counted on her deconstructing internal memoranda.

I'm waiting in the train station for the train to Tacoma for the game
tonight against the Warriors—about which, on Valentine's Day, Laurie
is undelighted. A black man is wearing a T-shirt that says *Don't Be
A Pussy*. A white woman is wearing a T-shirt that says *Don't Be A Dick*.
I catch myself looking at this couple for longer than I should; so do
they. They stare back daggers, and I can feel instantly the complica-
tions of such a relationship: how, even now, even in "liberal" Seattle,
you'd be aware of eyes watching you, and your eyes watching their eyes,
and your eyes watching each other. It would be a very watchful relationship, very viewed in a way that would be erotic and exhibitionistic and
exhausting.

"Love is a long close scrutiny," as my former writing teacher, John Hawkes, wrote in *The Lime Twig.*

Walking in the arena, I'm handed a poster with the logo *Partners in Crime:* Payton, standing against a brick wall thick with graffiti, brandishes a flashlight; flanking him are Gill, rope in hand, and McMillan, with a mesh bag of basketballs. All three players are wearing expressions of animosity and contempt, which, within the fiction of the advertisement, are meant to be directed at you, since they're fresh from burgling your house, but which are unmistakenly directed at the ad concept itself.

The Seattle Mariners' team mascot, the Moose, visits the Sonics' team mascot, Sasquatch, tonight. The Moose is ten times more amusing and adorable than his counterpart, but during a timeout the Moose gets on his hands and knees and pretends to shine the black ref's shoes. It makes the ref uneasy and it makes me uneasy. Maybe it was meant in an interesting way: *what would happen if we got down our hands and knees and shined your shoes for a while?* But it touches a wound too sore and recent and ongoing; too many shoeshine operators are black; it's too weird; it is one of the most uncomfortable thirty seconds I've ever witnessed. The ref is so embarrassed that even without my binoculars, I can see him blush.

The Sonics beat the Warriors. Payton scores 26 points. I bring home roses and apologies, which help very little.

2.15.95—I ask *ma chérie* to please reconsider my request to attend more than two games a month as a reporter. She notes that she's done so but has "decided to stay with our original decision." Furthermore, "please keep in mind that we will not be issuing playoff credentials to you for any games." She is the (quintessential) *belle dame sans merci.*

The Lakers play the Sonics in LA—the first game of a three-game West Coast trip. Payton always shakes hands with the players on the other team, except the guy who's going to be guarding him—tonight, Nick Van Exel—whom Gary always points a finger at, as if to say: *I got you in my sights.* Gary scores 24, but the Lakers win.

●　　●　　●

2.16.95—The *New York Times* prints a photograph of a black man and a black woman—it's not clear if they're a couple—walking past a white jazz trumpeter; the woman is looking straight ahead, while the man is looking at the trumpeter and slightly smiling. The caption reads, "Jesse Selengut, who recently received a master's degree in jazz studies from New York University, ignored yesterday's flurries to practice his trumpet at Spring and Crosby Streets in SoHo. He spends five hours a day on his technique." The photo wants to signify in the following way: *it's snowing out, but New Yorkers, regardless of race, can come together over hot jazz.* What the picture really says is: *Jesse Selengut is wearing glasses, a bulky parka, dress slacks, and a yarmulke. The woman walking past him is wearing cool sunglasses, the coolest boots, and an interesting white scarf. The man walking past him is wearing a black leather coat and a wool cap perched on his head at just the right angle. They are not playing jazz trumpet, but they have a relationship to jazz that Jesse Selengut is never going to have even if he spends fifteen hours a day on his technique.*

2.17.95—On the *Gary Payton Show,* New York Vinnie asks Payton, "Did you get a new haircut?"

Payton says, "Yeah."

Vinnie says, "What's the Z—anything in particular?"

Payton says, "No. Just something that my barber tried."

Vinnie: "See, I let my barber experiment on me, and I come out with blond hair. You let your barber experiment on you, and it looks good. Where's your barber? Maybe I'm gonna go to him now."

Payton: "You gotta try him out."

Vinnie: "My barber says, 'Let me try doing something different for you.' I come out, and I look like, I don't know, a girl. And a bad-looking girl at that. Not even good-looking. You get your hair cut and it kinda looks good. So it's nothing—not a secret message to anybody?"

Payton: "No, it's no message. It's just something that I tried, and it came out pretty good."

Vinnie: "It looks good. I was watching it. I kinda was fixated. I was saying, 'That looks good.' Listen, Gary, when you're lookin' sharp, you gotta let somebody know, right?"

Payton: "Yeah, you gotta do it sometimes."

Maybe it's as simple as this: Gary loves himself and Vinnie doesn't.

A caller named Hal says, "Congratulations on the great season you're having."

Payton says, "Thank you."

Hal: "But I just want you to know that the thing that really put you number one in my book was the Make-A-Wish act you did."

Payton: "Thank you."

Hal: "Absolutely great—to make a little guy's wish come true."

Payton: "Thank you very much."

Hal: "And good luck the rest of the season."

Payton: "Thank you."

Michael Knight says, "For those who don't know about that, tell them the story, Gary."

Payton says, "Well, a little kid made a wish that he wanted to come to the All-Star game and meet guys like us. He has bone cancer. He got his leg amputated Wednesday. And he came to the All-Star game and we got him a lot of stuff—balls and shoes and things—and he got to see the game and he got to see the dunk contest and it was very nice for him to see that kind of stuff before what he was going through happened."

He has perfect moral pitch, it seems to me, for when to play it straight, when to keep it simple, when not to fuck things up.

The Sonics lose to the Trailblazers in Portland, 114–109. Kemp scores 30; Payton, 18. Afterward, Karl says about the Blazers, "They played like men."

Act like a man.

Don't treat me like a boy.

First, act like a man.

First, don't treat me like a boy.

2.20.95—I fax *ma chérie* a letter letting her know that I'm working on a long profile of Gary Payton, "which I'm hoping will be a cover article for the *Weekly*," and that I'd like to schedule an interview with him some-time in the next week. She replies that she'll check with Payton regard-ing my interview request and asks me when the cover article is supposed to run so that if his schedule permits and he chooses to do the interview, she can arrange the interview in time. I tell her that I don't know whether my profile of Gary Payton will indeed be a cover article for the *Weekly,* but that it will certainly be long enough to merit the cover and that I have a reasonable hope the magazine will indeed run it as a cover piece. The longer and more thorough the article, I explain, the more likely it will land on the cover. I say that I hope to finish the article by the end of the month and I expect it to run the first or second week of next month. In actuality, I have about fifty pages of inchoate notes.

The Sonics are back "home" for the next four games. Tonight the Lakers are in town. From press row, with my binoculars I scope out the couple on a date sitting in "my seats." The Lakers-Sonics rivalry is becoming a big draw, so I got full value back on the tickets.

I continue my monomaniacal GP journal-keeping: GP has developed a nice scoop shot he uses on drives down the lane, a decent set shot (which he flicks rather than shoots) on open 3-pointers, and a little running push shot for shots on the move, but he has nothing resembling the most standard piece of a basketball player's repertoire—a jump shot. Just before the end of the first half, GP blows a dunk that would have put the Sonics in the lead at the half; Shawn tries to pat GP's head, but GP ducks away: *I ain't your boy.* After stealing the ball, GP glares, gloatingly, at Lakers coach Del Harris, who looks like a combination of Leslie Nielsen and Phil Donahue. GP grabs a rebound and, as a kind of parody of concentration, looks with exaggerated focus at the ball and at his own hands; he's mocking every coach's instruction he's ever received. GP seems obsessed with Nick Van Exel as his mirror double; the moment GP scores, he runs over to NVE to go rub it in (later, asked by the media what they were talking about, GP says, "Oh, we were just talking about the All-Star game"; *it's our camaraderie, not yours).* Called for a foul with which he disagrees, GP stands stock-still, with his hands wrapped behind his back, pseudo–good citizen. The Lakers' Cedric Ceballos, who is injured, sits courtside, and GP is constantly talking to Ceballos; he makes clear that his allegiance to his friends precedes his allegiance to his team. Before the ball is inbounded under the Sonics' basket, GP crouches down with a towel and wipes up the key just so; he goes about this task with an almost embarrassing fastidiousness. In the third quarter, GP strains his neck after driving to the basket and colliding with the Lakers' Antonio Harvey. He goes to the locker room; when he returns to the floor in the fourth quarter, I choke up a bit, which, I must admit, is very weird (he's just returned from the locker room, not Hades). It's a very strong, very strange, and utterly hallucinatory bond I feel with him. His emotions, what I imagine to be his emotions, move me. I imagine I can feel what he feels. I wish I were him, but precisely because I'm not—because in fact he's so different—his emotions hold me sway.

Payton scores 18 points and has 9 assists, but Van Exel scores 40. The Lakers beat the Sonics again.

Asked by a reporter whether he feels okay, Payton says, "Nope." Asked which hurts more, the loss or his neck, he doesn't say anything. He has a good sense of humor, but not at his own expense; he's not a good loser. He says, "We've got to learn how to play against these athletes [the Lakers, who are younger and more energetic than the Sonics]. They outworked us. When teams try to block our shots, we've got to punish them by dishing off." Asked if the similarities between the Lakers (whom the Sonics are likely to face in the first round of the playoffs) and the Nuggets (who beat the Sonics in the first round last year) are disturbing, Payton says, "It ain't disturbin'. Who cares?" *I care, but when you exaggerate how much I care, I don't care anymore.*

2.22.95—Before leaving for the Tacoma Dome tonight, I stand outside the car, waving to Natalie, who is sitting inside the house, waving back; we just keep waving goodbye and blowing kisses and mouthing "I love you" back and forth to each other. Pulling away, finally, I feel like faux-Father, off on a ridiculous invention of an errand.

Seattle vs. Minnesota: Having sold my tickets for half-price, I attend the game in the press box. Payton puts a little extra oomph on a pass to Schrempf; it's his way of letting Schrempf know he wants him to take it and drive to the basket. This is about as subtle and beautiful as communication gets, it seems to me. Marciulionis is getting tired, and Karl looks around to tell Payton to replace him, but before Karl even calls for Payton, Gary—like Radar O'Reilly—has already checked into the game.

Some sort of promotional announcement involving Kendall Gill goes "Superhuman: SuperSonic," which I first mishear as "Subhuman: Super-Sonic," and I think for a moment I'm losing my mind.

At halftime, I phone and tell Natalie over and over how much I miss her, which makes things worse all the way around.

Minnesota guard Isaiah Rider, Payton's friend from Oakland, implodes. He's thrown out of the game, but he won't leave the floor. A T-Wolves assistant coach—black, of course—has to escort him off the floor into the locker room. We finally get what we came for: the raw excitement of a talented, troubled black man misbehaving and being punished for misbehaving.

Gill scores 34 points on 15-for-19 shooting from the floor; Kemp scores 20; Payton, only 12 points on 4-for-10 from the floor, but he has 13 assists. The Sonics win easily. What's striking about the press conference afterward with Karl is its bizarrely funereal quality—its insane seriousness, the inane deference with which the reporters treat the coach. Bill Clinton isn't treated half as heroically. Print reporters condescend to TV reporters, who ask breathtakingly foolish questions; a sportscaster asks Karl, "So has this one victory over the T-Wolves totally fixed all the Sonics' problems?"

Later, concerning his relationship with Gill, Karl says, "We both admitted we should try and communicate rather than having the tension between each other. We're both proud people. I want him to believe in himself and believe in what I'm doing, too. He's been a very good player for us, and I think he can have great nights for us [e.g., tonight, with 34 points in 31 minutes]. Kendall and I need more time together; at least we're in that stage."

Asked what the keys are for him to maintain focus through such turbulence, Gill says, "Just letting time pass, just being quiet, and letting things blow over, like a storm. The situation is working itself out. It's a lot better than it was a month ago. We're communicating better. We both realize I'm going to be here for the rest of the season and he's going to be here. Arn [Tellem, Gill's agent] has been instructed not to say anything else the rest of the year."

Driving home, I listen to the post-game call-in show, and fans try to score points with Gastineau by criticizing the other callers for being whiners, crybabies, but that's what the show is there for: to dissect what you yourself couldn't do in a million years. "Language," as Lily Tomlin says, "was invented because of the deep human need to complain."

When I arrive home, I realize I feel pumped up and proud, as if I had contributed something crucial to the game, as if the slight thaw between Karl and Gill somehow reflects positively in some important way upon me.

2.24.95—At the T-Dome, Seattle beats Denver, barely. Payton has a lousy game (he makes only 3 of 14 shots from the floor), but in the last minute he forces Denver's Jalen Rose to make a bad pass; Kemp intercepts and gets fouled. Shawn misses his first free-throw attempt, and when he misses the second one as well, Payton leaps in and gets the rebound. At the very end of the game, Gary makes a final steal. When the horn sounds, as if suddenly decompressing, he goes into super-polite mode, handing the referee the ball, then folding his arms behind his back while waiting to be interviewed. I watched the game from press row through binoculars and listened to it on radio, and what interests me the most is how Marques Johnson can and does mock, for instance, Payton and Kemp in ways that Calabro wouldn't dream of doing, saying, for instance, that Shawn jumped up off the floor "just like a little kid"; imitating, for instance, how Payton says "ax" instead of "ask" and "fi'ty" instead of "fifty." Johnson is aware of this; he teases Calabro with this; Calabro sits in silence over this, certain only that he'd rather be silent than touch this very live wire.

On the post-game show, Johnson says, "I was working out last night at the LA Athletic Club, downtown Los Angeles [he lives in LA when he's not broadcasting Sonics games], and this guy that I play ball with sometimes—an older guy; he's a lawyer—told me that the *Wall Street Journal* computer, which has predicted the last two or three NCAA champions and the last two or three NBA champions, said the SuperSonics were going to win the NBA championship this year." Johnson still plays ball, but now at the LAAC and with lawyers who read the *Wall Street Journal* (and want to talk hoops with him). Dig it: he is (in his imagination or ours?) both black and white.

Calabro says, *"The Wall Street Journal?"* Calabro is imagining how mercilessly he would be razzed by Johnson if he, Calabro, brought up the *Wall Street Journal* computer, but he's trying not to tease Johnson too much lest he appear to be making fun of Marques' crossover move.

Johnson says, "Yeah. I have no idea what that is, what that's about." He's backpedaling, apologizing for buying some older lawyer's dream of reducing basketball to a computer printout.

Calabro, totally blasé, building up his courage to mock Marques and his lawyer-friend's computer: "Interesting."

Johnson: "But"—I adore this "but," because to me it means: *You, Kevin, by saying, "Interesting," are really saying, "You've got to be kidding. Pull it back, Marques. It's embarrassing how white you think you have to be to prove you belong. Don't do it, Marques. You're embarrassing yourself. You're cooler than this"*—"he made it sound like a big deal. It was interesting to me that the Sonics were picked I think last week to win the NBA championship this year." Johnson sounds idiotic here—it's a big deal that a computer picks the Sonics to win the NBA championship? Earth to Marques! Earth to Marques! You've got to be able to make fun of your friend, the older lawyer guy. "They feed all this stuff into the computer, and it all comes out." *I'm just telling you what this lawyer guy told me.*

Calabro, cruelly: "Ohhh-kay."

Apologetically, and a little hurt, Johnson says, "Just something to think about."

Calabro at his best—just a little nudge to bring Marques back; he's not going to let him twist slowly in the wind—"Well, I'd think they [the Sonics] would have as good a shot as anyone."

Johnson, recovering—*okay, I'll leave the LA Athletic Club, I'll leave the computer, I'll even leave my friend, the older lawyer guy; I'm not that stuffy, okay, I'll stop trying to sound pretentious, I'll get down, I'll go to Vegas*—"I don't know what the odds were in Vegas at the beginning of the year, what, 4-to-1, something like that."

Calabro, a little smug, a little too satisfied that he's brought Johnson back from the brink: "Sounds about right."

This is the Quentin Tarantino fantasy: a white man telling a black man he's not acting down enough.

•   •   •

2.25.95—Paul e-mails me: "A local spin on a universal theme: A friend of mine confessed to me the other day that when fighting a hair-trigger problem, while laying his new girlfriend, he tries to fix in his mind an unflickering image of a Payton/Kemp fast break." This is as nothing. Recently, under the covers with Laurie, I couldn't quite come. I thought about Charles Barkley saying he likes his teammate Kevin Johnson and that the only difference between them is Johnson likes to attend church while he, Barkley, prefers going to strip clubs; I imagined Barkley at a strip club; then I came.

A very buff black man in a skin-tight running suit was jogging down my block the other day. A bus full of middle-school girls rounded the corner. He puffed out his chest, let out his kick, put himself slightly on display. Rather than ooh or aah or whistle or applaud or ignore him, a group of girls sticking their heads out the windows in the back of the bus did the cruelest thing possible: they laughed.

2.26.95—A Nike commercial featuring Jason Kidd goes like this:
　　Voice-over: "Foot Action and Nike analyze Jason Kidd."
　　Shrink: "Jason, babe, what's your problem?"
　　Jason: "Well, Doctor—"
　　Shrink: "Yeah—"
　　Jason: "I'm obsessed with passing the rock." Video footage of Kidd making a great pass.
　　Shrink: "Uh-huh. Here's an inkblot. What do you see?"
　　Jason: "Oooh, me and my Ergo LWPs from Nike—school some chump with a no-look dish." Video footage of Kidd making another impossible pass.
　　Shrink: "I see the inner child is poking through."
　　Jason: "Hey, Doc, inner-child this."
　　Shrink (passive-aggressive): "Uh-huh. Uh-huh. Say, can I get some tickets?"
　　Voice-over: "Ergo LWP from Nike. Now at Foot Action."
　　It's an amazing commercial, which takes exact aim at, for instance, the method of this book: namely, the irrelevance of "analysis" to grace (what an agony of enthralldom we are in).

• • •

2.27.95—On the *Gary Payton Show,* New York Vinnie says, "Last year probably the most emotional game of the year for the Sonics—and I think the game that really brought the team together as a team—was that fiasco back in Charlotte when they [Charlotte Hornets fans] were getting on Kendall [who had been traded from Charlotte] and the team just kinda put their arm around him. It almost made you cry lookin' at it, you know, like a movie. Will the same thing or something similar to that happen this year with the team?" A ridiculous question—how could Payton possibly know? "It almost seems you would want to rally more around Kendall, who has been an emotional leader of this team in a lot of ways."

Payton: "I think that's not, you know, a big deal right now." I love when Gary dismisses long-winded, theoretical questions with a shrug. "I think it was more emotional last year. I think this year he should just play." *Don't melodrama me your melodramas; it's just basketball.*

I go to the Charlotte game with Neal, my physical therapist. He tells me what a genius his kid is and how much he sold his business for; he informs me that Michael Crichton is a great writer, that *Forrest Gump* is a great movie; doesn't offer to pay me back for his ticket. He's a classic alpha male. My stutter deepens around him, though it's worse before and after the game; during the game, it virtually vanishes.

At one point, one of the Sonics' ball boys, a white kid, is holding the ball. As if he were addressing a dog, Charlotte's Alonzo Mourning claps at him to give him the ball. There will never be enough money stuffed into the wounds to stop the bleeding. A black fan in the stands is wearing a shaved head, a huge gold chain, boots, black sweats. His whole getup is unreadable to me except as the costume of a very prosperous and very recently freed slave. Cf. Henry Louis Gates Jr.: "The black body has, of course, been demonized in Western culture: represented as ogreish, coarse, and highly, menacingly sexualized. But the black body has also been valorized, represented, perceived as darkly alluring—still highly, menacingly sexualized but, well, in a good way. And this, historically, is its ambiguous dual role in the Western imagination."

In the fourth quarter, Shawn throws down a spectacular dunk and cel-

ebrates for a second. The crowd loses its collective mind in frenzy. Ted
Bernhardt, one of the three referees, immediately gives him a technical
for taunting. I'm sitting in the stands, and along with nearly every other
fan in the T-Dome, I scream bloody murder at Bernhardt. I really do
resent how he has instantly and seemingly intentionally emptied the
moment of its ecstasy; the Sonics go on to lose.

2.28.95—A few weeks ago Mitch Levy came from Washington, DC, to
take over KJR's noon-to-3 slot from Brian Wheeler. Levy is a graduate of
Syracuse, so he presents himself as a New Yorker; when talking to a
caller (originally) from New York named Jay, Mitch says, "Homeboy
from New York. You're my boy." Because Mitch can tell that or at least
believes that Jay is black, he immediately changes it to "You're my man,"
but the very correction only underscores the awkwardness of the
moment, of Jay's silence. The conversation continues, but it never quite
recovers its equilibrium; Mitch is always trying too hard to make it up to
Jay, and Jay never lets him.

Wheeler grew up in Los Angeles, went to college in Chicago, and is
all careful, respectful, cliché-clogged WASP rectitude. Levy, who grew
up in Miami, is nothing but Jewish shtick. At first Wheeler couldn't stand
Levy, primarily because Levy took his job from him, but as Wheeler got
eased into a supporting role on the station, the two shared a mike for an
hour or so every afternoon, and what intrigues me about their relationship is how their mutual disregard transmuted within a fairly short time
into baffled admiration. Levy can't believe how repressed Wheeler is,
but he adores Wheeler's funny sense of decorum and his wonderful
laugh. Wheeler can't believe how uncorked Levy is, but he admires
Levy's ability to say the unsayable, especially regarding things sexual. It's
sort of an amazing marriage, these guys yammering at each other every
afternoon—otherness creating curiosity and affection for once rather
than hatred; but then, what the hell, maybe they don't have all that far to
travel.

3.2.95—After I read bedtime stories to Natalie, she offers me half of her
pillow to help me fall asleep. The simple grace of this gesture—its gen-
tleness—makes me feel like an imbecilic monster for expending emotion

on the exploits of aggressive men who are strangers. I want off the band-wagon: I don't watch or listen to the broadcast of the Sonics-Clippers game from Los Angeles. After Natalie is asleep, I get up and, out of habit, I suppose, flip on the radio to get a score: Sonics 116, Clippers 88.

3.3.95—In Phoenix, the Suns beat the Sonics. Schrempf misses a crucial shot at the end of the game, and I scream at TV-Detlef, as if he's actually done something importantly wrong, which upsets Natalie, which upsets me. Payton has a great game (I first wrote *time* instead of *game,* and maybe that's the point: he's very good at having a great time), playing 44 minutes, scoring 30 points, accumulating 8 assists.

3.5.95—In and around Seattle, you see kids wearing not only Sonics jer-seys (Payton and Kemp, mostly) but also jerseys of players from other teams—almost always guys who not only are great players but have a *fuck you* attitude: Nick Van Exel, Jason Kidd, Alonzo Mourning, Charles Barkley. Today, for instance, because for some reason there seems to be an amazing number of kids walking around wearing NBA jerseys, you can feel with a certain clarity what the whole thing is about: how much of these kids' swagger comes from the players, the sheer volume of hope/possibility/resistance these guys represent. Is it just my imagina-tion, or does even Natalie raise more hell than usual when she's wearing her Sonics outfit?

3.6.95—In a Harris poll, 61 percent of whites say O.J. is guilty; 68 per-cent of blacks say he's not guilty.

Laurie and I argue about this all the time. Laurie says she can't believe that two-thirds of black people think he's innocent. I say that two-thirds of black people know he did it but they say he's not guilty as a sort of protest vote. Laurie says that when a black woman at work says she thinks he didn't do it, she thinks he didn't do it; she isn't making any sort of protest vote. I say that it's subterranean, that no one is going to come out and say it's a protest vote; if they did, it wouldn't be a protest vote. "Then," she says (either finally seeing the light or mocking me, it's not entirely clear), "it wouldn't be subterranean."

· · ·

The Sonics' policy for the remainder of the season is that I'll be allowed to attend two games a month, so I call *ma chérie* to say I'd like to go to the Detroit and Sacramento games. She says no, I have to go to the Golden State and Miami games. I say I have the flu and can't go to the Golden State game tonight, so she says okay, Miami and Washington— two more dog-games than which it would be difficult to find.

I don't have the flu; I'm just tired of the season, everyone is tired of the season, we just want it to be over so we can get to the playoffs. I even find myself half-hoping that they get eliminated in the first round again, because I'm dead-broke and literally can't afford to buy tickets to any but a couple of playoff games—$85(!) a seat for the first round and progressively higher prices for each successive round. For $35, I sell the tickets for tonight's game to a coworker of Laurie's—the woman, in fact, who says she believes O.J. is innocent—and I watch the game against Golden State at home "with" Laurie and Natalie (they couldn't care less) on pay-per-view. Seattle is one of the relatively few teams in the NBA that charges— nearly $25—for fans to watch regular-season home games on TV.

McMillan always looks guiltily at the relevant ref whenever he's committed a foul; he's so not a poker player. Schrempf gets called for a foul and in his blunt Teutonic way points a finger right at a black ref; he gets called for a technical more quickly than I've ever seen anyone get called for a technical.

As bad as the Golden State Warriors are, they beat Seattle. Payton makes only 9 of 23 shots. There's no energy, no focus to the game. The Sonics have now lost three in a row, six of their last ten, and are five-and-a-half games out of first place. We all need a second wind, a seventh wind.

On the post-game show, Calabro interviews the Warriors' Latrell Sprewell. During the entire interview, Sprewell barely acknowledges Calabro, instead fondling the gift certificate he's been given—prematurely, it turns out—for participating in the interview. At first, Calabro keeps trying to connect with him, saying "Man," dropping his g's, but after a while Calabro gives up and an unusually tense, unusually uncivil interview winds down. I keep expecting Calabro to say, "Look, Spree, you don't want to talk to me; I don't want to talk with you. Let's just call the whole thing off."

• • •

3.7.95—A middle-aged man stands next to me at the bus stop, wearing a T-shirt that says *Love See No Color*. Is love the subject ("It is the nature of love to see no color")? If so, then the only reason the T-shirt doesn't say *Love Sees No Color* is to romanticize black vernacular. On the other hand, is love an imperative ("Love; see no color")? If so, who, commanded to love, has ever loved?

The bus arrives. A teenage girl, getting off the bus, says to her friend, "She's some color—I don't know what." The way she says "some color" conveys delirious depths of envy and longing. She makes me think of a punky white kid I saw wearing a Georgetown T-shirt, his Adam's apple visibly vibrating when he said the word *'hood* to his black friend; another white kid in front of me at the optometrist, saying "Sweet" when a replacement part was found for his glasses; frat boys at the University of Washington greeting each other by saying "What up"; a kid in the movie theater putting his baseball cap on with the bill in front, fixing the cap so it was on backward, then turning around and looking to see if he'd been found out.

3.8.95—In his column this week, my father criticizes the Women's Tennis Association for turning down $20 million from Tampax to sponsor the women's tour: "Get this: For more than twenty years, the WTA took the millions of another sponsor, the R.J. Reynolds Tobacco Company, makers of Virginia Slims cigarettes. So by its tortured reasoning, the WTA apparently thought it was okay to be pushing cigarettes, the certain cause of heart disease, emphysema, lung cancer, and allied ailments. But to be linked with a product women have used—one that can be bought over the counter in every pharmacy and tiny drugstore in the country—was too much for the Neanderthals of the WTA. The WTA officials caved in to those who think sex, or any aspect of it, is a dirty word never to be mentioned. You want to slam your fist against these small, hermetically sealed minds—the best minds of the eighteenth century." My father always takes the moral high ground, and he's always right, and I always agree with him, and whenever I explore the gray areas I assume the earth is going to fissure.

· · ·

The T-Wolves still aren't very good, and in the first of four consecutive road games, the Sonics beat them badly in Minneapolis. Schrempf scores 27 on five 3-pointers. Gill is benched. Karl says, "A lot of people write about my attitude toward Kendall. I tried to convey to him it's not that. It's not a reprimand. It's more like, 'How can I get you guys to be better for the second half of the season?' Gill's reaction is: "I don't have any reaction. I just play. The season will be over soon." Amen, brother: I'm flat busted.

3.9.95—The Hornets beat the Sonics in Charlotte. Payton has a solid if somewhat quiet game—44 minutes, 20 points, 5 assists, 4 boards.

Schrempf says, "When it comes down to crunch time, everybody has to be in sync, and everybody has to run the play and make sacrifices. Sometimes we don't do that." At the very beginning of the season, Karl said, "If they can't handle winning through sharing and sacrificing, then they probably can't handle winning." The entire season has thus become a proof of a theorem about black folks and responsibility.

Paul e-mails me: "Have you heard about the latest idea to print 'domestic violence warning labels' on all marriage licenses issued in the state of Washington? Now pending in the legislature! Also, did you see William Arnold's recent review in the *P-I* [*Post-Intelligencer*] of *My New Partner*—a pretty funny comedy about on-the-take cops in Paris—in which he concluded that the film was terrible because 'police corruption isn't funny'? And then there are the new public-service announcements urging people to report their friends and neighbors for any infractions or suspicious-seeming events, of which my own favorite is the Dial-000-HERO campaign, whereby we're encouraged to report observed commuter-lane violators on the freeways to the state police." All my friends love to struggle against the Seattle ethos, and what we love to struggle against is its assumption of the perfectibility of humankind. As the locally popular bumper sticker has it, *Mean People Suck;* someone finally came along with the necessary rejoinder: *Nice People Swallow.*

· · ·

3.11.95—In New York the Sonics beat the Knicks, 96–84. Kemp has a monster game—22 points, 19 boards. Payton has a great floor game—6 assists, no fouls, 7-for-14 from the floor, 19 points.

A notion still getting disseminated is that West Coast fans always arrive late and leave early, whereas East Coast fans arrive on time and stay till the bitter end: they have true forbearance, persistence, stick-to-it-iveness. In reality, Knicks fans are leaving in droves with four minutes to go. Everybody needs someone to beat up, and the East Coast defines itself as the East Coast by caricaturing the West Coast, which I didn't understand until I moved back to the West Coast a few years ago. It's simple but true: power is a fulcrum. East/West, North/South, white/black, male/female: Group X always needs Group Y to buff its own sense of superiority. *We are mind-haunted civilization; you are the physical beauty we'll contemplate.* In this view, the West Coast is—black people are—in a perpetual state of nature.

Afterward, Knicks coach Pat Riley says, "They [the Sonics] affected our offense probably as well as any team has all year, from taking away the things that we want. We struggled to get into the game. They forced our pick-and-roll game to the corner."

Although I strenuously resist the mythology of the Knicks, the mythology of Riley, the mythology of New York City, I must nevertheless acknowledge that for me, this statement coming from Riley carries more weight than it would coming from any other coach, makes me "proud" of the Supes in a way I would never be if it came from any other coach: *woo-hoo—we got good notices on Broadway!* My fandom, like a genuine drug, flows back into my veins.

3.12.95—I live across the street from a fundamentalist church, and after the Sonics' win last night over the Knicks, I'm filled for once with empathy for the church-goers. They go to church for the same reason fans go to games: adulthood didn't turn out to have quite as much glory as we thought it would; for an hour or two, we're in touch with transcendental things.

More pseudo-power, more meta-magic: in Detroit, the Sonics whomp the Pistons by 40, making me happy. Kemp has a great game, scoring 25 points. Payton scores 21 on 9-for-15 from the floor and 3-for-7 from the line. (Why is he such a consistently inconsistent free-throw shooter? Even this failing I tend to romanticize: free throws are too uncontested, too tediously masturbatory for him to practice with any diligence; he needs social interaction to flourish.) In the second quarter, Gary and Pistons rookie guard Lindsey Hunter get into a big trash-talking confrontation. Payton receives a technical foul for taunting Hunter after scoring on him. Payton whacks Hunter on the arm on the ensuing inbounds pass. Hunter gets two free throws but then receives a technical for talking back to Payton. Hunter commits four turnovers and winds up going 1-for-7 from the floor.

Afterward, Payton says, "I'm always getting hyper when somebody talks to me. If you want to talk, we can talk. It was the worst thing to start up with me, because I'm good at it, very good. He should have shut his mouth and kept playing." Gary's game is better than everyone else's because his language is better than everyone else's. My identification with him is total.

Byron Houston scores 14 points, including a torrid dunk. Asked about it later, Houston says, "I can jump when I want to. I just don't always want to." *They'd sit on the gallery and watch the niggers put it on brown.*

3.13.95—A caller to the *Gary Payton Show* says, "Lindsey Hunter said something, obviously, to Gary. What did he say, Gary?"

Payton says, "He said something he wasn't supposed to." *It's our camaraderie.* "He came out there yapping his lips a little bit, and it got me a little bit hyper, and I got into the game a little bit more. When we went into halftime, the guys was saying that they like doing that. Vincent [Askew] was the main one; he says that he like when I go to that level and we get to that level [when the game turns into a personal confrontation]. We need that sometimes to get us energized, and they call me the energizer, so I think I should have a little say-so when we need something to get us hyper. That was what happened yesterday. I got us into it. We started playing a little bit more defense and getting a lot of turnovers."

Knight says, "Det had you by the shoulders a couple times. You had something you wanted to say and you weren't quite finished saying it— to Lindsey Hunter and a couple other people, too."

Payton strenuously resists this scenario: "I know when to back off and not get the other tech so I won't get kicked out of the game. That's all Det was trying to tell me." *I'm not just a body; I possess consciousness; I don't need blond, blue-eyed Schrempf to imprint upon me the consequences of my actions.* Vinnie asks him, "What was the difference in Det coming over [to you] in that game [last night] and the other night when Shawn seemed to be getting out of hand? Are you an easier guy to approach than Shawn might be?" *When is it safe for a white person to approach a black person?*

Several weeks ago I borrowed from Bob Kloppenburg, who is the designer of the Sonics' defensive system and who got kicked upstairs this year, a videotape he produced about the particular style of defense he's developed. Today he calls and asks me to return the tape. On the air last night, Calabro had mentioned something about best wishes going out to Bob Kloppenburg's wife, so I say, "Sorry to hear about your wife; how's she doing?" Kloppenburg says, "We think we got it all"—removed the cancer. He seems unlike any coach I've ever heard or talked to: dour, confessional (much more so even than Karl), vulnerable (much more so even than Karl). During the few days between K.C. Jones being fired and Karl being hired in 1992, Kloppenburg was the interim coach, and when he won his first game as interim coach, the players all gathered around him, chanting, "Kloppy! Kloppy! Kloppy!" Kloppy cried his eyes out; he couldn't believe they liked him so much. I'm comfortable with people who wear their hearts on their sleeves, as Kloppy does and Karl does and Natalie does; as Laurie and G. Payton do not, making them more inscrutable to me. On the other hand, when Kloppy asks me whether I live on the "East Side"—i.e., perhaps he could swing by and get the videotape; he must really need it back—and I say no, I live in Wallingford, he seems absolutely flummoxed that anyone could or would reside anywhere else but in the suburban embrace of the East Side.

I telephone John Walter—the chairman of the American Ethnic Studies department at the University of Washington, who is compiling an oral history of black athletes who broke the color line in their sports—to confirm what time we're meeting for lunch at the Faculty Club.

"You can't miss me," he says. "I'll be the only black person there."

During lunch, I ask him why he thinks no one in the NBA wants to talk to me about race, and he says, "They don't want to talk to you about it because you're not black." He says that in 1975 if a black NBA player had a white girlfriend, his teammates would "try to beat him up, try to kill him," which strikes me as exceedingly unlikely. When, in response to a comparison he makes, I say, "That's a good analogy," he says, with mock-gratitude, "Thank you, David." Lunch is over, and we're walking to our cars; the last thing he says to me is, "Who gives a damn about the president? He's no fun. Clinton gonna make you happy? Michael Jordan's gonna make you happy." (A rumor has been circulating recently that Michael Jordan might be returning to the NBA. I am one of the very few people on the planet who don't adore Michael Jordan—his utter establishmentarianism repels me—but it's amazing how exciting this information is nevertheless.) John Walter keeps teasing me, tweaking me, testing me; I think I passed, though I can't be sure.

3.14.95—*Ma chérie* calls and leaves a message: "I have your interview request for Gary Payton. I have some people in ahead of you, and given the travel schedule and everything else, we'll certainly try to get that in and give you a call when I can schedule it. Thank you. Bye-bye."

The Sonics are back home. Tonight in Tacoma: Seattle vs. Boston (nobody wants to make the trek; I go alone). G. Payton has unusual stage presence. He'll foul a guy, then stare at the ref, daring him to call a foul against him, and frequently the ref won't call the foul. Not this time, though: Payton fouls Sherman Douglass hard to the floor, and Douglass doesn't let Payton help him up. It's a power play on Payton's part (*here, you poor dolt, you can't even stand up on your own two feet*), and it's wise of Douglass to refuse. Payton hits a 3-pointer, and as he runs back down the court along the sideline, a fan offers him a high-five, which Payton quite pointedly refuses; then, just as pointedly, he high-fives Kemp. *I ain't your fuckin' plaything*, I feel Gary telling the fan, *I ain't your buddy, you don't know me, don't go thinkin' you can slap my palm.*

Payton is constantly making clear to everyone in the arena how bored he is out there, which sets up a dynamic: *you're bored, too, and don't you*

want me to do something now completely new and amazing and danger-
ous to try to unwrap that seal of boredom right off your brain? I love
how he creates this mood of flat affectlessness in the building, which
then needs to be broken—by him. Payton finally gets the frisson he
wanted, to rock us out of our chairs: he gets thrown out by a referee
whom he hates and who hates him and whom all the fans hate, the ludi-
crously vainglorious Bernie Fryer.

Steve Scheffler, the last man on the Sonics' bench, is white and
ungainly and terrible and tries hard, and whenever the Sonics are way
ahead, as they are tonight, everyone shouts, as they do tonight, "We want
Scheff." What do fans see in Scheffler? It's not even a question; they see
themselves, obviously, in this big, hard-working, comparatively untal-
ented guy pulling down an NBA salary. Him we can empathize with. It
always pains me when fans chant, "We want Scheff, we want Scheff,"
because it makes utterly manifest that in reality they don't want any of
the other players, who are too talented and/or too black to be wanted in
quite this way. It's too interesting, too revealing, too much a statement of
fans' affirmation of our own middling, muddling, vanilla mediocrity.

Many, many years ago, I was living not far from St. Paul, Minnesota,
and so one Saturday night went to see the live performance of *A Prairie
Home Companion.* At the end of the show, the piano started up and Gar-
rison Keillor said, "I hope you enjoy the stories about Lake Wobegon.
They are meant for you to enjoy. But it gets harder and harder to tell
them, for a storyteller, because the more you tell them, the more you
realize how far wide of the mark you really are. I know that I've said
probably two or three things now in just about the last fifteen minutes
that will really bother me. Inaccurate things. I'll think about them tomorrow. I'll think about them all week."

Keillor inhaled deeply.

"It is sort of God's judgment on people who are ambitious about
telling lies, you see."

Some people laughed a little.

"It doesn't bother you when you start out telling lies, you know. You
are just grateful to be able to get through them without fainting up here."

People laughed a little more.

"But when you become as accomplished a liar as I am, then you are troubled by inaccuracies in your lies. Because, you see, the reason you tell lies about a wonderful place is that you believe that if you get every detail right—absolutely right—and every character in that story has exactly as many hairs on his or her head as she's supposed to have or him; that if you get it absolutely perfect, you will be lifted up out of this life and you will be set down in that wonderful place that you've told lies about and all your lies become true. Now, you see, what you don't realize, so many of you, is that not only is Lake Wobegon made up but Minnesota is made up, too."

The crowd roared; some clapped and whistled.

"I invented it. A lot of people invented it. There is no such state. I hate to be the first one to tell you. But I keep on telling stories about Minnesota in the hope that if I get it exactly right I'd be lifted out of here in East Los Angeles and be able to live there."

On "East Los Angeles"—*Watts*—the audience, including to my astonishment myself, went completely nuts. Whoop, whoop. Whoop, whoop, whoop. I'll never forget the sound of it.

3.15.95—On *Mitch at Mid-Day* on KJR, Mitch Levy says, "Shawn Kemp missed shootaround yesterday. Where was he? We're looking for Shawn Kemp sightings yesterday."

One caller says, "He was with what's-his-name's girlfriend."

Someone else says, "He was at Gene Juarez Salon in Northgate Mall, getting his nails done."

Another caller: "He was at home, watching *The Brady Bunch* [Levy's faux-favorite show]."

We live to move Shawn Kemp's body around like a battleship in a game of war.

3.16.95—Discussing why the Tacoma Dome is such a poor place to play, Steve Scheffler jokes to a reporter, "What's all this alternative stuff [Nirvana, Pearl Jam, Soundgarden] they play on the public-address system? They classify this stuff as music? If we had country, I think the fans would be rockin'."

All the people like us are We, / ...

Perkins says, "Country music? Disgusting. We just need a new soundtrack."

...And everyone else is They.

Driving down to Tacoma for the game tonight against Miami, I come to a four-way intersection. Everybody is waiting for everybody else, and although I was inarguably the last person to arrive at the intersection, I grab the gauntlet and whip on through. In the view of my fellow motorists, I've lost by winning, and they've won by losing. They're one with whatever it is that is beyond human traffic—nature, I suppose. I'm one with inconsequence.

I'm sitting in the press row tonight for the game against Miami (minimal return on the tickets) and I feel it as a huge relief to be out of fan mode. I'm weary right now of the Sturm und Drang of fandom and relieved to be in pseudo-objective journalist mode. I like going to this meaningless game in the middle of March against a mediocre team on a rainy night; I like—against the usefulness of the rest of my life—the completely excessive uselessness of the evening, its flagrant irrelevance, its aesthetic purity. I love the spaghetti dinner we get before the game: the salad, the bread, the brownies, the exquisite pleasure of anticipation before the game, the space gleaming down below with the promise of unknowable activity to come.

Gary gets a technical foul at 1:41 of the first quarter. You realize after a while it's sort of an act—Payton pretending to be talking to Karl but really complaining to the ref (the old "I-might-have-been-talking-about-you-but-I-wasn't-talking-to-you routine from junior high school). The ref techs him up.

A ball bounces into the first row. A fan wants to hand Payton the ball so he'll return it to the ref and so the fan can have that communion with Gary. Payton turns his back, will have no part of it; it's not his job to retrieve the ball. He's a relentlessly proud (excessively vain) human. During a break in the action to reset the clock, Payton sits in a chair, shooting the shit with people; this he'll do—interact on his own terms, when he wants to, with a little wit.

My non-fan mode comes quickly undone. Ervin Johnson plays well in the first quarter; when he dunks off a Payton feed and gets fouled, then receives multiple vicious chest-bumps of congratulations from Payton and Kemp, I focus the binoculars on him but can't see through the lenses because my eyes are so foggy. It's weird enough how moved I am by the game of basketball, but what's much, much weirder is how suddenly the game can move me, like a virus I catch upon contact; in a fraction of a second, I'm running streaks down my face. (Yesterday, while eating breakfast, I listened to a short promotional highlight on KJR—Calabro describing Payton twisting 360 degrees to score on a layup, and then saying, "You gotta be kidding me"—and immediately started tearing up. The lift in Calabro's voice, me remembering the play Calabro is describing— there's a direct link between Calabro's voice and Payton's body and my heart that is inextinguishable and inexplicable. Why do I care so much? That's what I would like to know. It's a safe love, this love, this semi-self-love, this fandom; it's a frenzy in a vacuum, a completely imaginary love affair in which the beloved is forever larger than life.)

What I hate about Sasquatch is that he's so pathetic you can never really relax around him. As he begs for our appreciation and admiration, all I'm thinking is that I hope he doesn't embarrass or hurt himself. He is exactly the opposite of how a mascot should be: instead of drawing us out of ourselves into a public play, as Payton does, he pushes us back into our own delicate psyches.

In the third quarter, the Sonics are way ahead, and as is his wont, Karl chooses this moment to instigate a squabble with a ref. The Sonics still get to win, and Karl can say, in effect, *See? I was quarreling with the refs even though we were winning. It's just the spirit of the game I care about. I wish the players and refs would still be paying attention even though we're up by twenty.* He gets upset about a call made against Vince Askew, who was battling the Heat's Keith Askins for a rebound. Sitting on the scorer's table, Karl barks at ref Monty McCutchen and receives two straight techs—automatic ejection, at which point he races onto the floor to stand toe-to-toe with McCutchen, screaming at him. McMillan and assistant coach Terry Stotts pull Karl away. He'll be fined at least $1,000 for ejection, possibly much more. The Sonics win by 25. Scheffler has 4 points: he is us.

After the game, Karl emerges with his arms draped around his son and Cheri White. He sits down at the table without making a comment.

Mike Kahn, of the *Tacoma News Tribune,* says, "It's really great that you came out [for the press conference] after getting kicked out. We appreciate it. Thanks. So what happened?"

Karl can't stand Kahn's ingratiating style and says, "No comment."

Jim Moore, of the *Post-Intelligencer,* breaks the ice by saying, "Why did you run out and get in his [McCutchen's] face? Did you say that you think that he should be shot?" This last line, referring to Karl's comment a couple of weeks ago that another referee should be shot, is a great joke, and everybody laughs, because it's a great joke. It even draws Karl out a little; he acknowledges that he kicked the table and that "the second [technical] was deserved."

Asked what Karl said, Kemp says, "He said, 'You're a very nice guy. I thought you made a bad call and I hope you make a better one next time.'" *It's our camaraderie.*

As if in conscious contrast to all this bad behavior: Ervin Johnson, the Sonics' God-fearing center, who had 7 rebounds and 15 points, when asked whether he wishes he were playing more, says, "I'm not worried about my minutes; that's the coach's job. I just try to make the most of my opportunities." And when he says this, I'm struck anew by the fact that we all find Ervin Johnson utterly bereft of interest precisely because he is so respectful, well-mannered, polite. We get plenty of that service with a smile in our own lives; we come to the game for the same reason we go to Nirvana concerts or used to go to Nirvana concerts: we want intimations of excitement/danger/evil, of something sad or bad in ourselves we would express if we had the talent or the nerve. We will do anything to leave our lives, even for a minute.

8

CAN YOU FEEL
NOW WHAT POWER
FEELS LIKE?

3.18.95—KJR has fired Kevin Wall and reduced Brian Wheeler's role to utility infielder—both boring WASPs with no real identity—and brought in Jews with attitude: Mitch Levy and now Rob Tepper, who calls himself "T-Man," is like Wolfman Jack crossed with Howard Stern, and whom, I must admit, I immediately adore (his voice's confident maleness, his extraordinarily quick and brutal repartee).

A caller asks T-Man, "What nationality are you?"

Although Tepper, like Levy, is a direct descendant of Jewish stand-up, he says, "I can't get into that." A black "preacher" named Reverend Daimen—a friend of Tepper's, I assume, just doing a bit with his Barry White–like bass—shows up for a concluding monologue virtually every evening on Tepper's show. Daimen's monologues always end with an ode to the fact that whether we're white or black or yellow or red or brown or blue, we're all God's creatures. This is the unmistakable, corny, and irresistible message of T-Man's show, so he "can't get into that"; he's going to try to emphasize how we're all alike rather than how we're different. When I read in the University of Washington Baha'i Club newsletter, "Humankind is one," I think, *Nah,* but when Reverend Daimen says it, I get goose bumps.

I need the money, so I sell my tickets to the Sonics-Pistons game and listen to it on the radio. Schrempf has a nearly perfect night, going 9-for-10 from the floor, 3-for-3 from the line, scoring 25 points, collecting 6 rebounds and 8 assists. Afterward, Karl praises Schrempf's "family, politics, taste in clothes, the perfect little way he smiles," and concludes, in appreciation: "C'mon, have a flaw." The German player is, in the German-American coach's opinion, flawless.

3.19.95—A woman walks into my local bookstore and asks the owner to recommend a book for her friend. The owner asks the customer what her friend's interests are.

"Well," she says, "he's gay and he's Afro-American and very ecology-minded."

The owner is thinking, thinking.

"Oh," the customer says, "and he's HIV-positive."

The customer's friend isn't a person to her; he's a collection of appreciated categories.

3.20.95—The Spurs beat the Sonics, in San Antonio. Afterward, Karl says, "The top five teams in the West are ready to play playoff basketball. The next eighteen games will prove basically nothing." They're tired. I, personally, am utterly exhausted, and all I do is watch the games. It is one long fucking season. I never remotely understood this before.

3.21.95—In Houston, the Sonics squeak out a win over the Rockets. Payton goes 7 for 16 from the floor and has 6 assists—a typical game for him, in many ways: statistically not overwhelming, but he completely controls the flow of the game at both ends of the floor.

3.23.95—The Washington Bullets are in Tacoma for a game tonight against the Sonics. On his occasional radio show, Detlef Schrempf was expecting to talk with two Bullets, Jawon Howard and Chris Webber, but they never show. Schrempf says that he can't understand where they might be; he knows they've blown him off, but he has to profess bafflement.

Having sold my seats for a song, I sit in press row. During the national anthem, I only half-stand; this was my father's mini-rebellion against the military-industrial complex whenever we went to games when I was a boy.

An amazing play occurs early on: Shawn leaps, catches the ball, *in midair fakes a pass,* comes down, puts it in, and scores. The midair fake completely throws off the defender. His reputation is that he is not a particularly clever player, but this play seems to me brilliantly conceived as well as brilliantly executed.

At halftime, I watch, on the TV in the press box, the last few minutes of an NCAA tournament basketball game—North Carolina versus Georgetown—and am chagrined to find myself rooting for the squares (Dean Smith's clean-cut Tarheels) against the hipsters (Georgetown hats and jerseys are nearly as ubiquitous among black teens as X paraphernalia).

Late in the third quarter, the Sonics are losing to the Bullets when one of the nets shreds. A seamstress takes fifteen minutes to repair the net, after which the Sonics go on a 32–17 run and win. Payton plays spectacularly, shooting 11-for-17 from the field and scoring 24 points, with 9 assists and 3 steals. The rhythm of the game, as with so many other games, is this: Gary spends the entire evening trying to get the Sonics to play, and they finally do. With 16 seconds left in the fourth quarter, Gill scores the winning basket; Payton tries to high-five him, but Gill either isn't looking or ignores it.

I attend Karl's press conference. "I'm listening," he barks out as he slumps in the chair at a table before about a dozen reporters and cameramen, sipping Coke and popping Tylenol—the tough-love high-school principal calling a group of chronic underachievers into his office.

Someone tries to establish a light tone by saying, "The key to the game was the net lady."

Karl doesn't laugh. The reporters are forever trying to enter a club to which they are, by definition, denied access. It's strange to me how much they want him to approve of their questions, when in fact no question could possibly win his approval (if people ask powder-puff questions, he snorts; if people try to ask technical questions, he guffaws). There is no way to ask a good question except not to ask a question.

3.26.95—The Sonics, who have won nine of their last ten, have a record of 48-and-20, and are now just a game and a half behind the Suns with a little less than a month remaining in the regular season, are home for four straight. During the Sonics-Knicks game tonight at Tacoma (I sold one ticket to someone who not only paid me $100—it's New York!—but never showed), Payton picks up the resin bag and throws it so the resin rises up into Marques Johnson's face. On the air, Johnson laughs it off, calling it an "accident," but this, too, is a kind of test, isn't it? The Knicks' enforcer, Charles Oakley, keeps talking to Payton, who, sitting on the bench for the moment, cups his hand over his ear—*I'm sorry, I didn't hear that; what did you say?*—and repeatedly juts his chin straight out, trying to taunt Oakley into getting his second technical. Called in off the bench to re-enter the game, Payton immediately hits a 3-pointer, nodding at Oakley all the way down the court. Gary is so cool, and the cool consists of precisely this: being comfortable being a complete asshole. Schrempf needs to foul Anthony Mason to prevent him from scoring a layup, but there's been a lot of fighting between the two teams all night long, and—I feel Schrempf actually calculates things like this but could never say so—as the lone white guy out there, Schrempf doesn't want to be the person who makes things worse, so he doesn't foul Mason as hard as he should, and the result is that Mason gets both the basket and the foul.

I'm watching the game with my Walkman on, and at one point, apropos of how much Payton loves Snoop Doggy Dogg, Calabro says, "I went into a country-and-western bar in Dallas—the whole country bar scene. And they were dancing country to Snoop Doggy Dogg. Only in Dallas." This is a compressed parable of: *only connect.*

Marques replies, "I went into a redneck bar and they all turned around to look at me. The whole place went silent, and I said, 'Somebody call a cab?'" This is compressed parable of: *spare me your "only connect" parables.*

If an exchange exists that registers more exactly the current state of American race relations, I'd like to hear it.

For the second time in two weeks, the Sonics beat the Knicks, which matters way too much to me, as if this fact somehow constituted final proof that it doesn't matter where you live (i.e., not in New York); all that matters is how much game you got. Payton plays 41 minutes, scores 26 points, has 8 boards and 4 assists.

Ervin Johnson also plays a rare good game, and on the post-game show he says, "Practice makes perfect." He says, "If you continue to practice and work hard and keep a positive attitude, then things will work out for you." He says, "I'm just trying to work hard and keep a positive attitude." He says, "I'd just like to thank God for giving me the opportunity, Coach Karl for giving me the opportunity, to play game in and game out." He says, "We've just got to take one game at a time and work hard and continue to win ballgames; we don't want to get above ourselves." More than any player I've ever heard, Ervin appears to think that the discourse is composed entirely of clichés, that he needs to hit one every few seconds, like a slalom skier passing through certain gates every few seconds, and that if he doesn't hit these gate-clichés the conversation might veer spookily out of control. To me, it's an open question whether Ervin believes these clichés or not. I have no idea if it's just rhetorical sleight-of-hand so he doesn't have to think when speaking to reporters, or whether these are his actual thoughts; there's no real way to know.

New York guard John Starks, who missed 14 of the 16 shots he took, tells reporters, "The lighting here [in the Tacoma Dome] is terrible. When you look to shoot, you're looking at a lot of different things instead of the basket. You've got to be used to shooting in this gym, and we only come here once a year. It's a bad gym for shooters."

Knicks point-guard Derek Harper says, "The shots were there; they were there all night."

New York won't admit that Seattle's defense had anything to do with their poor shooting night, which irritates the Sonics (and me) a little.

On the post-game show, Marques Johnson says, "The Sonics just beat you up on defense. They just try to wear you down, get you to the point where you want to put on a dress or something, like 'Leave me alone. Please quit. Stop.' They just maul you, they just come out, attack, attack, attack, and hope you'll eventually put up the white flag." In Johnson's analogy, sports becomes sex becomes rape becomes war. Johnson is an unreconstructed chauvinist, but Calabro, who isn't, would no more broach this subject with him than critique his wardrobe, as no white man I know feels comfortable criticizing a black man in the physical realm; it's too loaded.

SST: Sonic Show Time, a weekly review, is on late every Sunday night on the channel that broadcasts most Sonics games, and tonight, for once, I catch it. Payton has a special taped segment every week in which he usually interviews a player from an opposing team who's a friend of his and with whom he can word-war. Tonight his guest is Calabro, and Gary asks him, "People always want to know, where do you get all those words?" *How do you talk so good?*

Calabro says, "Hangin' out with you, G., hangin' in the posse." This is (barely) okay up to here; Calabro is dropping his *g*'s a little too much and a black thing is entering his diction, but at least he knows that with a compliment you have to mock it, knock it back, turn it inside out. Then he says, "In the ghetto." This is a reference to what Payton calls the back of the Sonics' private plane, where he and the more loquacious players hold court. There's no way to explain this, though, in the context of the interview without sounding moronic: *"Ghetto" is what we call the back of the plane, where we*...etc. Payton, dumbfounded by Calabro's faux pas, scowls at him; Calabro looks abashed.

Payton semi-rescues him by saying, "We won't go into that." They keep talking, but the interview is, for all practical purposes, over before it's begun. You can tell Calabro would give anything not to have said this, but he did.

3.27.95—On the *Gary Payton Show,* the guest host, television sportscaster Rod Simons, asks Payton, "What were you saying to Charles Oakley last night by the bench? You had come out of the game for a couple of minutes, and he was working on Kendall Gill. You had some words of encouragement for Mr. Oakley."

Payton says, "He was going off of whatever was happenin' in the paper—a lot of quotes from the team." How would Payton know this unless he himself read the paper, which he claims he only occasionally peruses? "I guess he had an attitude problem and he came over and wanted to take it out on us. I got to let him know, you know, you not gonna just come in here and punk nobody." *I'm defending my boy Kendall Gill, who—and this is a little pathetic—can't defend himself.* "It's not no East Coast team, so you gotta take that back to New York." I love how unimpressed he is by New York bluster, how unambivalent he is about the West Coast. "I'm a West Coast guy," he says all the time. "I hate the cold weather."

Simons says, "Then you're back in the game. You sting a 3 [3-pointer] and you go back and you turn around and you let Derek Harper know you really don't like him that much."

Payton: "Me and Harper, we been going at it since I got in the league. We're close friends, but we yap a lot out there." *It's not antagonism, you idiot, it's conversation.* "I kept telling him if he kept doublin' down, every time they kick it to me, I was gonna hit a jumper on him or hit a 3, and he stopped doublin' down after that."

Simons: "I gotta ask you. Let's face it, John Starks sucked last night." This locution is ubiquitous, but particularly in sports: *you suck* means *you're a woman* or *you're a faggot,* because *you suck cock,* which is to say *you're servicing someone rather than getting serviced,* which is to say *servicing someone is no fun; getting serviced is the only fun;* which is to say *all that matters is who's doing whom, all that matters is who worships whom, all that matters is who's in control.* "He says it's the lights. You got 26 points last night; did you have contact lenses on or what, Gary? What's the deal?"

Payton says, "People gotta understand: you can't have a great night every night, so he gotta let that one go. He just didn't have a good night." Gary will initiate the trash-talk when he wants to, not when Rod Simons tells him to.

Simons, as instructed, gets his foot off Starks' back. "Five films: *Pulp Fiction, Shawshank, Forrest Gump, Madness of King George, Four Weddings and a Funeral*—which one do you think gets it?" The Academy Awards are tonight.

Payton: *"Pulp Fiction."*

Vinnie: "That's a wild movie, huh?"

Payton: "I haven't seen it, but I heard it was good."

Simons: "Samuel L. Jackson is too live in this film. He's the best."

More currying of Payton's favor on Simons' part. His incessant use of what he thinks must be G-speak—"too live"—nauseates me and, I think, nauseates Payton.

Vinnie: "I don't know. I like John Travolta in this movie." In this context, Vinnie's honest acknowledgment that he likes his *paesan* seems admirably unforced; I imagine that he, too, is embarrassed by Simons.

Simons: "Samuel L. Jackson had some brilliant lines"—which, apparently, he came up with on the spot.

Vinnie: "Jodie Foster, Susan Sarandon, Miranda Richardson, Winona Ryder, Jessica Lange—who do you think [will win the Academy Award for best actress]?"

The way Payton answers "Jodie Foster," it has the quality of answering the question *Which of these women would you most like to fuck?*

Vinnie says, "I kinda like Miranda Richardson, but I can't get *The Crying Game* out of my head."

Simons: "Weird movie."

Payton: "Crazy movie."

Vinnie: "You know, that movie restored my faith in America, because that was the best-kept secret—"

Payton: "It still should be secret." Payton is adamant about this: he's no gender-bending bohemian.

Vinnie: "They wouldn't tell you the middle of *The Crying*—"

Payton: "That's why we should just keep that one on the shelf and don't bring it back." Payton doesn't dig it. He doesn't want any confusion of the realms; his conservatism on this matter disappoints me, but why should it? He never pretended to be the Artist Formerly Known as Prince.

The conversation segues somehow to Vinnie's bumping into Payton's former teammate Derrick McKey in Miami: "He was in Hooters [the restaurant chain featuring waitresses in low-cut white T-shirts and orange hot pants], eating chicken. I'll tell you, I never seen anybody that could suck meat off the bone like Derrick McKey."

Vinnie's trying to send this in the direction of radio double-entendre land, but Gary gives him instead Anthro 101: "Derrick from the South, so you know he could do that."

Vinnie, who must weigh 300 pounds, says, "He's skinny as a rail."

Payton: "But he can eat, though."

Simons: "Glove, do you have an appetite?" More supposed Gary-isms: "Glove," etc.

Payton: "Yeah, I can throw down some food, too. I watch my weight. Y'all gotta look at my figure now." Last year Payton said, "Coach looks at me and sees himself, only younger, skinnier, and better-looking."

Simons, completely overzealous: "Man, you are skinny as a rail, too. What's your waist size, like 26 or something?"

Payton (in falsetto): "Thirty-two, man. Come on. Twenty-six; you want me to be like a girl now." GP, taking us right into the heart of darkness.

Vinnie: "Twenty-six. You would have a girl's figure at 26."

Simons: "Twenty-eight. Thirty, then."

Vinnie: "Thirty-two."

Simons: "He is skinny as a rail."

Payton says, "Me and my little son, Gary, be wearin' the same clothes at 26. At 26 I could Hula Hoop with a Cheerio."

Not a minute of this edition of the *Gary Payton Show* has not been about the various ways in which shy white people understand Gary Payton to be an authority on the human body.

On the *George Karl Show*, Mitch Levy says to Karl, "Do you have an opinion on best picture tonight?"

Karl says, "I don't even know who's running." *I'm such a workaholic I wouldn't know something trivial like that.*

Levy: "*Forrest Gump.* Did you see *Gump?*"

Karl: "Loved it."

Levy: "How about *Pulp Fiction?*"

Karl: "My assistants want me to go see it, because they think I absolutely would love it. I think it's *Gump* or *Pulp Fiction.* My assistants see a lot of movies." *They don't work as hard as I do.* "And they like *Pulp Fiction.*" *They're ironists rather than sentimental slobs like me.* "But I think *Gump's* gonna win." *Sentimentality always wins out over irony.*

3.29.95—Natalie has the chicken pox, so we mainly sit around with her watching and rewinding and watching and rewinding and watching *The Black Stallion.* The two moments that interest me the most occur toward the very end. When the black stallion is warming up before the big race, a fur-draped society woman oohs and aahs, with undisguised sexual yearning, at the horse. And when the black stallion wins the big race, the racetrack announcer, who throughout has been the embodiment of effete officialdom, goes completely, giddily nuts. The movie is about the relationship between civilization, phrased as money, and the primitive, phrased as a big beautiful black beast.

I sell my Sonics-Timberwolves tickets for $45, a loss of 50 percent. I'm in the press box in Tacoma, listening to the game on the radio. Dave Harshman says, "The problem with young kids is that there are so many who want to look good rather than try to be good." He also informs us that players no longer wear jock straps; they wear "form-fitting compression shorts." *Things once used to be simple and good; now even our balls have been harnessed in euphemism.* In a lopsided victory, Payton scores 33 points (tying his career high), going 14 for 21 from the floor and 3 for 3 from the free-throw line.

Apropos of the NCAA Final Four college basketball tournament, which is being held in Seattle in a few days, a white fan calls Rob Tepper (T-Man) on KJR and says about North Carolina's Rasheed Wallace, "The boy can play ball."

T-Man is very quick to say, "Refer to him as a man. He's a man."

Fan: "He's a man."

T-Man: "He is *the* Man."

Fan: "He's *the* Man."

This is all very sentimental and easy. What's interesting is the next thing T-Man says: "He refers to you as a boy." *Can you feel now what power feels like?*

3.30.95—A large black woman gets on the bus. Trying to pay the bus fare, she steps over her kid. "Take care of your child first," the white male bus driver says. He means this kindly, I think—*don't worry about the bus fare; deal with your kid.* But she says, "I am taking care of my child. Can I pay my fare first, please?" She says this semi-politely, but over the next fifteen minutes she does a slow burn. An acquaintance of hers, who's blonde, skinny, and wearing a nose ring and a New York Knicks number

33 jersey, asks her son, TJ, if he wants to sit on her lap, as he apparently did yesterday on the bus. An older white lady commiserates by telling the black woman "the same thing" once happened to her on the ferry. The black mother says, "I got food for him and clothes on him. I must be doing something right." TJ tries to engage her in some sort of game. "No, TJ," she says. "Not now. I'm not in the mood." Patrick Ewing, number 33, hovers over the moment, like greatness over suffering.

3.31.95—On the *Gary Payton Show*, Payton, asked about shooting so well against the T-Wolves a couple of nights ago, says, "It was just something that happened. How you all doing?" *Why do I always have to be the point of interest? Why can't you ever do something interesting?*

Vinnie says, "We're dancing to your music here"—it's "Livin' Legal and Large"—"but not as good as you were Wednesday night." Sometimes what being a fan seems to be most about is self-defeat.

Rod Simons says, "Gary, do you know who's walking around the studio? John Wayne Bobbitt."

Payton: "Who's that?"

Simons: "The guy who lost his ha-ha. His wife—the knife? The guy who lost his ha-ha?"

Payton: "Oh, that dude. Stop it."

Simons: "No, he is."

Payton: "Why is he in your-all's studio?"

Simons: "You know what? All of us needed to get ours hacked off and get all this publicity, too."

Payton: "No, no, if someone hacked mine off, the last thing I would be doing is going on radio, telling people about it." Payton is very unironic about penises; this has become clear. "I wouldn't even come around no more—for real. Because I be so mad."

Simons: "I mean, here's a guy puttin' an ad in the paper, saying, 'Come watch me dance with some topless girls.'"

Payton: "Didn't he make, like, a video or something?"

Simons: "He did a porno thing."

Payton, his voice going screechingly high: "Did he? See how you get publicity in a stupid way, you see that? It's crazy." Payton actually sounds quite exercised about this—the part of him that is Benjamin Franklin.

Simons: "Well, he ain't gonna be a rocket scientist, Gary." It couldn't be more obvious: we all need someone to lord it over, and John Wayne Bobbitt is it for almost everyone.

I can't get anyone to go with me to Tacoma to watch the Sonics play Sacramento. One friend, the moment I say hello, laughs and says, "David, I bet I know why you're calling."

Payton spends the whole game arguing with ref Ted Bernhardt, who does seem to disfavor the Sonics. Tonight he calls a technical on Kemp, then T's up Payton, who argues, points his finger at him, won't back down, curses him, tells Karl to shut up and stop butting in, has to get in the last word. Payton knows Bernhardt knows that he did a poor job of officiating the Sonics-Hornets game last month, that he shouldn't have given Shawn a T during that game, so Gary is exploiting this, stretching Bernhardt to his very limit in this game, knowing Bernhardt is determined not to over-react again, that he owes the Sonics one, and so Gary just keeps talking at him and pointing at him and cursing him and standing about three inches away from him, embarrassing him to death in that Bernhardt can't eject Gary but neither can he walk away. He just has to stand there and take it, and Gary is going to make him eat shit for as long as he possibly can.

Payton scores 27 points. Schrempf scores 26. The Supes, winning tonight, have now won six in a row and are just a half-game behind the Suns.

Nate McMillan, asked for his prediction of who will win the Final Four this weekend, says, "North Carolina. Coach Smith's coaching ability will get them through the finals and win it." This is painfully ass-kissy on McMillan's part (Karl, who played for North Carolina twenty years ago, idolizes Dean Smith); as Marques would say, "You missed a spot." Think, though, how exhausting it would be to be a black man in America: your relationship to the majority culture is always under observation; you're either in constant conflict or in suspiciously easy harmony.

4.1.95—Ma chérie calls and leaves a message that "given Gary's travel schedule and our schedule, we won't be able to arrange an interview with you." I don't experience the slightest disappointment; the predictability of the response even delivers a sort of low-grade pleasure.

• • •

In his column this week, my father discusses the phenomenon of high-school and college players turning pro, and he concludes, "It would make better sense for a player to finish his education, get a degree, and then decide what professional sports offer to accept. By the time they're twenty-two, they will be bigger, stronger, and more mature than they are now—better able to cope with the rigors and demands of the tough world of professional sports." My father and his belief in problem-solving solutions...

4.2.95—The *Seattle Times'* Sunday magazine is its annual health-and-fitness issue; the model on the cover, over the title "The Body Perfect," is a nearly naked black man holding a barbell to his skull in the pose of Rodin's *The Thinker.* Am I the only *Seattle Times* subscriber who finds this terribly strange? Is it me or is it "them"?

I go to the Seattle-Atlanta game with Paul, who keeps saying that his new roommate is "the only genius I've ever known." I keep questioning him as to what exactly constitutes his roommate's supposed genius, because I'm pissed that I, his former teacher, am not, in his eyes, a genius. Sometimes I get tired of paying homage to all the geniuses out there on the court. Just once I'd like the whole arena to invert itself and applaud me and all my amazing feats; I can't imagine everyone in the audience doesn't feel the same way often enough. Who wants to always be just an appreciator of other people's performances?

I suddenly hate being here, hate being a fan, hate the Tacoma Dome: the lurid neon, the pathetic PA system, the ticky-tack scoreboard, the horrific food, the petulant players, the weirdly grandiose refs, the money, the cheerleaders, Sasquatch with his megaphone, the kids with their baseball caps on backward, the businessmen in the stands, the rotating ads, the endless promotions, the corporate sponsorship of every inert object, the wall-to-wall bullshit of the entire operation, the money, the money, the money.

The ref makes a call a fan behind me doesn't like, so the fan yells at the (diminutive) ref, "You just wish you were taller." It really is so much (and so manifestly) about who is and who isn't a big man, about John

Wayne Bobbitt, about "uncut and uncensored," about *The Crying Game,* about GP's 32-inch waist and the Z in his hair, about "an awful lot of life in that young man's body," about "the hottest spot in the universe," about the microphone under his bed.

A half hour later the same ref puts his whistle in his mouth to call a technical on Atlanta's Mookie Blaylock for protesting a call too loudly and too long. Everybody in Seattle loves Mookie, because the local band Pearl Jam was originally called Mookie Blaylock. Nevertheless, when the referee puts his whistle into his mouth and waits for an eternal second or two before blowing the whistle and calling the T, there's a delicious moment of anticipation, of knowing what is coming next, and knowing that what is going to come next is almost certainly going to deliver a visceral twinge of justice and triumph.

On another play, the whistle has already sounded, but Schrempf keeps running down the court with the ball. As he goes up to shoot, Payton pretends to try to block his shot, and as their bodies intertwine like leaping porpoises, I get a very sudden and strong sense of the acute pleasure their bodies give them. Myself, I spent the afternoon spring-cleaning the basement and was amazed to discover that I still possess a body and that it is satisfying to put it to use now and then.

Payton, scoring a basket, eschews a teammate's high-five; he hates slapping hands after every good play, understands how fundamentally uncool this is. Payton scores 21 points, has 6 assists and 4 steals. The Sonics win by 20.

4.3.95—On the *Gary Payton Show,* a caller named Heather says, "You and George have pretty much smoothed out the rough spots, at least for appearance's sake. You've really mellowed out, and I've seen you've been really calm in some pretty intense situations. Do you think Kendall Gill is in the same spot, where he's really frustrated and he's waiting for George to give him some respect, and George, on the other hand, is saying you need to earn it? Do you think that's where they're at?"

Payton says, "That's very, uh…" He seems like he's on the verge of saying, "That's very smart" or "That's very sharp," but then has to mess up the grammar to conform to his *Gary Payton Show* persona: "I think you lookin' at the game pretty good. It's somethin' like that. All Kendall has to do is come out and play. People think it's a big problem, but it's not. He wants to play and Coach wants to coach. I think both of them just need to step up and give each other respect and/or a little leeway."

Rayleen, who calls nearly every week and has a searing crush on Payton, says, "On Friday I met the cutest little boy in the elevator. When I said, 'Hey, cutie,' he just kind of looked out the side of his face and gave his mom this smirky smile. 'Are you three?' He said, 'No, I'm two' and then held up three fingers."

Payton: "Who was that?"

Rayleen: "He said his name was Gary. I said, 'Oh, you are just so cute,' and I said, 'You're big,' and his mom said he's gonna be tall. She said his dad is 6'4". I didn't want to ask her, but I knew. I knew it was you. It was little G." The story rings false to me, for some reason; I think Rayleen made it up. She sounds really, really scary to me—Kathy Bates in *Misery*.

Laurie has made chocolate chip cookies, and all morning I can't stop eating them. "Life isn't good enough for no cigarette," Leonard Michaels once wrote; this is precisely how I've come to view my relationship to sugar. *Today was a disaster,* I tell myself at least twice a week, stopping in at a café that makes the most perfect Rice Krispies Treats, *but this tastes delicious.* Eat Dessert First, as the bumper sticker says, Life Is Uncertain. Quentin Tarantino, asked why he eats Cap'n Crunch, replied, "Because it tastes good and is easy to fix." Cap'n Crunch, Rice Krispies Treats: I'm addicted to refined sugar in its less refined forms—breakfast cereal, cookies, ice cream, root beer, licorice, peanut brittle, et al., ad nauseam. Kid stuff. When I'm happy, I consume sweets to celebrate. When I'm upset, I eat treats as consolation. I'm never without a reason to be in the throes of sugar shock. I don't drink. I don't smoke. I don't do drugs. I do sugar, in massive doses. So what? Who doesn't? What's the harm? Where's the interest? Due to my stutter, much of the glory of sugar is the way it seems like succor to my tired mouth muscles; to me, sugar consumption is (as sports fandom also is) a gorgeous allegory about intractable reality and very temporary transcendence.

Gill is diagnosed with "symptoms of clinical depression" and will be out of action indefinitely. Issuing a press release through his agent, he says,

"I hope to feel better and contribute on the court as soon as possible, but right now, finding a treatment and recovering must take precedence over basketball."

Karl says, "It's a difficult thing to understand. I think it's something that's actually in the game of basketball more than we understand." Karl is like George Bush or Ronald Reagan or Dwight Eisenhower in that he's incapable of uttering a sentence that's not a syntactical snarl. Half the time he talks I find it exceedingly difficult to determine exactly what it is he's trying to say.

Sonics general manager Wally Walker says, "Our biggest concern right now is Kendall Gill and his well-being. Kendall is a member of our family, and we will do whatever we can to aid the process."

On the other hand, T-Man, the new KJR talk-show host, says, "I pose the question: if Kendall Gill were averaging twenty points a game, averaging forty-two minutes a game, hearing the fans cheer, making the thunder roar, being an integral part of the Sonics winning basketball games—would we be here today talking about clinical depression? The Sonics put out a press release that no sports reporter in this town will touch with a 10-foot pole. You'd have to be nuts, crazy, a lunatic. It's way too sensitive an issue. It's taboo. Taboo is very dangerous; stay away from taboo.

"So why am I the idiot? I know why. Because I, unlike every other person in this business, refuse to let any thought in my head be repressed, for the sake of being criticized. All these thoughts have popped into every other Seattle reporter's head; I'm the only idiot who's willing to go on the air and tell you that it's a little too convenient to me for this to come out at this time. I'm the only one stupid enough to go on the air and say that what the media release does is tie up all these problems Kendall Gill has had all year, in a nice, neat little package with a bow on top and make them go away for the time being. Because what dipstick is gonna tackle a sensitive issue like clinical depression? Well, I'll tell you what, Seattle, there's a new dipstick in town, and his name is the T-Man. I've never said anything to appease anybody. If I believe it, I'll say it. If I lose all my fans, fine. I'll go push a souvlaki cart on Fifth Avenue." I suppose this is all terribly self-congratulatory on T-Man's part, but *refuse to let any thought in my head be repressed* is pretty much the banner under which I fly as well, and his monologue is a strong surge of adrenaline for me. I couldn't agree more with him about Gill: the "clinical depression" narrative is a transparent ruse, and the fact that no one else has the temerity to express any skepticism about it even seems to me quite racist, in a guilty-liberal sort of way.

After an upbeat homiletic discourse about how "all the little chilluns—the black ones and white ones and brown ones and yellow ones and red ones and green ones—are the same in God's eyes," Reverend Daimen says about T-Man: "He is the T-Man; there ain't nothin' else; he is the T-Man; goo-goo-g'joob." It's a compelling fictional universe T-Man creates, in which not only our masculinity but our humanity get fluffed up and flattered. The world is sick; Daimen is the cure. The world is sick; T-Man created Daimen, who is the cure. Reverend Daimen is God, but really T-Man is God

4.4.95—At Utah, the Jazz rout the Sonics. Afterward, Payton says, "It was just a game, that's all this is. This was just a game you throw out the door. Things happen around our town and you've just got to bounce back and play." Professional athletes are better than almost anyone else at not pursuing self-destructive thought patterns: regret, second-guessing, etc. It's one of the main and best things you can try to learn from them. I'm in awe of Payton's ability to shut down lines of consciousness that aren't to his advantage, as opposed especially to Schrempf, who always has something to bemoan: "We didn't get any calls, and I think that influenced the whole game. They set the tempo and after that we never found it."

Karl says, "We were unfocused, didn't meet the challenge—whatever cliché you want to use." This is an interesting intellectual position to be in—knowing that what you're saying is a cliché, having no access to language other than clichés, and so using clichés even as you acknowledge their well-worn quality. Karl does this often (as does Marques Johnson). It conveys to me something of his exhaustion, his complexity, his self-consciousness; it makes me like him.

4.5.95—Asked to comment about Kendall Gill's clinical depression, Brian Williams, of the Denver Nuggets, says, "I think people just don't believe sports figures can have any other problems outside of physical injury directly related to sports. I think they feel that we do just one thing, and that's play basketball. So that's why I think people didn't accept, or didn't want to accept, that I really suffered from clinical depression. You know: 'How can he have it when he makes this amount of money, he has such a glamour job, he has a comfortable life? He, of all people, why should he be depressed?'" We will do anything to keep our icons iconic.

4.6.95—For the *Weekly,* I'm reviewing *Full Court Pressure,* the book about the Sonics' '93–'94 season. The author, Curt Sampson, is a golfing buddy of Karl's, so he had unusual access to the team, which yields some funny moments, my favorite of which is this: Karl's wife, Cathy, approaches Payton's five-year-old daughter at the sink in the players' wives' bathroom and says, "Hello, Raquel, do you know who I am?" Raquel says, "You're Coach Karl's wife." Cathy Karl says, "Well, when this season's over, I'm going to come see you at your house. Would you like that?" Raquel says, "No. My daddy don't like Coach Karl." However, what Sampson gains in proximity he sacrifices in objectivity, and the book reduces to panegyric: "Clearly, Karl was a man out of his time. He'd defied a convention by building a defensive team, a team with no center and no offensive star. He'd asked for selflessness in a league so money-obsessed that even the games had become commercials. The experiment had failed; the Sonics not only lost to the Nuggets, they beat their coach."

I conduct a phone interview with Sampson, who says, "I was talking to Detlef about [the tennis player] Boris Becker, and I said Boris' behavior is bizarre. And he said, 'What do you mean?' I said, 'Well, his wife.' Detlef said, 'What do you mean? I like his wife.' I said, 'I mean his wife and him posing nude for this German magazine.' As you know, Boris Becker's wife is black"—I didn't know this; how was I supposed to know this?—"and Schrempf's wife is mulatto or whatever the phrase is." The subtext, of course, of the Sampson-Schrempf exchange is that Schrempf at first thought Sampson was calling Becker bizarre for marrying a black woman. "It's dynamite, isn't it, just talking about it?" Sampson says. We're both breathing heavily with the thrill of white men talking, obliquely and for a millisecond, about race.

•   •   •

Karl says about himself and Gill, who has left Seattle for his parents' house in suburban Chicago, "We had a voice-mail exchange. I called him, and he called back. But we both were in and out. He was coaching, talking about the game against Utah and how he was going to pick up the Denver game on satellite." Karl can't stand it when players try to act like coaches. "He's got to do some conditioning. I don't think he's working out right now. But I definitely think he's one of our top eight players." This is a dig, since Gill thinks he's one of the Sonics' top three or four players.

4.7.95—The baseball player Andre Dawson, asked by Ron Barr how he deals with racist fans, says, "Not absorbing any other person's hatred of you by reacting to it is essential. For you are then leaving the disease right where it belongs, with the one who has it and is the only one who can do anything about it." Listening to him, I'm struck by two things: (1) it's too twelve-stepish a formulation—he's been instructed to say this; and (2) in a million years, I couldn't be that restrained.

4.9.95—Ponsella, posting to the Sonics newsgroup, writes: "I have faith that Kendall will return with the same fire and flair that Jordan did." As rumored, Jordan did indeed return to the NBA, about a week ago; in a recent game against the Knicks, he scored 55 points. "It takes a strong brother to admit that he has a problem and to seek help. More power to you, Kendall!!!!"

In bed at night, Laurie mentions that she had a dream about Gary Payton a few nights ago.

I go find my tape recorder, climb back into bed, and say, "What was the date?"

She thinks for a while and says, "The early morning of April sixth."

I say, "The night of April fifth?"

She says, "Yes, but it was definitely after midnight."

I say, "So, technically, April sixth."

She says, "I feel like I'm on the stand."

"When did the dog start barking?" I ask.

"D—" she says.

"Was the ice cream melting?" I say—O.J. details...

"Anyway, what I remember is that it was at the beach in Lake Forest [her hometown, an opulent suburb on the North Shore of Chicago, where hers was one of the few merely middle-class families]. "There were huge waves there this day—huge, like you'd see off the coast of Hawaii. And they were coming up the hill that you have to drive down to get to the beach. I kept coming down the hill."

"With whom?" I ask.

"With different people each time," she says. "I remember I drove down one time with my father in the car; I think he was driving, and when the waves hit the car, it would knock the car around like a little boat, but then the waves would recede and the cars would drive on, and people were just doing this."

"Was it frightening?"

"It was while it was happening, but it was just what you had to go through to get to the beach; it was a fun day at the beach because the big waves were there." Laurie has always understood better than I have that obstacles amplify rather than diminish enjoyment. "It was like surfing. Then there was another time when I was coming down the hill in the car; there were four people in the car, and I can't remember who they all were, but one of them was Gary Payton. Our car got down to the beach. I remember there was a kind of cave, where you could get away from the waves, but they'd still crash all around it. Several people were going into the cave; one of them was Gary Payton, and he was in a little bathing suit, with his nice figure. I just remember he was walking around in there. There were other people in there, too, but that's really all I can remember. It felt like it was a long dream, but I can't remember that much of it."

"What role did he play in the dream?" I ask. "Did he have any particular presence?"

"It's just that he was at the beach in Lake Forest." There are no two more discrete entities in the universe than Gary Payton and Lake Forest, Illinois. "I don't think he ever even talked to me, but I remember I noticed him as a man whose attention you might want to get."

The extremely casual way Laurie tosses off the last sentence causes me to pout a little; noticing this, she puts the moves on and says, "Come here, my GP wanna-be," by which she means, I think, to cheer me up but which has the surprising or perhaps not so surprising effect of making my whole body go cold. *Can you feel now what power feels like?*

9

HISTORY IS NOT JUST A RUMOR SOMEWHERE OUT THERE

4.10.95—A young woman named Lavonne, asked by T-Man where she's originally from, says, "South Central LA. Can I say that on the air?"

T-Man says, "What are you doing up here?"

Lavonne says, "Came up here for film school."

T-Man says, "You want to be the next—"

Lavonne: "Don't say Spike Lee."

T-Man: "I was going to say Steven Spielberg." No, he wasn't.

Lavonne: "Stanley Kubrick."

T-Man: "Who the hell is that? How about John Singleton?"

Lavonne: "He's okay."

T-Man: "Oliver Stone?"

Lavonne: "A little bombastic."

T-Man whistles, but he has no idea what she's trying to tell him: *I am not a figure in the frieze of your imagination.*

• • •

In his review in the *New Yorker* of Daniel Wolff's biography of Sam Cooke, Terrence Rafferty says: "Throughout, the book suggests that its subject's mainstream success was the product of compromise—of keeping the 'black' elements of his music safely contained. The irony of *You Send Me: The Life and Times of Sam Cooke* is that by bringing racial style to the fore, Wolff puts his subject in a different box. In this account, Cooke, the wayward black pilgrim in search of his identity, is emphatically not special: he's just a cultural emblem. Wolff may know plenty about history, but he doesn't appear to know why he loves Sam Cooke: you sense that he's drawn to the music despite, rather than because, of its variety, its unclassifiabilty, its unearthly combination of soothing textures and profound emotional urgency. The demon that frightens the writer of this biography is the sheer ambiguity of its subject's popular art, the soulfulness that can't be reduced to black and white. Sam Cooke crossed over; Daniel Wolff sends him back." It's an easy position for Rafferty to adopt, covering himself in moral clover, but still I take it as a useful cautionary tale—Gary Payton is not a figure in the frieze of my imagination.

4.11.95—At a press conference in Seattle, Gill announces that he's rejoining the Sonics and will begin practicing with the team tomorrow, but that he'll need a few days until he's ready to play. He says that he was diagnosed with a metabolic imbalance, that he doesn't know how long he's been suffering from the condition, and that he prefers not to say what treatment he's receiving. He's daring anyone to call his bluff. "I have a fresh look on everything. I've never felt better physically and mentally in my life. The problems I have had will never happen again. That incident with George [shouting at him in his office a couple of weeks ago]: I normally don't react that way. I apologize to George for what has happened. I may even take George to lunch."

Peace.

Karl says, "I'm not gonna stand up here and say I'm an authority on clinical depression, but"—*I am an authority on clinical depression*—"it's a situation that can be fixed very quickly [with drugs] and it can free you up. I don't think we can win a championship without Kendall Gill," which is an oblique apology to Gill after saying he was only one of the

Sonics' top eight players a few days ago. "My hope is that we can turn this experience into a positive. We can establish better communication, develop more of an intensity, a camaraderie. But I'm still going to coach the game. I'm not going to manage egos."

No peace.

Tonight, in Tacoma, during pre-game warmups before the game against Phoenix, Gary makes a point, it seems to me, of taking his pre-game warm-up shots directly behind the TNT reporter on the floor to make sure he'll be on TV. Sasquatch comes up to shake Gary's hand; G. slaps his hand, kicks him in the ass, tells him to go away. No one else could do this with his weird mix of threat and warmth. If anyone else did this, it would either seem too mean or too benign. My brief ode to things like this that Gary does appeared in the *Weekly* today—to what degree would this hold his interest, affect his mood? *We don't have a philosophy.*

Barkley is kissing up to referee Jake O'Donnell and winds up patting him on the back; I'm practically shouting at O'Donnell not to fall for all this pseudo-friendliness. It seems to me that a lot of what makes Barkley so magnetic is that you can't tell to what degree it's natural garrulousness, to what degree it's playful showmanship, and to what degree it's a very concerted effort to orchestrate the game. Barkley gets into an argument with Jake O'Donnell, and Joe Kline, the Suns' 7-foot white center, tries to argue on Barkey's behalf. Barkley literally shoves Kline out of the way: *I can argue my own arguments, thank you very much.* Leaving the court at halftime, Payton gives Barkley a hug. Fans want to see these guys as sworn enemies, but they're not. They adore each other; how explicit do they have to make it till people get it?

Paul is at the game with me, but he says he doesn't seem to feel like talking much—he's been unusually subdued and quiet all evening—so I listen to the game on the radio. Toward the end of the first half, Calabro says, "The game has no kind of flow."

Marques Johnson says, "We call it rhythm."

Calabro can't tell if Johnson is kidding or serious. There's a long silence, which Calabro finally breaks by launching into a song: "I got rhythm, I got music."

During halftime, a guy plays familiar tunes by bouncing colored plastic balls on an enormous keyboard placed on the floor at center court. In the audience, most white people are applauding mightily; black people sit there, stunned, stunned that this is apparently what white people find lyrical.

Marques says, "Now that's rhythm right there."

Kevin says, "Mozart was doing that at age four."

Marques: "Stevie Wonder at age three."

Kevin: "So Mozart was an underachiever, huh?"

Is race racing through Calabro's mind every time he talks to Johnson, or am I just imagining it? Is race on my brain, and am I screwed up? Or is it on everyone else's brain, and am I just taking notes? No one ever acknowledges the true subject of our discussions; it can never get expressed directly, it simply can't be, won't be, isn't allowed to be talked about openly, and so it comes out in a thousand indirect inflections.

An exhibitionistic young woman—who has beautiful olive skin, long dark hair, blue eyes, and usually wears tight black jeans and T-shirts— always stands and cheers in such a way, always walks from the aisle to her seat in such a way, that all the men in our entire section seem to have their tongues perpetually hanging out. Tonight, in the third quarter, as a song plays during a timeout, she sashays so suggestively that the three men sitting directly behind her bow to her and say, "Thank you," which somehow captures for me the relation of fans to players, the mixture of reverence and contempt.

The Sonics miss nearly two-thirds of their shots; Payton and Schrempf shoot particularly poorly; Gill doesn't play or even show; the Suns win. Schrempf is in foul trouble for most of the game, about which Karl says, "Here's a great player getting rookie calls in a big game. I'm dumbfounded." No, he's not; in Schrempf is gathered the reverb from a racist society cordoning off one arena in which the people it has oppressed will succeed.

Driving home, I ask Paul why he was so silent tonight, and he says that his jaw hurts. I ask why his jaw hurts, and he says he was in Pioneer Square last night with his new girlfriend, Meredith. A young black man wearing a red bandana walked past them and mumbled something. Paul, being Paul, said, "What?" The man mumbled some more. Paul, being

Paul, said, "I'm sorry—what—excuse me?" Paul finally understood that what the guy had been saying was: "Apologize to me right now." Before Paul could say anything, the man hit Paul in the back of his head with his hand. Paul fell to the ground. Meredith screamed. The man ran. What do you want to be attacked for—for not apologizing or for acknowledging that you have something to apologize for?

4.13.95—Payton has a strained left hamstring and is listed at only 50–50 probability before the Dallas-Seattle game tonight at the T-Dome (to which I have a press pass and so to which I've sold my seats). However, Payton says, "You never have to worry about me not playing."

Karl says, "He plays great when he's hurt. I like him sore." *They'd sit on the gallery and watch the niggers put it on brown.*

As I walk into press row, *ma chérie* makes a specific point of coming up to me and saying, "Hi, David." She must have finally seen in this week's *Weekly* my ode to G. Payton, which, although not cut from the cloth she'd prefer, at least may have demonstrated that I'm not an utter charlatan.

At the start of the game, I expect Gill to be sitting on the bench in street clothes but don't see him anywhere.

Midway through the second quarter, Sasquatch, as a kind of joke, steals the ball from the black referee. I'm very aware that this bit can't go on too long before it becomes problematic, and virtually all of its problematicalness derives from the fact that the ref is black, so after ten seconds or so Squatch returns the ball to the ref. If the ref were white, the shtick could and would have gone on for, say, twenty seconds, and this difference of ten seconds is a measurement of history, of blood over time.

During halftime, a group of guys who specialize in supposedly spectacular dunks take the floor, although they're none too spectacular. Some are black; some are white. It seems quite calculated to me that toward the end of their performance, when they hold a kind of elimination tournament, it winds up with one black dunker and one white dunker: two black dunkers would have too emphatically reinforced the stereotype (white men can't jump, etc.), and two white dunkers would have seemed like affirmative action, but having one black finalist and one white finalist is an attempt to empty out the racial code of the thing, which is immediately reintroduced when the white dunker proves to be painfully, comically bad compared to the black dunker.

Just as he did in December, when he scored 30 points against Houston a few hours after he injured his back in a fall on his icy driveway, Payton has a great game tonight despite his strained left hamstring; he makes 7 steals and scores 24 points. With the victory, Seattle's record goes to 54-and-22—still just a half-game behind Phoenix.

After the game, as he heads to the locker room, Sam Perkins throws his used towel into the crowd; fans go crazy. What must the players think of us, that we worship their dirty laundry?

In the first quarter, Jason Kidd, Payton's friend from Oakland, blocked one of his shots. Asked in the post-game locker room what he said to rub it in, Kidd says, "I don't quite remember." *It's our camaraderie, not yours.* McMillan says, "Kidd got Gary upset. Whatever he said, he shouldn't have. I like for players to talk to Payton. That's a way of getting him into the game"—Payton's weirdly primary, proprietary relation to language. "He didn't start it [the trash-talking] tonight. He will finish it, put it that way." McMillan admires Payton for some of the same reasons I do: he's as bad as we'd like to be, if we ever got good at being bad.

Payton, asked what Kidd said, says, of course, "It was nothing. It's cool. Just a little humor. That's my boy. He's like a little brother to me." Like an astronaut with the right stuff, he makes whatever transpired seem more dramatic by downplaying it. The Sonics, however, are a little concerned about the fact that sometime during the game—no one seems to know just when—Payton appears to have sprained the ring finger on his left hand.

After the game, I'm hanging around in the corridor outside the Sonics' locker room. Karl comes up to me and, shaking my hand, says, "I hope you know that it wasn't me; I wanted to do it," i.e., it wasn't his decision to nix the Sonics' cooperation with my book project; he would have welcomed me officially spending the year with the team. (Necessity is the proverbial mother of invention; denied access to the gods, I'm writing this other book—about being a fan in the faraway stands and ogling the gods.) Whatever spin-doctoring he's doing, I'm still stupidly flattered that Karl would go out of his way to reassure me; it suggests a certain insecurity on his part but also, undeniably, a certain capacity to empathize, which very few coaches are keen about exhibiting.

4.14.95—The Sonics are playing the Golden State Warriors tomorrow, and on the *Gary Payton Show* Michael Knight and New York Vinnie can't comprehend why Payton says he'd rather play for Sacramento than Golden State. Vinnie and Michael used to work in San Francisco, and like nearly everyone who has lived in San Francisco except me, they're hopelessly nostalgic for the Bay Area. Gary finally explains to them that "Sacramento is a better situation than Golden State," which is to say that what matters is not place but what you're doing in that place. Vinnie and Michael can't understand this, but I understand this—I've always felt this way—and in a sudden upsurge of feeling my grumbling dissatisfaction with Seattle vanishes, via GP.

X-rays reveal that Payton suffered a broken left ring finger; videotape shows that Payton suffered the fracture when Jamal Mashburn of the Mavericks slapped at the ball in the third quarter of last night's game. The playoffs start in two weeks; Karl, trapped in the first stage of grief (denial), says, "I thought it was just displaced in the joint."

4.15.95—Last night I had a dream about Gary: as his backcourt mate, I play particularly well, knocking down jumpers every time he passes me the ball. I'm earning his begrudging approval and admiration, but I'm nervous because I know the real test is still to come—the repartee between plays.

In Oakland, in pre-game warmups, Payton is constantly trying to bring Gill out of his shell, trying to make him laugh, but to little effect. During the game, Gill is oddly effective, scoring 10 points and making 3 assists. Due to his broken finger, Payton looks a little awkward at times, but he plays 34 minutes, makes more than half his shots, scores 24 points, and has 10 assists. The Sonics easily defeat the Warriors. This was Payton's 287th consecutive game—a streak covering nearly four seasons.

Gary is the youngest of five children, and when he played against his father, Al would never let him win, throwing elbows, boxing him out. Al's vanity plate reads MR. MEAN. Gary is fanatical about never missing a game, about never letting an injury prevent him from playing, about never being not as tough as Mr. Mean taught him to be. Asked by reporters why he rarely used his left hand during the game, he says, with transparent defensiveness, "I could've, but what's the purpose? I didn't want to force the issue if I didn't have to." His bluffing machismo I suddenly find off-putting, since it would obviously do the team more good if he had the broken bone repaired now and sat out the last couple of weeks of the season to let the finger heal completely, so that he could be ready for the playoffs. I want him to do the wise thing rather than the heroic thing, but he's not willing to. When a reporter tells him that no one remembers who holds the record for most consecutive games played, Payton says, "They'll remember me. This is the NBA. I'll get the finger fixed after the season. When we go to the [championship] parade, I'll just have a cast on."

Karl says, "We're still in the process of making a decision, but Gary wants to play. It's his decision. We're not forcing him one way or another. I could, and it would be an interesting battle on the sideline."

Asked who would win such a battle, Payton says, "You all know who's running the team," and then he bangs himself on the chest.

After watching the Sonics-Warriors game on TV, Daniel, my basketball pal from graduate school who now lives in San Francisco, phones me and says about Karl, "When you look at George Karl, you see someone who appears to be struggling to control himself. The other coaches have tempers, but he seems to be actually in the middle of the struggle, like he hasn't really resolved how to do it. And he tries to force himself—to convince himself—to act as if he's not feeling what he's really feeling. And that's why it seems that he's smiling all the time, like a fighter who's been punched really hard, just smiling and brushing it off, like 'It wasn't that hard.' I get the feeling with Karl that he's doing that, and I wonder what effect that has on his team. There's something about that guy; there's something not right. You know the expression 'What you see is what you get'? With him what you see is definitely not what you get. He's always smiling, but you can tell something else is going on." This captures something I've always felt but never quite been able to articulate about Karl—

the deep disconnect in him between what his mouth says and what his eyes show.

4.16.95—At Safeway, a black man and white woman are ahead of me and Natalie. The bagger is black. The black man and the bagger are talking about Michael Jordan's 50-point performance against the Knicks earlier today. (The amount of excitement surrounding his return has been otherworldly, as if all season long we'd been arguing with each other because we'd been without our one transcendental signifier, our one universal beloved.) The customer says, "There will never be another like him." The bagger says, "He practices, like, six hours a day." The woman keeps looking from one man to the other, watching their conversation go back and forth as they groove on Michael Jordan. After the bagger hands me my bag, he says, with brutal condescension, "Have an *exciting* afternoon."

Natalie and I do have an exciting afternoon. We go to a new movie called *A Goofy Movie,* about the Disney character Goofy. Goofy believes that the only way he can prove his worth to himself, his father, and his girlfriend is to be seen on stage with Power Line (a dead ringer for Michael Jackson). Goofy sneaks on stage, dances with Power Line, and although later he tells his girlfriend that he doesn't really know Power Line, she says she likes him, anyway. Regardless, the point remains that for him the only way he could possibly come alive (become authentic, male, alluring, sexual) is to be seen on the same stage with Power Line. The ostensible moral is that he learns he doesn't need Power Line in order to come alive. The real moral is that he does.

4.17.95—On the *Gary Payton Show,* Michael Knight says, "Congratulations on your inspiring performance against the Warriors. How did you do it with one hand?"

Payton says, "I just concentrated. It wasn't that hard to do; I could catch the ball. I could do a lot of things. But it was basically all right."

Asked how opposing players might try to exploit his injured hand, Payton says, "A lot of people will be trying a lot of different things. They might want to hit me, make me put the ball in my left hand, but that's good. I'll show them that there's nothing wrong with me, that it's no different. I'll just go out there and play basketball. I don't think [Rod] Strickland [of Portland] or [Nick] Van Exel [of Los Angeles] is going to try to force the issue with me."

Asked whether he's thinking about the playoffs yet, Gary says—and I'll never be able to convey the degree to which this is in triplicate quotes: saying the cliché, mocking the cliché, mocking mocking the cliché—"We just go out and take one game at a time."

Vinnie asks, "Tough to signal a right turn when you're going down the street?"

Payton says, "Nah. I got my three other hands operatin' the signal and stuff like that." His three other hands? Anybody's guess.

Vinnie: "You know you are 27-and-1 against people who are on your record album [Basketball's Best Kept Secret]?"

Payton: "Is that right?"

Vinnie: "I mean CD; you can't call it 'album' anymore"—Vinnie's recurrent anxiety about being judged out of it by Gary. "What do you think about facing the Lakers first?" If current playoff positions within the Western Conference hold through the last week and a half of the season, Seattle and Los Angeles will face each other in the playoffs.

Payton: "Let's get it over with. Everybody's talkin' about how we don't want to play them. Let's get it over with. Bring it on." Ever since his injury, his macho pose never manages to seem to me like anything more than whistling past the graveyard.

Vinnie: "This recent business of Rod Strickland telling his coach, 'No thank you, I don't want to play for you, I don't like you, I don't want to be with you, I got a few games left, and then our days are over,' then he comes back and says, 'Well, what I meant was, 'I'll be glad to play for this team'—did he wake up to the fact that maybe he would be better to stay with Portland than maybe end up with the Clippers?"

Vinnie's trying to get Payton to indict Strickland for insubordination, but Payton won't do it: "It was probably a heated moment when Rod said what he said. I think he caught hisself when he thought about it for a coupla days—came back and apologized. I know Rod pretty well. He is an outspoken person; he lets things off his chest. At the time, he was probably a little bit upset and he came back and did what he was supposed to do. I think he'll be fine. I think they'll work it out." *It's not you and me in a dialogue discussing that crazy nigger.*

Vinnie: "Get your taxes done?"

Payton: "Fortunately, they are."

Vinnie: "You feel good to have to give up all that money?"

Payton: "Yeah, at least they won't have to be knockin' on my door."

Vinnie: "And they're always big, ugly people."

Payton: "And lots of them, too"—feeding our fantasies that what he and we are doing is still somehow slightly illegal. A T-shirt I saw someone wearing yesterday had on the front *Sex, Drugs, and Rock n' Roll* x'd out in red, and on the back *Basketball—The Last Vice.*

A fan calls and says, "Hey, GP, love ya. I love Kendall Gill, too. It seems like his attitude is totally different; looking at his face, he looks happy."

Payton: "Kendall is very happy. He came back very joyful. He's taking everything a little bit serious and a little bit more of a fun way. And I think that's the way he gots to approach things—just having fun every day." Payton actually thinks of his life as being about having fun every day. I don't think of my life this way, and I don't know anyone who does.

A woman named Ricole calls and says, "Hi, Gary Payton, I just want to say hi, I love you so much, and I'm by your side all the time. You're my favorite basketball player." I love how she says, "Hi, Gary Payton." "Gary" seems presumptuous. "Mr. Payton" is too formal. "Gary Payton" sounds right. I also love the perfect love in her voice: you can feel how absolutely she worships Payton. What would it do to you to be adored like this everywhere you go?

In the last game of the year I'll be allowed to watch from the press box (I got $50 total for both tickets), Portland beats Seattle, 97–93. Payton, playing with his fractured ring finger taped to his middle finger, seems drastically limited by the injury. He misses two-thirds of his shots from the field, attempts no free throws, attempts no 3-pointers. His counterpart on Portland, Rod Strickland, scores 21 points and makes the game-winning basket against him with a few seconds left. Gill hits a 3-pointer; fans cheer wildly, but it's a forced gaiety. Overall, Gill plays terribly, and you can tell that Karl wants to remove Gill from the game even earlier than he does, but he waits as long as possible to avoid re-creating that ruckus.

Toward the end of the game a black kid asks me for my accumulated stat sheets, and I still want to look at them some more, so I say sorry. After the game, I see him in the bleachers, and I'm about to offer him the stat sheets, but it's too late, the moment feels wrong, and so I pass by.

Karl, speaking to reporters, defends Payton, sort of: "He's going to have good games, great games, and games like tonight when he misses shots, and you're going to ask, 'Is it his hand?' We have to get him better opportunities. Right now the game plan is for him to try to play through the pain and the discomfort. It's going to be a learning process for him. He's got to figure it out, and we've got to figure it out. I don't think many doctors would recommend playing as therapy." What's become apparent is that Karl has almost no authority to enforce his wish that Payton rest so that his hand can heal.

If Payton received from his father the stubborn refusal to ever acknowledge that he might need a little R and R, he also received from him the equally unusual ability to say, *I fucked up.* In the locker room after the loss, Payton tells the media, "I lost that game. My fault. I messed up. I was tripping and made some bad decisions. I forced a lot of things. I did things I wasn't supposed to do. I didn't let the game come to me."

The Blazers' coach, P.J. Carlesimo, wears loafers, a monogrammed shirt, and a perfectly trimmed beard, and he maintains excellent eye contact; there's something way too practiced about him. When I ask him what he did to "repair things with Rod Strickland," before going off on a long evasive answer, he says, "I'm not being smart," i.e., *I'm not being a smart-aleck in my disingenuous response to your question,* as if "smart" were the worst epithet in the world. I ask him what the Blazers did to take advantage of Payton's damaged finger; again he says, "I'm not being smart, but…" and goes off on another long and rambling evasion. To be smart is, to P.J. Carlesimo, a kind of crime.

Sonics assistant coach Terry Stotts comes up to him and says, "Good game, Coach."

Carlesimo says, "Terry, please: P.J." *Only the players have to call me Coach.*

Nothing Kendall Gill does works, it seems to me; he walks out of the locker room wearing glasses, which are supposed to look fashionable, but they just make him look like Mickey Mouse with a small head, big ears, and glasses. Sam Perkins exits, wearing a black beret and jeans. Sonics assistant coach Bob Weiss is, I swear to God, wearing a sweatsuit.

Outside, Gary's fiancée, Monique, goes squealing out of the parking lot in her black Mercedes 5000 SL, with *4MO* plates.

On the post-game call-in show, Jeremy, from Northgate, says to T-Man, "I'm a Sonic guy. I'm a best fan. I hope I speak for many fans. They [the Sonics front office] are running us ragged, man. Forty-one games in Tacoma. Then we get our order forms for the playoffs: in ten days we need $3,000. 'Unless you're a corporation, give us a credit card, dude.' By the time I found out that my playoff stuff was in my PO box, I had two days to turn it in. 'By the way, would you like to get your seats for next year?' Look, this isn't a corporate thing, man; there are some blue-collar fans and hopefully you have to have some blue-collar fans, because that's what sports is all about. These people have to realize some of us just don't have millions of dollars to drop at the blink of a hat. I drove all over town today to try to find the game—all the way from Everett to Bothell to Northgate—and I finally found the game on satellite. What I'm saying is we're really good right now, everybody's hot on us, we're cool, and God knows I've been busting my butt so we can win this damn championship, but the point is that in five or six years we won't be good, just like the Lakers weren't any good there for a while, and the Celtics. You get in slumps. Where are they gonna be without us in five years? They gotta remember us. We are the people; they have to remember us. Next year they won't have 18,000 people in their beautiful new building; they'll have people like you and me and guys who care. They better take care of us now. Because we're the fans. We're good fans. And in a sense we made them."

This is so sad I vow to never again look for meaning and myth anywhere else except in the interstices of my own life.

T-Man says about Portland, "They're like an Eastern Conference team. They play tough, physical, hard." Why can't he just say that Portland played tough, physical, and hard? Why does he need to ascribe these qualities to the East?

A man named Matt calls and asks T-Man, "What do you call a gay guy
with a vasectomy?"

T-Man says, "You call it Matt," then immediately dumps the call,
which underlines the point T-Man has been trying to make over and over
and over: grooving on rather than demonizing difference (except when it
comes to the East Coast/West Coast hierarchy).

T-Man plays a tape of a roving reporter named Jennifer Pebbles asking Payton: "You have to forgive me, but the T-Man asked me to ask you
if you be lovin' the big-butted womens." This is a favorite expression of
T-Man's: "I be lovin' the big-butted womens," which he always says in
faintly black dialect. He appears to want it to mean, and I actually take it
to mean, *I love the sisters. I love this language celebrating the sisters.*
With almost anyone else, it would come across as an insult; with T-Man,
somehow it doesn't. Exhibit A: several Sonics players supposedly listen
to his show. They don't listen to anybody else's show.

Payton, stalling for time, says, "The big who?"

Pebbles: "Do you be lovin' the big-butted womens?"

Payton: "Yeah, that's all good. You know, anybody with a big butt, she
all right with me." I love how he engages the question, thinks it's a perfectly legitimate area of inquiry. "I ain't gonna discriminate." Now, realizing how ridiculous he sounds being too PC about the whole thing, he
suddenly starts being honest: "But if there's a flap on anyone"—by which
he means "If she's fat..."; then he changes his mind again—"and she look
good, she all right with me."

Pebbles translates: "You could just look at her from the front."

Payton: "Yeah, that's all." Payton is done with the conversation.

Pebbles, trying to re-energize the discussion, says, "You could compromise with it, I guess"—*she'd have a pretty face but a fat ass.*

But Payton is done.

On *Sports By-Line,* his syndicated show, Ron Barr, interviewing Arthur
Agee, one of the two protagonists of *Hoop Dreams,* says, "I've had the
opportunity to watch some inner-city basketball games and I find it fascinating. I spent some of my youth in Washington, DC, and I remember
what it was like on a hot, humid evening, watching basketball in the

nation's capital. Take me into Chicago, right there, in the middle of the city on a summer night at about ten o'clock with a group of guys out there on the asphalt." *Exoticize yourself for me; glamorize yourself for me; make yourself strange and fascinating; treat yourself as raw anthropological data.*

4.18.95—The Sonics play the Lakers in Los Angeles tonight for what in all likelihood is a tuneup for their playoff matchup in ten days. At halftime, Seattle leads, 64–34. I dig Payton's concentrated determination to play well despite his broken finger; he scores 28 points on 12-for-17 shooting. The Sonics win. At the start of a post-game TV interview with Marques Johnson, Payton gets the kinks out of his neck by slowly swiveling his head from one shoulder to the other; all over Seattle, every day of the week, I see different kinds of people doing this, consciously or unconsciously imitating this characteristic GP gesture, and I dig this, too. Johnson says, "You forced the issue versus Portland." Gary nods and says, "Yes, I did"—I dig this as well. Even how he chews his gum—in a sort of faux-furious cow-cud style—I dig.

Later, Payton asks the assembled media: "Did it look like there was anything wrong with the finger tonight? That's what I keep telling everyone. But they keep asking. Everyone else is more worried about it than I am. They'd have to kill me before I'll miss a game, and they're not about to."

Karl says, "You doubt [the wisdom of his decision], but he wants to play. [Telling him he couldn't play] would be a bigger negative than the finger. He wants to lead. He wants to fight through it."

Payton asks a reporter, "You think I'm going to let someone slap the shit out of my hand?"

"What if someone tried?" the reporter asks him.

"I'd slap the shit out of him first."

It raises an interesting question: I think he's doing the wrong thing, but maybe he just is sort of superhuman. Me, I can't concentrate if I have water in my ear, and he's going to play in the playoffs with a broken ring finger on his left hand. He's different from me; he's different from me; he's different from me.

． ． ．

Posting to the Sonics newsgroup, Howard writes, "Seattle has talent and can crank out the highlight-show clips, but they have little heart. When I think of flashy teams of the past (the 76ers of the early '80s, the Lakers of the '80s), I remember great players competing with class and guts. Now I have to watch Kemp grab his dick to gloat whenever he dunks over an opponent." Cf. Richard Pryor: "Niggers be holdin' them dicks, too, jack. White people goin', 'Why you guys hold your things?' 'Cause you done took everything else, motherfucker. Nigger be checkin'."

In an Amsterdam sex shop a few years ago I watched a videotape that consisted of nothing but a blonde woman repeatedly fondling and kissing and stroking and posting up and down on and generally worshiping an enormous dark-colored dildo. One could feel in the woman's impossibly worshipful gaze how precisely the tape had been niche-marketed for consumption by dark-colored men all over the planet.

4.19.95—Doctors advise Payton to insert a screw in the broken bone and take a two-week vacation, but he chooses instead to keep playing with a leather splint on the broken finger, which just seems nuts. "It would probably mess me up," he tells reporters. "When I came back, I wouldn't know how to deal with it. If it was affecting my play, I'd understand all of this. When I have a bad shooting night, they say it's the finger. Everyone is making a big thing out of nothing. Everybody's saying, 'What if? What if you hadn't broke your foot in the playoffs?' [Last year, Payton broke a bone in his foot in the Sonics' final and losing game against Denver in the first round of the playoffs.] Every time you go out there, you risk breaking something. I can't worry about getting hurt. Why worry about it now? If 'if' was a fifth, we'd all be drunk." Is this last line a quote from something, or is this aphorism his own? Is he as brilliant as I wish him to be? "But everybody has a finger that's crooked, so fuck it." The finger is broken between the knuckle and the first joint, and though it will probably never be as straight as it once was, it will ultimately heal on its own. "I just like to play basketball. That's what I get paid for." His Benjamin Franklin side—giving good weight. "This isn't an injury to take me out of anything. Doctors can't tell me what to do." He just seems nuts.

4.20.95—The Sonics-Rockets game at the T-Dome: I go by myself, sell the other ticket to a guy dressed in Rockets paraphernalia. Warming up, Gill seems *too* upbeat; he's wearing a brittle smile, a faint charm that's been applied across his face like fairy dust. During the first quarter, when Gill is on the bench, Vinny Askew throws him the towel as he heads back onto the court, and Gill refuses to catch the towel. *I'm not your towel boy,* you can practically hear Gill thinking, *take care of your own goddamn towel.* If Payton had done this, I would no doubt have found it amusing, but when Gill does it, it just seems petty.

With Houston ahead by 8 points, Karl starts to call timeout, but Payton beats him to it.

Karl has a question for Gill, who sprints over to Karl's side, in an unconscious parody of allegiance.

Gill misses 9 of 12 shots. Payton scores 25 points, goes 6-for-6 from the free-throw line, has 5 rebounds, 7 assists.

No one believes that Gill was suffering from clinical depression. No one can believe that Payton is playing with a broken finger. We denigrate Gill because he reminds us of ourselves in our ordinary confusion. We worship Gary because he seems to be, truly, a brother from another planet.

Seattle wins, tying them for the division lead with a record of 57-and-23. At the end of the game, Payton cups the Rockets guard Sam Cassell's head in his hand in a half-hug. Cassell doesn't like this, squirms away. Gary goes over and makes a point of hugging Houston's much maligned Vernon Maxwell.

Toward the end of the game, Hakeem Olajuwon decked Schrempf with an elbow. Speaking to reporters afterward, Schrempf says, "It wasn't intentional like he was trying to hurt me. But it was intentional in that he was trying to get a lick in. He was trying to bump me out of the way." Earlier, Schrempf had held down Hakeem, preventing him from dunking—an utterly routine play. Black players definitely hold Schrempf to a different standard, because he's so white in this black world.

•   •   •

4.21.95—In the next-to-last game of the regular season—the Sonics-Kings game in Sacramento—for the first time I've ever seen in thirty years of watching basketball, an NBA player successfully argues a referee into reversing a technical foul, and that person is of course Detlef Schrempf. Attempting to irritate Spud Webb of the Kings, Payton stands right next to him, chomping gum. Sacramento wins. If the Sonics had won tonight, they would have had a chance to win the Pacific Division by beating the Suns in the final game of the regular reason the day after tomorrow. Payton has a decent game—17 points, 5 assists—but his hand is clearly bothering him. I first wrote "bothering me," which it clearly is.

On the post-game show, somebody calls up T-Man, speaking with a strong (east) Indian accent. "Your voice reminds me of New York," T-Man says, waxing nostalgic about various Indian cab drivers, at which point the caller immediately stops doing his Indian voice and says in a bland-on-bland tone, "This is John, from Seattle University." It's a brutal moment: T-Man waxing nostalgic for a faux-ethnic voice; the delicacy of these arrangements and affiliations getting laid bare; T-Man's hunger to embrace his brethren from the mysterious East getting laid bare.

4.22.95—Laurie, Natalie, and I are watching a videotape of the Jim Carrey movie *Ace Ventura: Pet Detective*. In an early scene, the apartment manager asks Ace for the rent; Ace says he'll pay him later. The apartment manager accuses him of having animals in his apartment. Ace takes him around the apartment and shows him that there are no animals. The apartment manager leaves, Ace whistles, and an astonishing menagerie of animals comes rushing out of the woodwork. Animals love him; he loves animals; he's Tarzan, in touch with his animal selves; we love him because we, too, want to be in touch with our animal selves. Natalie loves plastic animals, zoo animals, all manner of animals; she loves the scene, and we play it back over and over and over again, and every time she points out the animals, she stutters badly on the word *animals*. Laurie and I look at each other. For the last few days, Natalie has been stumbling over words a little as she learns to talk, and we've thought nothing of it. This, though, seems different; is my disorder fated to become my daughter's?

•   •   •

4.23.95—*Ma chérie* leaves a phone message: "David, just confirming that we'll not be able to credential you for the playoffs, staying with my original decision reached at the end of February. Thank you."

In the meaningless final game of the regular season—they can't win the Pacific Division; instead, they'll finish second in the division, fourth in the Western Conference, and in a week will begin a three-out-of-five series against Los Angeles in the first round of the playoffs—the Sonics play Phoenix in Phoenix. My favorite moment of the game occurs when Payton does this funny mock-helpful thing whereby he grabs the ball after he makes a basket and hands it to Kevin Johnson, ostensibly to save him the trouble of retrieving the ball but actually to rub it in. Payton goes 8 for 16 from the floor but still looks extremely uncomfortable. Phoenix wins, 105–100, and wins the division over Seattle by three games; the Sonics' final regular-season record is 57-and-25, which is very good but six wins shy of their record last year.

On the post-game show, Marques Johnson says about the Sonics: "They can't knock down the open jumper. They seem tense and nervous and self-conscious." It's true: they have the terrible self-consciousness of someone trying very, very hard not to fuck up again.

McMillan tells reporters, "If we don't play better, we'll be through in a week [i.e., eliminated again in the first round of the playoffs]."

Payton, disappointed that the Sonics have scrapped plans for a two-day mini-camp in Santa Barbara intended to focus concentration and develop (at this late date) family feeling, asks, "Why should we stay around Seattle and read all that Denver shit?"—predictions that the Sonics are going to repeat their collapse of last year, this time against Los Angeles.

4.24.95—Larry Doby, the first black player in the American League, has been named special assistant to the president of the American League. In his column this week, my father writes: "Baseball has come a long way, baby, since the mid-1940s [when Doby broke the color line in the American League and four of his teammates refused to shake his hand], but there are still more roads to travel, including moving minority personnel into top-level managerial and front-office jobs." My admirable dad's indefatigable idealism.

. . .

A writer-friend from Brooklyn comes to Seattle to give a reading at the Elliott Bay Bookstore. He stays at a hotel downtown, and when I meet him for a drink before the reading, he says, as a kind of accusation, "Walking around today, I hardly saw any black people," the subtext of which is *you're living in Mayberry*. At the bookstore, to an audience that includes a black couple wearing Rastafarian dreadlocks, he reads a mock-Melville story about a black deckhand that, in the published version I'm holding in my hand, contains the phrases "you little black turd" and "nigger cabinboys." Both of these phrases evaporate in his oral recitation, and afterward, I ask him why he felt compelled to elide them, the subtext of which is *you're not as urbane as you think you are*.

Concerned about Natalie's speech, I phone my former speech therapist, who reminds me that most two-year-olds hit a few speed bumps when they're first putting words together; that's probably all Natalie is going through, and in a month or two she's likely to be fine. Nevertheless, she recommends that when talking with Natalie, Laurie and I try to use simple, short sentences; model slow and easy speech, "like Mr. Rogers"; make statements ("Look at the brown dog") rather than putting her on the spot by asking quiz questions ("What color is that dog?"); allow conversations to have long pauses and silences; give Natalie the chance to initiate conversations; incorporate singing and fingerplay, making communication more fun; when she's talking, be sure to acknowledge and value what she's saying; make sure not to interrupt her and, if she happens to stutter, not to correct her or tell her to slow down or show surprise but, instead, respond by using the troublesome word in a sentence, saying it slowly and easily. Whenever I stutter, I'm advised to repeat the word fluently, then say, "Sometimes we make mistakes when we speak. I pushed really hard making that sound." For all the anxiety, dread, pity, and self-pity this creates, it also makes me feel thrillingly close to Natalie. She is, apparently, vulnerable exactly where I am; she's flesh of my flesh—I "get" this in a way I simply didn't before, although I wish I didn't need this sense of a potentially shared affliction in order for me to arrive here.

. . .

Howard Cosell dies. The *New York Times* obituary mentions the infamous incident when Cosell referred, during a telecast, to a black football player as "that little monkey," but cautions that Cosell's "civil rights credentials were secure in any event."

Mitch Levy asks Karl: "Howard Cosell—loved him or hated him?"

Karl: "I enjoyed him. I thought he was a very bright. He brought a different perspective, an intellectual perspective, to sport, which I think more people should have." Karl's Cosell-ness: when Seattle hired him a couple of years ago, Snoopy Graham, whom Karl coached in the CBA and who credits Karl for helping him make it to the NBA, said, "George'll do great. But one thing bothers players. It's not that he knows more than we do. It's that he has to *tell* you that."

McMillan says, "In the playoffs, we need to stay together. When things go bad, we need to figure out how to change things and do it together. When things are going good, we can blow teams out."

Schrempf says, "Last year is always going to be there until we go past the first round. If we play hard and stay together, we should win."

Payton says, "We're all right. The playoffs are here." The Sonics' series against the Lakers starts in Tacoma in three days. "This is the real McCoy. We'll be ready."

I can't shake my impression that they're protesting much too much, that they're creating perfectly self-fulfilling prophecies of doom.

In the last couple of minutes of every show, callers attempt to replicate down to the last inflection T-Man's signature sign-off: "I am the T-Man—there ain't nothing else. I am the T-Man—goo goo g'joob." If a caller gets anything even slightly wrong, T-Man always says with droll condescension, "Close enough," which always means *not even close*. Tonight, an old guy (whom I'm almost certain T-Man is certain is black) tries but muddles it badly; T-Man should treat him with the same droll condescension he treats everyone else with and say, "Close enough," but, meaning well, meaning not to offend, T-Man says, "You nailed it," which, in its murderous pity, creates horrible dead air for a second or two.

· · ·

4.25.95—Karl says, "There is no disgrace to what happened last year"—
losing to eighth-seeded Denver in the first round of the playoffs. "We
have come back with a year of improvement. We tell people, 'Get over
it, it's history and move forward.'" This is, to me, the crucial incompre-
hension of the season. History is not something you get over. History is
what you keep reliving. If you stutter, your daughter might stutter.

The *Post-Intelligencer*'s Jim Moore, analyzing the Sonics-Lakers playoff series, which starts two days from now in Tacoma, says, "Payton has
to muzzle [the Lakers' point-guard Nick] Van Exel as well as himself. He
too often engages in extracurricular conversations with players and referees. The Sonics don't need any unnecessary technical fouls. Although
the chatter supposedly fires him up, Payton should save the backtalk for
the playground this summer. He must remember to start the offense and
defense instead of trouble." Payton will risk everything for the sound of
words—my hero.

Another *P-I* sportswriter, Art Thiel, says that the only person on the
Sonics who wants to win a championship as badly as Karl Malone and
Charles Barkley do is George Karl, "and he's twenty years out of uniform."

Marciulionis says, "It could happen that we lose the first game. It's
very important to stay together and not make it somebody's fault. We
can't play for ourselves. We must support each other."

Karl says, "We have a solid commitment to be selfless. We're more
oriented to sacrifice."

The season has come perfectly full circle and we're right back where
Karl said we started from: *if they can come together, they can win; if they
can't, we're not meant to come together, anyway.*

Laurie tells me that when she was putting Natalie to bed, Natalie got
stuck again on the word *animal,* grimacing badly and blinking her eyes—
two of the signs the therapist said to look for. Natalie and I even seem to
share the tendency to have trouble on words beginning with vowels; does
the genetic code get spliced that thin? Is this what I'll pass on to her? I
cry harder than I've ever cried in my life.

4.26.95—Payton says, "I think I'm meant to be the type of player who
does things to help make his teammates better: to draw the double-

teams and pass the ball to open shooters, or to draw the contact so the team can get rebounds. Part of it is the team I'm on. Part of it is that I'm proud of being an unselfish player. I just want to be consistent. That's my main goal now. People recognize consistency. Me and Shawn weren't playing well early in the year. That was the truth. I told Shawn that we couldn't be the ones giving Coach any problems. We had to be the ones who stepped up and chilled out. I wanted to come in and be a team leader. With all the turmoil going on around the team, I wanted to be the one who got everyone settled. The biggest part was just sucking it up and taking all the blame; don't trip off everything else. Everybody's got an ego, but for me, it was time to grow up." *The season has been a growth chart, all arrows pointing upward.*

10

THE SPACE BETWEEN US

4.27.95—The Sonics' first playoff game is tonight. Payton, in his guest column for the *Seattle Times,* predicts, "It'll be somebody and Utah for the Western Conference championship, and that somebody else will win it. I'm not going to say who that somebody is. I'll give you a hint. It's green and gold [the Sonics' colors]." His bravado now rings in my ears as utterly pro forma and false.

As Paul and I are getting out of the car in the parking lot outside the Tacoma Dome, I realize I've forgotten the tickets. Laurie sweetly agrees, despite the relentless rain, to meet us halfway between Seattle and Tacoma at the Seattle-Tacoma Airport, where she gives us the $85 tickets and I hug Natalie, who informs me that she wants to fly high in the sky like a birdie. Paul and I virtually hydroplane back to the Tacoma Dome, missing only the first couple of minutes of the first quarter. It feels wonderful to experience in our own bodies—rather than vicariously through other people's bodies—the adrenaline rush of going from gloom to joy.

At the insistence of the NBA, NBC, and TNT, the T-Dome's overhead klieg lights have been turned off and twenty-four lamps have been added courtside; the effect is to make the court seem the site of imminent, momentous thrills. After wearing white shoes all season, the Supes wear black shoes for the playoffs—*we're going to be* bad.

I tune in to get the radio broadcast on my headphones. Marques Johnson says, "The Sonics are gonna come out, at least in the first round, as Jim Carrey would say, smokin'."

Calabro, quoting from another Jim Carrey movie, says, "Do not go in there."

Marques, quickly moving on to refer to a yet more recent Jim Carrey movie, says, "He's dumb, I'm dumber."

They both laugh—one of my favorite moments of the season. Playing as it does with people's preconceptions, Johnson's joke works only because it's so obviously untrue.

A sign in the stands says *Just Remember Ted Bundy Was A* [University of Washington] *Husky.* Another sign says *Gary's Our General, Our Man, Our Barometer.* A fan yells to Anthony Peeler of the Lakers, "You convict." He does look like a convict, whatever a convict looks like. "You little brute." Little he's not. "You're an animal." This topic has, I think, been amply addressed by now.

Magic Johnson, who's now vice president of the Lakers, is sitting just a few seats down from me and Paul, and everybody watches Magic watch the game. (It's mainly what I do, in any case—I watch Magic watch the game more than I watch the game.) A bodyguard stands right next to him. A soda vendor offers him a free soda as a way to express to Magic some small gratitude for all the pleasure Magic has given to him over the years, but Magic says, "No, thanks," which breaks my heart all the way around; maybe for medical reasons he doesn't want to drink Coke, but why couldn't he just accept the gift and say thanks and put it under his seat?

Magic is wearing a black suit, white shirt, purple tie. Very pretty women come up to him, but none of them flirt; because Magic is HIV-positive, it's all quite asexual, like kissing the hand of the Pope, which gives it its sadness. All game long, kids come up to touch him; it's impossible to overstate what he means to these kids, how much they adore him. A mother and her kid come up to Magic; Magic lets the white bodyguard turn away most white kids, but this black kid and his mom he lets through, signs an autograph for. People stare at Magic constantly, as if he were an exhibit in a wax museum. Sitting with Mitch Kupchak, the

Lakers' general manager, Magic overreacts to virtually every play; the TNT camera can't get enough of him. There is a fascinating anger and hunger in the building—LA is everything Seattle wants and despises: money, glamour, fame, etc.

Toward the end of the first half, the Sonics are playing particularly well. Payton pats Van Exel on the head, trying to patronize him, trying to get dominion over him, like Natalie over her dolls. Van Exel says something to Payton; Gary blows a bubble at him, says nothing. He is cool, cool, cool. Without consulting the Lakers' coach, Del Harris, Van Exel calls timeout. Harris is furious at him. On the first play after the timeout, Vinny Askew blocks Van Exel's shot, strips the ball from Van Exel, and smiles, which I take as a good sign. The Sonics seem to have a killer instinct tonight.

With the Lakers playing well in the third quarter, Karl refuses to call timeout to stop their momentum. When the Sonics are playing well, on the other hand, he often will call timeout, which has the effect of stalling their good momentum. It's almost as if he calls timeouts at inopportune, idiosyncratic times in order to call attention to his own strategizing, to get people to wonder what he's up to, to contemplate the unfathomable genius of Coach's consciousness. In the George Karl cartoon commercial, Karl—wearing a wired apparatus on his head that showcases his brain—emerges from a group of black players. The announcer says, "At the center of sweat and tendons, blood and muscles: Coach Karl." Karl's brain emits waves. The announcer shouts: "The Brain!" Karl stands in front of an enormous computer, into which his brain apparatus is wired. Sweat drips off his face; he's deep in concentration. The computer blows up. Gill says, "Look, Coach Karl beat the computer." Karl, standing by the dismantled computer, looks smug. The announcer says, "And what's this, telepathy?" Karl then telepathically communicates with the players to pass the ball to one another and directs the ball into the hoop—Mind's dominion over Nature.

Van Exel scores 29 points, but no other Laker scores in double figures. Payton scores only 18 points and is obviously hampered by his hand. Kemp scores 21, though, Schrempf has 20, and Gill plays surprisingly well, too, shooting 6 for 10 from the field and 4–4 from the line. The Sonics win the first game of the series, 96–71.

After the game, Karl says, "Kendall's a pro. Before the game he looked as relaxed as I've seen him all year. We chatted about what a long year it's been, and I told him that it was time to have some fun."

Gill says, "It's money time: this is the playoffs. This is when I flourish. I love these games. I love playing in them. It's been like that since high school. Everything off the court doesn't matter. I'm not even thinking about [my feud with Karl]."

Perkins says, "Kendall came back in good spirits, instead of staying to himself, and that helped a lot. Definitely, everybody had a good focus on, trying to help each other. We're good when we're like that."

Askew says, "We believe in each other more [than we did last year], at least I know I do. It's a different atmosphere."

T-Man has challenged Gill to a game of 21; the game would start with T-Man ahead, 19–0. After the game, on T-Man's show, Reverend Daimen advises listeners, "Take the T-Man, take the points, and bet it all."

Gill replies, "You tell T-Man I want to play him a game of one-on-one at the end of the season. Tell him I got a score to settle with him. Tell him it's me and him." But it's all just in good fun. In the warm afterglow of the win, all is forgiven, all is forgotten, ego is dead, team is transcendent, everybody is happy, we are family.

4.28.95—On the *Gary Payton Show,* New York Vinnie says, "That one shot in the first quarter, when you went under the basket and kinda flipped it up over your head—did you believe you got that thing in?"

Payton, snickering, says, "Shawn did that, not me."

Michael Knight semi-rescues Vinnie from what, in Payton's eyes, is a fatal mistake—paying insufficiently close attention to what Gary Payton was doing: "That was Shawn who had people holding their heads; they couldn't believe what they had seen."

Vinnie, attempting, ineffectually, to recover—it's such a lesson: when you make a mistake, just acknowledge it, don't try to cover it up—says, "There was one shot that you had, though, that was kinda wild. I remember turning to someone who was behind me and saying, 'Damn.'"

Michael, continuing to offer Vinnie a life jacket, says, "There was that 3 [3-point shot] right at the top of the game."

Vinnie: "Yeah, maybe that was it, who knows? Who knows what was going on? See"—and this seems even less well-considered, following up the snafu with yet more sycophancy—"I'm crediting you for things you didn't even do, Gary."

Payton, blowing him off, says, "Yeah. Whatever." It's a brutal exchange, and I feel for Vinnie. *Excuse me, Gary, if I'm not utterly tele-pathic in appreciation of your every moment on the court.*

A fan named Jeremy calls and says, "You looked like a cat last night. You were a big ol' cat, playing Van Exel like a mouse: 'yeah, yeah, you can do that, you can do that, nope, can't do that,' like that. Very good work here."

Because there's so much to hate in the comment—the "very good work here" condescension, the inaccuracy of the analogy (Van Exel com-pletely outplayed Payton, as he has in most of their head-to-head meet-ings this year, so clearly Payton wasn't toying with him like a mouse), and animal analogies in general tend not to amuse Payton—he doesn't answer.

Jeremy, blithely oblivious, continues, "I want to ask you a question: do you remember way back in 1978 when you were playing in the Bay Area—this was pre-high-school ball—did you ever play a team from Alameda called St. Barnabus?"

Gary reanimates: "Yeah, sure did."

Jeremy says, "The St. Barnabus Bricks, right? I was on that team."

Gary laughs.

Jeremy: "We were so bad, it's like, you know, when your coach will take you out for pizza when you win your first game? He took us out when we lost by less than 20."

Gary truly laughs this time. Jeremy has recovered beautifully by trad-ing his condescension for subservience.

Asked by Vinnie how his broken finger affected his performance, Pay-ton says, "It didn't do anything for me. It was just one of them nights. It was just something that happened."

Vinnie, realizing he needs to make yet more amends, says, "You're almost pretty well healed on that thing. I seen your hand the other day, and it just has a little leather sleeve over the finger, right? It usually takes two to three weeks for a finger to heal up, and you're about two-and-a-half weeks into it already, right?"

Quite curtly—the topic is no longer under discussion—Payton says, "It's not affecting me anymore."

Vinnie says, "You can still grip the Coupe de Ville wheel and the Corvette wheel, right?"

Niggers and their driving machines—Payton doesn't go for this at all. With transparently phony agreeability, he says, "Right."

A caller named Ellen, who sounds about twelve, says she wants to go to Payton's basketball camp this summer but she's nervous about the prospect.

With tender solicitation, breaking through a dozen walls separating himself from her, he asks, "Why you nervous?"

She says, "You're the greatest."

He knows this, feels no need to respond. "You gonna come to the camp?"

She says, "No."

Payton says, "Why not?"

Ellen says, "You wouldn't want to see me."

Payton: "Why?"

"I don't have a shot like you do," she says, then suddenly hangs up.

Vinnie says, "I think that's great, what you're doing for the kids."

Payton: "It's okay. I try to do as much as possible." He is anti-sentimental but affectionate: he does what he can to connect with Ellen but refuses to lay it on with a trowel about "doing it for the kids."

In the new installment of his guest column for the *Seattle Times,* Payton says, "People see us on the court and automatically judge us by our demeanor on the court. Like Vernon [Maxwell]. People think he's a crazy wild guy. But off the court he's the coolest person I know. I can relate to him. People don't understand that we might be tough on the court, but off the court we're a lot nicer than what they think." *It's all just theater: we're not the lunatic niggers you want to think we are.*

4.29.95—Before Laurie and I drop Natalie off to play at a friend's house (we're going together to the second playoff game), the speech therapist encourages me to keep things in perspective by comparing the anxiety

I'm feeling about Natalie to the anguish of the parents whose children were killed a few days ago in the Oklahoma City bombing. Theoretically, this might be good advice; in practice, it's not how we live our lives. We're all trapped inside our own space helmets.

Before the game begins, Michael Richards, Kramer on *Seinfeld,* throws out the ceremonial ball, then on his way to his seat tries to shake several of the Lakers' hands. None of them acknowledges him. He's our icon, not theirs.

Magic Johnson is sitting in the same seat he was for the first game, a few rows in front of us. An endless parade of kids comes up to shake his hand, high-five him, hug him; he's the repository for them of an absolutely amazing amount of feeling. A kid comes up to Magic's silk suit and paws it; Magic gives him a bemused look.

Sam Perkins hits a 3. "I told them to watch Perkins," Magic screeches to the man who's sitting next to him again, Mitch Kupchak, the Lakers' GM. Magic is constantly stretching, standing up, pacing up and down the aisle, hollering, waving, grimacing, covering his face, making himself the relentless object of everybody's attention. NBC's "roving reporter," Hannah Storm, chatting up Magic before the camera comes on, is anomalously flirtatious with him; she looks and pouts like nothing so much as an expensive callgirl. Even Laurie, who usually disagrees with me, especially about things like this, thinks so.

As a goofy goodwill gesture, the Sonics fan sitting to Magic's left hands him a sign—*Beat LA* with the *B* removed, which turns it into *Eat LA,* which turns it into a sexual metaphor, which references Magic's HIV status, which makes the whole moment really uncomfortable, which makes me wonder how could anybody be so oblivious. Magic pretends to smile.

A fan calls out to the Lakers' reserve center Sam Bowie, "Do you think Portland made a mistake, Sam?"—i.e., choosing him over Michael Jordan in the NBA draft ten years ago? What a life, what an exhaustingly public life it must be for them.

In the first quarter, Payton kicks a ball out of bounds; Karl smiles back at him, trying (a bit too hard) to convey *everything's cool.* After scoring to put the Sonics ahead, Payton catches the ball as it goes through the net, then throws a behind-the-back pass to Van Exel: *here, here's the ball;*

eat it. Payton hits a 3 and leaves his hand in the air an implausibly long time to celebrate and taunt Van Exel. In the third quarter, Van Exel hits a 3-pointer to give the Lakers the lead and heads downcourt shadow-boxing, then doing his infamous and infuriating "mummy walk." With a little less than three minutes left in the game and the Lakers leading by 8 points, literal lightning literally strikes, creating a power surge and causing the Tacoma Dome to go dark for twenty minutes. Once the lights cool and come back on, the Sonics outscore the Lakers, 9–3, but they still lose, 84–82.

Karl, on post-game spin patrol, tells the media, "In all playoff series you get tested. This is a good test. Just a test. There's no problem. We just have to do it."

Schrempf says, "They did to us what we did to them in the first game. They doubled us in the low post and made us shoot from the outside. We didn't shoot very well today [only 31 percent; Payton was 7 for 19 from the field]. We dug ourselves in a hole. This loss has nothing to do with Denver. Against Denver we fell apart as a team. I don't think that's going to happen here. We had a tough game today, but we stuck together, worked hard, and supported each other. That's the bottom line."

But it's not Denver. Denver is history. And history is over.

At midnight, on Bruce Shine's nationally syndicated sports-talk show, a caller says, "I think we've given athletes too much power in our lives." Bruce Shine doesn't disagree so much as offer the only defense he can of his livelihood, his life, the lives of people listening to this show at midnight: "It's a way for people to come together."

4.30.95—In an essay appearing in the *New York Times* sports section, Eileen Robinson, the mother of an eight-year-old girl in Pleasant Grove, Utah, who's obsessed with the New York Knicks' center Patrick Ewing, explains how through Ewing her dyslexic daughter, Rina, has learned "that it takes hard work to accomplish goals. She heard him say he couldn't play basketball very well in the beginning. She heard him say school was hard for him when he came to this country from Jamaica, but that he didn't give up and that he would ask the teacher to explain until he understood. Patrick Ewing's life story made a real impression on my daughter. He and the New York Knicks and basketball have given her something to be interested in, to be excited about, to look forward to, to believe in, to love." So all glory to Rina Robinson; one wants (despite all evidence to the contrary) to believe that Bruce Shine is right, that it's a way for people to come together. A few days ago I saw a black teenager who was wearing a Gary Payton jersey jaywalk right in front of a cop. The cop was so stunned he didn't respond until the kid was nearly across the street. Then, although such an offense is usually punishable in Seattle by lethal injection, the cop stopped him and said, "Hey, next time wait till the light turns green, number 20." The cop just couldn't bring himself to cite a kid wearing a Gary Payton jersey. So far as I can tell, this is all to the good.

Natalie and I walk across the street to Wallingford Park to go swinging. I encourage her to kick her legs out and pump as she swings forward and tuck her legs underneath her as she swings back. She doesn't quite get it yet; it's really just something to talk about as I push her. As requested, I repeatedly "do underdog"—give her a big push and then run under the swing. Flying high in the sky, she becomes a birdie. I'm very conscious of doing the things my speech therapist advised: speaking slowly and easily myself, not interrupting her when she speaks, applauding her efforts. Another little girl—a little older than Natalie—swings next to us, listening with apparently fascinated curiosity to our singsong dialogue. Language seems to surround Natalie now; the very air is thick with unexploded syllables. I'm now wired into her words the same way I've been wired into Gary's.

Payton's coach, teammates, and agent are reduced to speaking for Payton, who has stopped speaking to reporters. The battery that powered Payton and the team all season—Gary's language—is now dead. Karl says, "The last X-ray [of his broken finger] didn't show any healing, but we didn't see any separation of the fracture. It takes a lot of courage to play through this. It's gotta be painful." Perkins says, in defense of Payton, "When the playoffs come, the last thing to worry about is what a guy's shooting or what his stats are." McMillan, asked by a reporter about

Payton's physical and mental states, says, "I guess I'm supposed to answer questions for him, then, huh?" Even McMillan is getting a bit testy. The reporter replies, "I guess that's a 'no comment.'" Eric Goodwin, Payton's agent, says, "Gary isn't angry with the media or anything. He's up for the playoffs. In terms of his broken left ring finger, he's playing with pain. But he was real positive about Saturday's game. I thought he'd be real down, but he wasn't." More bluffing on Payton's part.

5.1.95—On the *Gary Payton Show,* Payton says, "Everybody always predict something. You miss a layup, you miss a coupla shots: people want to say there's somethin' wrong with you all the time. I don't know why people do that." Of course he does: because we love him a lot, but not enough. "Our team is fine; we just had a bad shooting night. Things didn't fall for us, that's just the way things went."

Asked why the Sonics' best players—with the exception of Kemp—can't seem to find their groove against the Lakers, Payton says, "It's just something that happens; you got to try to fight through it, try to find better ways to get everybody else into the game."

Why did the Sonics lose the second game after winning the first game so easily?

Payton says, "Game one, they [the Lakers] didn't make shots, but they did in game two." *Philosophize me no philosophies.*

Michael Knight says, "The finger's not giving you any fits?"

Payton says, "No, everybody's making big things out of nothing; they don't know what's going on. Everybody always wants to predict what's going on, and they don't know what's happenin'." *It's all just theater; my real life is elsewhere.* "Nothing wrong with me; people always want to make up excuses or something, but Gary the only one know what going on and it's nothing going on, so I'm fine."

Knight, somewhat peskily, says, "Do you feel like yourself in these games, now that you're struggling with the double-team?"

Payton says, "Nah, I don't feel like I'm struggling. If they gonna double me like that, I just have to adjust my game to other things. If they don't let me score, then I gotta help my teammates in other ways, and that's fine with me."

I find tedious, in a way I never did before, his purposefully bland reassurances, because the macho mask has slipped so low you can almost see
his face.

In the latest installment of his guest newspaper column, Payton, after
mentioning that he did two commercials for the local department store
Bon Marché, says, "As for my own clothes, I get them everywhere"—*you
didn't think I really shopped at the Bon, did you?* "But the main place I
get them in Seattle is Choices, a clothing store right off First. The owner,
Kevin, makes a lot of clothes for me, or has clothes sent. For my shoes,
I go to Atlanta. My jeans come from Los Angeles. But my suits and dress-
up clothes come from Choices." Not a good sign, so far as the Sonics' for-
tunes go, that he's much more animated on this topic than on any of the
basketball-related topics broached earlier. "Once the playoffs are over,
I'll be doing a lot of things this summer. I plan on going to the Virgin
Islands. I'm also going to Hawaii and Santa Barbara to work some [bas-
ketball] camps." Not a good sign, either: he's already on vacation.

The third game of the series is in LA. On the Sonics' first possession,
Schrempf throws away a pass, leading to two Laker free throws and
somehow setting a tone for the rest of the evening (Seattle winds up
committing 17 turnovers). After a few minutes, the Sonics trail, 12–2;
halfway through the second quarter, they're behind, 44–26. Both Payton
and Karl seem affectless, and their affectlessness seem to feed, in a curious way, off each other. At one point, during a timeout, Payton stands by
himself on the sideline with his arms folded demurely behind his back.
Ordinarily, this would be a mock-meek GP gesture; tonight (because he's
protecting his broken finger?), he actually seems genuinely quiet and
withdrawn. In the second half, the Lakers tire and get in foul trouble,
their bench plays poorly, and the Sonics finally come clawing back. Also,
Payton seems energized in a way he hadn't yet been in the entire series:
he winds up scoring 20 points on 10-for-21 shooting. Kemp scores 30
points and has a brilliant all-around game; Schrempf scores 19; Perkins
18; but the Sonics expend all their energy climbing uphill and finally
lose, 105–101, in a game that never feels quite that close.

After the game, Karl tells reporters, "We got shocked early. Our fight didn't start until we got 15 to 18 points down. But it's not over. We've been here before and it's going to take a lot of work, but we've done it before. We were in the same position two years ago in Utah, down 2–1, and we came back to win. I believe in this team. I love this team. We've got to find an answer on the court. Winning two games in a row, we can do that." Otherwise, the series and the Sonics' season are over. "This team will come ready to play Thursday. We are in the process of building a championship character." His reassurances are as flagrantly moot as Payton's. Asked why Gill didn't play in the second half, Karl says, "I just liked my other players."

The Sonics are now in nearly open mutiny against Karl. Payton tells a reporter, "Everybody's fucked up. People and things in the Sonic organization change once playoff time comes. I can't play against six motherfuckers by myself. What am I supposed to do, go up against their whole team every time and try to score? I'm going to be me." Marciulionis says, "It sucks. It's hard to understand. I thought they traded for me for the playoffs. The first three or four months of the season, I kept hearing that song. Now it might be too late." Gill, pseudo-stoic, says, "Yeah, I'm disappointed. I want to play. I want to help my team win. But it's Coach's decision. No matter what, I'm with the team. I'm just trying to stay positive."

On the post-game call-in show, T-Man says, "All night Karl looked like a beaten man. How many shots during the broadcast did you see of Coach Karl slumped back in his chair? It made me sick. The first sign of adversity, the Sonics fold like a house of cards, and why is that? Because their coach is leading the way; he looks clueless. If Pat Riley was coaching this team, the series would be over [with the Sonics having won in three straight games]. Show me some fortitude here, please. I was supposed to be off the air at midnight, and it is now 12:28. The twelve o'clock limit has been waived by me personally. I will go until I'm tired tonight. We're gonna talk to you, the fans, until we find some answers. We could go until 12:30; we could go until six A.M.; I don't know. I'll go until I run out of steam. We are here for Sonic therapy. The management of this fine station is obviously sound asleep and is unaware that I'm going to go as long as I want. Ron Barr, that boring doofus, will not be heard tonight; you can write your congressman if you have a problem with that. I'm going with you, the people here in the big city, talking about the city, trying to find some answers. I'm just upset. Softy [his producer], call out for pizza." *We're going to hunker down until we find answers to the problems that plague us here in the big city.*

Gas Man, joining T-Man on the air from Los Angeles, says, "I know you know that to keep a finely honed athletic body like mine in shape, I spend a lot of time working out: I got off the Stairmaster this afternoon and ran into Bobby Medina, the strength coach of the Sonics, and he said, 'Hey, how you doin', Mike?' and I said, 'Good,' and he said, 'Wow, you got your playoff face on; you oughta walk by the bench tonight with that face.' If it gets to the point that they need the Gas Man to walk by the bench to rev them up, then the Sonics, ladies and gentlemen, are in a world of trouble."

T-Man says, "Go enjoy the LA night. Go boogie."

Gas Man says, "Oh yeah, we're really going to roll out into Inglewood at midnight." The LA Forum—the Lakers' arena—is in Inglewood, a black ghetto. "We'll be stopping at the first club we see." In the NBA, black men rule (sort of), so we admire them (sort of); everywhere else in America we're afraid of them.

Posting to the Sonics newsgroup, James writes: "When you have a team with players that always talk shit, what do you expect? Now that they're down 2-to-1, they'll probably start arguing among each other. What a waste of such a talented team."

Murray, who at the beginning of the season traded notes with me about bumping into Payton in an electronics store, writes back to James, defending the Sonics: "I'm not sure where people get their ideas that Seattle is a trash-talking team. Payton used to talk a lot but not as much anymore. I really see no problem with talking, anyway."

James replies, "Hey, Murray, I don't know how many of the Sonics games you've been to this year, but the games I've been to this year, they were flapping their gums the whole time. My seats are second row center court, so hearing this isn't a problem. I suppose the info you're getting is from the media or you're sitting in nosebleed country where you need binoculars to see the game."

Your life isn't real to me, because it's not my life.

. . .

5.2.95—In the *Post-Intelligencer,* Jim Moore calls a play McMillan made "boneheaded." In the *Los Angeles Daily News,* Michael Ventre says the Sonics are devoid of "heart or character." They're back on the yellow brick road, looking for Dorothy.

Speaking to reporters, Karl says, "My assistant, Bobby Weiss, tells this story. He says if the Pope visited Seattle and his hat fell in the lake and I walked on water to fetch it and slapped it right back on his head, the headline in Seattle would be, 'George Karl Can't Swim.'"

Payton, asked if he's nervous about the Sonics' predicament, says, "Nervous for what? I ain't got time to be nervous." Asked why the Sonics are struggling, he says, "Everybody is playing fucked up."

This is exactly the difference between them: Karl wallows in (his own) pain, which reminds us too much of ourselves; Payton pretends to be beyond it, knowing that we know he feels it.

Gas Man listens to caller after caller excoriate the Sonics, then says, "I've been doing sports-talk shows for a number of years now, and you realize some fans like to see their team struggle. It's kind of strange. Sports fans are a strange breed." As John Hawkes once said to me, "The only subject is failure."

Calabro, asked by Gas Man what he did this morning, says he "went golfing in Simi Valley [where a jury acquitted the LAPD of beating Rodney King] and got whapped over the head by some members of the FOP."

Gas Man says, "FOP?"

"Friends of the police."

Gas Man has no idea where to go with this, and I'm not sure I do, either. Is Calabro kidding? Did he really go golfing? Is he trying to demonstrate how much he's learned this season from Marques Johnson?

Laurie and I take Natalie to the zoo to ride her favorite pony. A sullen teenage girl guides the pony, with Natalie sitting atop him, slowly around the ring. I tell the girl that Major is Natalie's favorite pony. "Major's a doofus," the girl says. Everybody's a critic.

. . .

The NBA releases a video today entitled *Shawn Kemp: The Reignman.* I'm the first person on my block to rent it. Shawn explains that his life thus far "isn't very long, so the video doesn't take very long." The most interesting moment in the film occurs when Karl, exhorting the Sonics to play hard at the end of a game, says, "Rock 'n' roll, gentlemen, rock 'n' roll." "Gentlemen" is meant to be mock-genteel, I understand that, but "rock 'n' roll"? How could anyone be that tone-deaf to nuance?

Paul e-mails me: "I think I'm taking b-ball stuff too seriously. I'm going through this weird anticipatory grieving thing. It isn't pretty."
    Me? I'm withdrawing, distancing myself, detaching...

A late-middle-aged white man is wearing a hat that has *America's Cup* '95 on the brim, a gold watch, Dockers, a flowered shirt. The post-office supervisor—a short, stocky, middle-aged black woman—explains to him that the postal scales are calibrated every month.
    "But you're charging the public money," he says. "If the scales aren't correct, it isn't right."
    She asks him to come with her into her office, so he won't hold up the rest of the line, but he says, "I'd just as soon be out here." Who knows what nefariousness she might have planned for him back there? "You should certify the scales," he reiterates.
    "We do certify them," she explains again.
    "Someone else should certify them—an independent agent, not a government employee. That's a flaw in the system, when you're charging the public money."
    Finally, he asks for her card and her name and the name of her supervisor.
    "I'm the supervisor," she says. "I am in charge of this postal branch."
    They stare bullets at each other for an eternity until she pivots to return to her office. The man slams the glass door against a garbage can on his way out, nearly shattering the glass. When he's gone, everybody waiting in line breaks into applause for the supervisor. I find that, at least for the moment, I really do sort of love Seattle.

·   ·   ·

"Where you from originally?" T-Man asks a particularly agitated Sonics fan.

"Bed-Stuy," the caller says.

T-Man replies, "No wonder you got the fire." *All energy flows from one city. One thing is real. Everything else isn't.*

A television commercial juxtaposes tennis shoes worn by a black man and Pirelli tires. The tag line is: "Power is nothing without control." It's difficult to imagine a more explicit and concise expression of white people's reverence for, resentment toward, and colonization of black people's bodies.

5.3.95—At practice this morning, the seven players in Karl's rotation—Payton, Kemp, Schrempf, Perkins, McMillan, Askew, Johnson—shoot at one basket. Gill, Marciulionis, Cartwright, Scheffler, and Houston shoot at the other basket. The two camps don't communicate.

Afterward, McMillan, the team captain, calls a players-only meeting. The players reportedly decide to wrest control of the team back from their coach and win the game for themselves rather than, in any sense, for Karl. They also complain about Karl's never explaining why he's doing what he's doing—shortening the rotation, effectively excluding Gill, Marciulionis, and Cartwright from the game; they complain that Karl's coaching scared. An anonymous player tells a reporter: "Part of the problem is George is scared of Gary and pretty much lets Shawn do whatever he wants. Those guys have him, and in the end they won't help him." That's it: his guilt, their rage—the difficulty of building bridges across such a wide abyss.

Del Harris, the Lakers' coach, is named the coach of the year by the *Sporting News.* "In the pros it involves a lot of give and take of the egos involved," he says. "Unlike in high school or college, you [the coach] can't be the number one guy. If you set yourself up to have everyone feed your ego, you'll fail. The more you give in these regards, the more it will tend to work. You've got to be able to give respect to the player, to give and receive input and listen, because there's no respect if there's no input." Sentence by sentence, it's as if he's glossing exactly what's gone wrong with the Sonics' season; e.g., Marciulionis says, "Kendall asked me today, 'When was the last time you talked to George?' I don't even remember. A coach should have enough respect for his players to talk to them about this."

On the *George Karl Show*, Karl says, "We play our best basketball when there's a sense of urgency, and there's definitely a sense of urgency. It's not pressure, the fans and media want to turn it into pressure, but that's the challenge of athletics, that's why we play sport; you play sport to play in the big games. That's what you want to do. There's going to be nights when your heart's flittering and flattering, but when the game starts, this is why you play, this is what you do, this is why you want to be there." No one remotely believes this. From the sound of his voice, not even Karl believes it, especially when it's followed immediately by the defeated fatalism of "My desire to be a celebrity or a spokesman dwindles every day. I mean, I'm tired of making sure I say the right things to make thirty-five other people happy. Some of this other stuff—I've had it. I've—kind of like the Mountain Dew commercial—'done it.' Well, I'm not sure I want to do it again. I want to be able to laugh."

Asked what's the matter with the Sonics, Payton says, "Ain't nothin' wrong. Ain't nothin' different. You all can evaluate my play the way you want to evaluate it. I ain't trippin'." At the same time, he says, "I've been blank. I haven't been into the games the way I need to be. But that's going to change. Tonight, I'm going to say, 'Fuck it,' and be the way I need to be. Everything's fine; we just need to play smarter. If we lose, I'll keep breathing." Why does Payton's detachment seem interesting some- how, whereas Karl's seems only defensive? Why do I romanticize Payton's contradictions but not Karl's? In the sports world, these are what are known as rhetorical questions.

Laurie says that our neighbor from across the street is putting up a chain- link fence so that his next-door neighbor, a Cuban woman, will stop cut- ting across his lawn.

"That's so Nordic," I say. "Why doesn't he just tell her to stop walking across his lawn?"

Because—especially in Seattle, I suppose—everybody's afraid to say anything to anybody when the subtext is difference. Laurie says, "It's like what I would have done before I realized what I was doing. I mean, before you pointed out how Nordic I was being." She makes me happy when she says this; I serve a crucial function for her in a way that I'm not sure I understood before. To Laurie, I represent something other, something subtly dark. Playing George Karl, she allows me to play Gary Payton. For better or worse—mainly better, I've come to see—this is the erotics of our marriage: other calling to other.

5.4.95—The Alabama Department of Corrections puts chain gangs back into use. An AP photo appearing in the *Seattle Times* shows a chain gang—all but one of whom is black—cleaning a public highway, watched over by rifle-carrying guards, all of whom are white. Seventy-three percent of Alabamans support the program. Rod Jones, the commissioner of Alabama's corrections department, says, "You can't equate this with slavery. People in slavery had no choice. People in prisons made a choice: they broke the law. The message is clear: we don't want you committing crime in our state." *There,* we're supposed to think, reading the article and looking at the picture, *over there is racism.*

In a pre-game interview, Karl, asked if he's concerned about his future, says, "Of course I'm concerned, concerned about my family and their financial future. I'm not going to tell you there aren't moments when it's unnerving and unsettling. It's unsettling to me and it's unsettling to my family." Asked the laughably leading question as to whether getting fired would be fair, Karl lets himself answer, indulging in deep, deep self-pity: "To try and judge this business on fairness would be lunacy. I've done everything I can do. I've worked my tail off. I can't do much more than that." *It's over.*

"I watch a lot of cartoons," Payton writes in his guest column today. "I like cartoons a lot. I'll be watching *Space Ghost* or *Secret Squirrel* [this afternoon in the hotel room]. I got the Cartoon Network at home. I watch them all day." Unlike most people I know, he's completely comfortable with who he is and what he loves. "I'm going to come out and be aggressive, play a normal game, a simple game. And if they double-team me, I'll kick it out to the players who are open for an outside shot. I believed in them all year; why stop believing in them now?" *It's really over.* "I can't play against five people myself." *It's really, really over.* "I'm going to get it to the open man. And if that's the way we're going to lose, that's the way we're going to lose." *It's really, really, really over.*

He knows they're going to lose; they know they're going to lose; I know they're going to lose. There is, somehow, something oddly thrilling about, as they say in the sports world, the wheels coming off.

Nicholas, from Magnolia, tells Gas Man, "You can't treat players like puppets and expect them to dance whenever you take them out of the closet." As Ervin Johnson, the Sonics' backup center, said earlier in the day, "It's impossible to feel comfortable in this situation, but that's just my opinion. You can't play guys one way one game, another way the next, and expect them to be consistent. I try to come prepared the same way every night, but it doesn't always work out like that. That's what happens when you keep changing the lineup." Suddenly all his clichés have vanished on him; they *were* just a ruse.

A poster on a city bus says, "Condoms—they go where you go. Condoms have improved since your parents used them. If they had sex, that is." In the ad, a black man and black woman are both wearing glasses. It's unmistakable to me that their blackness is meant to represent their sexuality; it's also unmistakable that their glasses are meant to represent being smart about sex. The ad wouldn't make sense if they weren't wearing glasses or if they weren't black. Embedded in the ad is the history of our country.

Game four on the tube from LA: Before the tipoff, Payton and Van Exel slap and shake each other's hands; Payton seems respectful rather than antagonistic—not, to me, a good sign (he seems in too accommodating a mood). Another not very good sign: in the first quarter, at the end of a play, Payton lands in the lap of a fan and stops to inquire whether the fan is okay. I wonder, why suddenly so polite? Payton gets two quick fouls in the first quarter and makes immediate eye contact with Karl, letting Karl know it's his—Payton's—decision: he's not coming out of the game. Gary makes a circus shot; Gary and Shawn do a low-five; they both seem to gather some momentum from the moment.

The Sonics lead almost the entire game, by 12 points in the second quarter and by 8 at the end of the third quarter. But, as they have so often throughout the year, they self-destruct under stress, committing five turnovers in the last seven minutes of the game. The Sonics still lead, 108–107, with two minutes to go. Then, rather than calling plays for Payton (27 points) and Kemp (26 points, 18 rebounds), Karl calls plays for the two veterans he holds in highest regard—Schrempf and Perkins, neither of whom comes close to delivering. The Lakers wind up winning, 114–110.

On the post-game show, Marques Johnson says, "My feeling is, I just don't think you win championships in the NBA by committee. Maybe on the NCAA level you can, but not on this level. Here you need to get the feeling that someone is the guy." Karl refuses to anoint any one player the star; his system of interchangeable cogs is the star.

Calabro says, "You need to give Gary Payton or Shawn Kemp that responsibility."

Johnson says, "I've heard George talk more than any NBA coach about how negative the players are, how money-conscious the players are; they're not the same breed of tough-nosed players he used to play with. True or not true, when he does that, it's perceived that he's talking about the players he coaches—who else does he spend all his time with? It would be hard for me to respect my coach if he's telling me at the same time that he doesn't respect me."

Calabro says, surprisingly sharply, "My reaction is, the system will stay; Kendall Gill will go."

Thus, after building their friendship all season long, Calabro and Johnson in effect turn and walk in opposite directions.

Gill, removing his jersey before getting to the locker room, says to reporters, "Next year, if things are the way they were this year, I don't want to come back. I have to move on. I'm going to ask for a trade. Last year was bad. This year was worse. It's a shame that all the guys have busted their butts all year long, put up with all kinds of controversy, and it ends like this. I thought our consolation for going through all this was going to be a championship. It hurts like a son-of-a-bitch. I don't want to stay in this type of system any more, platooning players in and out, because I don't believe it works. I tried my best to do it these past two years, but it gets really tedious when you don't know what your role is on the team and you don't know how much you're going to play. When you've got players, let 'em play. You don't yank 'em in and out. You don't play games with them. You let them play and they form a bond, like the Lakers."

Schrempf says, "We didn't pull together. We went our separate ways again. Something like this has been going on for two years. We go off on our own, we aren't very well-disciplined, we're a very relaxed group, we don't work on things we need to work on, we don't practice hard when we need to, and when it gets down to it, when it's crunch time, when you need to execute right, that backfires on us every time."

Marciulionis, throwing his warmup top on the locker room floor, says, "I don't think he [Karl] was on the same page with the team. He closed his eyes to many things. We hurt ourselves all season because we didn't talk about what we had in our hearts. We were afraid of each other, afraid to talk to each other, to express our thoughts, to offer support. Instead of that, people just said, 'Okay, just keep going, work hard, play defense.' It's very sad." The cartoon commercial featuring Sarunas portrays him as a space alien who, attached to an escape pod by an umbilical cord, uncurls from the fetal position and becomes a ball with spikes sticking out of it in order to defend the distant, ludicrous planet of Marciulonia. *Everyone else is They.*

Karl says, "We're a better basketball team than we showed the last two years. Everybody in that room [the Sonics' locker] knows that. I'm not embarrassed by how we played. My hat is off to LA. It's such a shock. It's time to face our embarrassment, feel the humility of sport, and go on and try to figure out some things. The common denominator the last two years is that we played young teams and gave them confidence." Asked if he feels his team let him down, Karl shrugs, then says, "I don't know the answer. For two years now, we haven't been able to find the bonding or the commitment to find answers to playoff basketball. We do it a lot during the year, but we've gotten caught twice by teams that, deep down inside, I think we should have beaten." Asked to compare being eliminated by Los Angeles in the first round this year to being eliminated by Denver in the first round last year, he says, "This one hurts even more. Because in coaching you're supposed to learn from your mistakes. I don't think we did. Last year was more of an emotional shock. This season has been more of a controlling, Band-Aiding, fixing, ego-managing season, and the bottom line probably is that we weren't together enough to win the first round. This is not a bad basketball team. This is a good basketball team. I don't think I've changed. Except I get tired of the bullshit. I get tired of managing the baloney, rather than coaching character and toughness and discipline." All those great words.

Payton, emerging from a room across the hall, yells at Karl. The two of them hug, then turn and—with their arms around each other—walk a hundred feet down a long corridor, not saying anything. At the end of the corridor, they start speaking loudly to each other, waving their arms. Reporters can hear them talking, but no one can tell what they're saying. After a couple of minutes, Karl, with red-rimmed eyes, walks back into the locker room.

Karl declines comment. Payton tells TV reporters, "It ain't just Coach Karl's fault. All twelve people who stepped on the floor lost this playoff game. It's not all about blaming one person. Blame me—I care less. When we step on the floor, we should be able to want to play, and we didn't step up, so I think it's all twelve guys' fault, and that's the way it is. When we step on the floor, it should be on the floor. When we play on the basketball court, nobody should have no problems; we have no problems with each other on or off the floor, either. People are tryin' to stop problems with each other or start something without our team, and that ain't gonna happen with this team. It ain't gonna be like that. We supportin' George; that's our coach. I don't care what people say; we supportin' him."

Asked whether he thinks the coach should be the same next year, Payton says, "Yeah. Yeah. Why not? What is it? It's the twelve people who players who did this. He give us a plan; if we didn't execute it, that's our problem. It's not Coach's fault; he ain't out there playing for us, and that's just the way I feel about it. Everybody got to evaluate ourselves; we haven't been stepping it up in the playoffs. George Karl is gonna stay our coach, and I'm gonna support him till the end. When he came here, he changed my whole game. Now to back out on him and say it's his fault, that ain't right, and it ain't his fault. Like I said, it's the twelve guys, and I'm gonna keep saying that."

A reporter asks him, "What did you tell George?"

Stalling for time, Payton says, "Say what?"

"What did you tell George?"

"That's between us."

Warren G. and Snoop Doggy Dogg—rappers, Lakers fans, friends of Payton's—pass by outside the locker room, shouting encouragement to him. Gary shouts right back to them, "All right, okay, baby, take care, it easy." He's not going to mope before Snoop and Warren G.; it's not about one kind of performance (winning/losing); it's about another kind of performance (coming through slaughter with grace).

On the post-game call-in show, Howard, from Bainbridge Island, says, "The one thing I feel bad about for Karl is that I think he put a lot of trust in people like Askew and Perkins, guys who he thought would take him through the wilderness, and they just didn't do it."

Kenny, from Queen Anne, says, "What frustrates me about Karl is that he seems to know X's and O's, but he doesn't really relate well to his players, and I think that's the essence of leadership. He's constantly blaming the players for this or that, some failing or other, but it seems he always gets into a personality conflict with one or the other of them and he should take a step back and realize leadership is not necessarily being in control."

Gene, from Lynnwood, says, "Wally [Walker] needs to take his *cojones* out of his mama's purse and get [Pat] Riley in here. Riley will take the boys in the locker room at halftime, slap 'em around a little, spit on 'em, all that stuff."

Timothy, from Ballard, says, "Sam Perkins can be thrown into a garbage can, for all I care. That guy sucks."

Doug, from Spanaway, says, "Askew and George had a thing going on. Trade Askew for Dennis Rodman and then George can have a thing with Rodman."

You can hear the relief in fans' voices, calling in to affirm how frayed our little republic had been all along. *They weren't together; we and they are definitely not together; we're atoms in a centrifuge; we're separate and apart; we knew the hope we clung to was an illusion, and now we really know it.*

Joey, from Tacoma, tells T-Man, "I don't have a comment about the Sonics. I have a question about Karl Malone [of the Utah Jazz]: what is the secret saying he whispers to himself every time he shoots a free throw?"

T-Man says, "I know what he says, but I can't reveal that information. It's information that us here in the trade have to keep amongst ourselves, because it's really that perverted. I could tell you, but you'll never have the same respect for the Mailman ever again."

Joey says, "Oh, man, I would give anything to know what he says at the foul line."

T-Man says, "I'll tell you what. Next time, try to read his lips. Think dirty and you'll understand it."

Joey: "I do. Every time I watch the Jazz I try to read his lips."

T-Man: "You're not thinking dirty enough. It's not something we can air. What Karl Malone says under his breath, before every foul shot, is so nasty that I can't even tell you. I know—everyone in the sports trade knows—but we don't tell anyone, because of the fear that we might be shut down as a business. It is that perverted." T-Man's joking, and Joey doesn't get it, but I feel like I finally do: only because we're so strange to ourselves do we find everyone else so strange.

Defending Payton, Andrew posts to the Sonics newsgroup, "Just remember that Gary played the last few games of the season and the entire playoffs with a broken finger. You play with a broken finger and see how well you play."

Sherman replies, "Geez, I wonder if he broke his finger from sticking it up his ass too many times. The guy is a class-A loser and always will be. Why don't you go back to sucking Payton's dick and get back to me when you have something constructive to say?"

We resent that we need them so badly, that we live through them so completely; we're embarrassed that we've created a religion with such fallible gods.

T-Man says about Softy, his producer: "He's the best producer on this side of the Mississippi, but on the East Coast he sucks." Then he says (and now he's not kidding, which makes me question everything I've wanted to see in T-Man), "Gary Payton is the whole problem of this team. They tried to separate Shawn Kemp from Gary Payton; they tried to trade Shawn Kemp. After they lost game three to Denver last year in the play-offs, Payton said he knew they were going to lose game five. If I had a boss that allowed me to do whatever I wanted, of course I'd support him. Karl lets Payton get away with a lot of stuff. He's not much of a disciplinarian. There's something to be said for discipline and Pat Riley. Karl's not going to be a good coach with this team. There has to be a change of scenery in the coaching spot. Maybe it's not fair. Maybe Coach Karl is a great guy and possibly will prove to be a good coach, but not in this city. Something's gotta change at this position. How will fans get excited next year if Coach Karl is in that position, walking that sideline? Sorry, Gary, you may not be able to fool around with the next coach as much as you have with Coach Karl, but maybe it will be for the best. You get the right guy in here who can control these players a little bit better and tighten the reins a little bit; maybe Gary Payton won't be as happy that he doesn't get as much freedom, but so be it. Maybe that's the best thing."

T-Man then plays a tape of TNT's Kevin Kiley interviewing Karl earlier tonight. On the tape, Kiley says, "I talked to these guys after the game. Players—Payton especially—have nothing but nice things to say about you, and they're worried you're gonna leave."

Karl starts choking up. T-Man imitates Karl sniffling and says, pseudo-sympathetically, "Take your time."

Kiley, mercilessly, continues: "How tough is this for you? I know the pressure's been unbelievable. I know you've given it your all; your team played magnificently for three quarters tonight but came apart at the end. I mean, what are you feeling?"

Karl says, "Coaching is the only thing I do really well. I'm not gonna leave that."

Kiley persists: "Can you do it anymore in Seattle?"

Karl can't not go where he doesn't want to go, so he says, "I don't want to do it anywhere else. I got a family that likes Seattle, I got a team I like, I got disappointment that I want to overcome, and I don't understand all the bunch of baloney that people say to try to make people's lives awful and miserable. I think it's disgusting; I think it's becoming a problem in our country. It's become a problem in my life. I don't handle it really well all the time, but I am proud of who I am and what I do. And I want to continue doing that, and I will."

Cheri White sees what Kiley is doing—trying to get Karl to have a nervous breakdown on national television—and she swiftly steps in, cutting off the interview, saying, "That's it. Thank you, gentlemen. We're done."

Karl—thanking Kevin Kiley for torturing him? thanking *ma chérie* for rescuing him?—says, "Thank you."

T-Man says about the interview: "Who was that? Ooh, who was that? I mean, there's your next coach; there's a tough lady right there. That's the Sonic PR director—what's her name, Cheryl White? There's toughness right there; she's your next Sonic coach. Cheryl White gets right in the face of Kevin Kiley and says, 'That's it, it's over, get the hell out of here before I grab you by the nose and throw you out, Kevin, you girly man.' That's what we need on this team. Where has she been hiding? The next Sonic coach right under our nose. Gary Payton steps out of line: we got Cheryl White to step in and say, 'No, you'll get to practice on time, young man. You'll get there. You'll learn to shut your mouth. You'll learn to behave. You'll do as I say.'"

Power is nothing without control.

5.5.95—Overwhelming the front page of the *Seattle Times* sports section is an enormous color photograph of last night's colloquy between Payton and Karl at the far end of a long corridor. Payton (gesturing with his broken finger) and Karl (slumped against a wall, staring forlornly at the ceiling) are relatively small figures in the photo; most of the picture is just the open space surrounding them. All that space is the space between us.

DAVID SHIELDS is the author of the novels *Dead Languages* and *Heroes;* a collection of linked stories, *A Handbook for Drowning;* and, most recently, a work of autobiographical nonfiction, *Remote.* His stories and essays have appeared in the *New York Times Magazine, Harper's, Vogue, Details,* and the *Village Voice.* The recipient of two National Endowment for the Arts fellowships, a PEN/Revson Foundation fellowship, and a New York Foundation for the Arts fellowship, he lives with his wife and daughter in Seattle, where he is a professor in the English department at the University of Washington.